D1590367

THE BEST OF
RALPH McGILL

RALPH McGILL

This portrait of the famed editor and publisher of *The Atlanta Constitution*, by Robert Templeton, is the focal point of the McGill Collection at Emory University's Robert W. Woodruff Library.

THE BEST OF

Ralph McGill

SELECTED COLUMNS

By

Michael Strickland
Harry Davis
Jeff Strickland

ATLANTA

CHEROKEE PUBLISHING COMPANY

1980

Library of Congress Catalog Card No.: 80–66816
International Standard Book No.: 0–87797–052–1

Copies of *The Best of Ralph McGill* may be obtained through leading book-sellers or by ordering from Cherokee Publishing Company's sales office: P. O. Box 1081, Covington, Ga. 30209. On mail orders send $12.50 plus 81¢ postage. Georgia residents add 38¢ state sales tax and, where applicable, 13¢ MARTA or local option tax.

PRINTED IN THE UNITED STATES OF AMERICA

To Rudy

and His Memory

Contents

Acknowledgements   xi
Illustrations   xiii
Foreword   xv
Ralph McGill (*A biographical sketch*)   xvii
Introduction   xxi

THE SOUTH

THE SMALL TOWN LIFE   3
LET'S LEAVE JUST ONE DIRT ROAD   4
THE SAD DECLINE IN SOUTHERN ARTS   6
FOX HOUNDS AND AN OLD MYSTERY   8
DOGS AND GRASS AND FIELDS   11
JOURNEY IN SEARCH OF SPRING   13
"GONE WITH THE WIND"   14
THE DELTA IS A STATE OF MIND   17
A SOUTHERNER REMEMBERS   18
"MY OLD MULE IS GONE"   20

PEOPLE AND AMERICAN LIFE

CHRISTMAS EVE   25
TAKE ME OUT TO THE BALL GAME   26
TUTANKHAMEN WAS GOOD LITTLE GUY   28
THE LEPRECHAUNS LOOK AFTER LEFT-HANDERS   31
WAITING AT THE MINE'S MOUTH   33
THE PLUCKED PEACOCKS OF NAZIDOM   35
MAGGOTS EAT IN CADAVERS AND MINDS   37
THIS WAS TOM WOLFE'S TOWN   39
"TIGER, TIGER, BURNING BRIGHT"   41
A SIN LOCKED IN A ROOM   42

THE LAST JOKE ON JOHN LYNN   44
THE BUST-UP OF JOE AND MARILYN   45
HOMECOMING GAMES AND PAIN   47
HE IS THE ONE WITH RIFLE SLUNG   49
THE DERBY MERRY-GO-ROUND   50
"AMERICA, I LOVE YOU . . ."   52
A STORY FOR CHILDREN   54
TO BE READ TO A CHILD   55
BYRON REECE — "AS I LIE DOWN"   57
THE "DRUNK" LEGENDS   59
BOBBY JONES; BEN FRANKLIN   61
DID YOU EVER SEE CHURCHILL PLAIN?   62
DID YOU EVER DIP A TIGER?   64
THE GEORGIAS AND THE TECHS   66
SALUTE TO MAN AT HIS BEST   67
HEMINGWAY: OUR BEST!   69
GRISSOM AND THE FIRE GODS   70
WHAT IS THE "WILL OF GOD"?   72
A SMALL BOY'S HURT FEELINGS?   74
THEY STILL WRITE ABOUT MRS. FDR   75
"FREE COUNTRY, AIN'T IT?"   77
"NOW I KNOW ABOUT THE GUY"   79
A SALUTE TO 40 YEARS   80
CARL SANDBURG TURNS 88   82
"HONEY AND SALT"   83
MAN FOR ALL THE WORLD   85
SCARLET LETTERS OUT OF DATE   87
LINDA REFUSED GUILT BURDEN   88
THE KENNEDYS: STYLE AND GUTS   90
AN ESSAY ON "SEPARATION"   91
TESTIMONY OF THE OLD DAYS   93

CIVIL RIGHTS

THE CRITICISMS COMING TO SOUTH   97
A TRADITION IS BADLY TREATED   98
AT MIDNIGHT THERE WAS A CALL   100
THERE ARE TIMES WHEN A MAN —   102
MEN WHO SHAME OUR STATE AND FLAG   104
THE YELLOW RATS OF UNDADILLA   107
ONE DAY IT WILL BE MONDAY   108
ONCE A BISCUIT IS OPENED —   110

A CHURCH, A SCHOOL 112
GOV. BATTLE WARNED, BUT — 113
THE FACE OF THE SOUTH 115
SOUTH NEEDS NEW MOOD 117
WANTED — A NEW IMAGE! 119
AN ESSAY ON DR. M. L. KING 120
HATRED REAPS ITS HARVEST 122
AN IDYL OF THE KKK 123
THE PATH IS OF THE PICKETS 125
"CRY, BELOVED COUNTRY" 127
WE CANNOT ESCAPE HISTORY 128
A STRING OF BEADS 130
A MATTER OF COSTS 131
BULL CONNOR HELPS INSIGHT 133
SHADOW ON THE SCHOOL HOUSE 135
HONEST TO GOD 136
EMANCIPATING THE SOUTHERNER 138
NOBEL PRIZE REMINDS US 139
NOT SO MUCH OF "OLD UGLY" 141
CANCER OF "SOUTHERNNESS" 142
LOOK AWAY, LOOK AWAY 144
A FREE MAN KILLED BY WHITE SLAVES 145
"MANY FINGERS ON THE TRIGGER" 147
THE HARVEST OF HATE 148
THEY MOURNED LOST RIGHTS 149

THE PRESIDENCY

YOUNG QUEEN OF CAPITALS 154
THE HOME OF JEFFERSON 155
ASKING THE PARDON OF ANDREW JACKSON 158
RACHEL REACHES WHITE HOUSE 160
PORTRAIT IN A NIGHTSHIRT 162
HOOVER, A STORY OF USEFULNESS 163
THE TREE HAS BEEN DOWN SIX YEARS 165
CAPITAL BRACES FOR BIG SHOW 167
"HERE GOES PRIVATE TRUMAN" 168
A PRESIDENT WITH STEEL 170
THE SYMBOL OF A GRAVE 172

CAMPAIGNS AND CONVENTIONS

". . . SO GAUDY AND HILARIOUS"   176
NEW FRONTIERS BY FAST TRAVEL   177
NIXON'S CHOICE: SOUTH OR NORTH   179
IN DIXIE LAND HE TAKES A STAND   180
NIXON — AT HIS BEST OR WORST?   182
KENNEDY—NIXON CAMPAIGN FAR CRY
    FROM McKINLEY'S   184
DEMOCRATIC HEART THROBS IN FLORIDA   185
KENNEDY BELIEVES IN FUTURE OF U.S.   187
DEMOCRATS SENSE CHANCE AT VICTORY   189
THE "NEW NIXON" IS ON THE SPOT   190

McGILL ON McGILL

AN EXPERT IN ONE FIELD   194
DEAR OLD RULE DAYS?   196
OLD STEPS, OLD MEMORIES   197
"WHAT HAPPENED TO HIM?"   199
A GOOD THOROUGH EXAMINATION   201
"THIS WAS IT, THIS VERY ROOM"   203
THOUGHTS AFTER CLIMBING FUJI   204
OBJECTIVITY? OR THE WHOLE TRUTH   206
THINGS CHANGE, CHARLIE —   208

Photo Credits   *210*
Index   *211*

ACKNOWLEDGMENTS

In compiling this collection of columns by the late Ralph McGill, we have received help and support from numerous individuals.

Of primary importance was the cooperation and assistance provided by personnel of Atlanta Newspapers, Inc., which organization kindly granted permission for us to reproduce the columns by Mr. McGill which were copyrighted by *The Atlanta Constitution.*

The editor's widow, now Mrs. Bernard Smith, graciously assisted in various ways and evidenced continuing interest in the undertaking. We are especially indebted to her for introducing us to two persons who did everything possible to make our task easier.

The first of these, Miss Grace Lundy, who was for many years Mr. McGill's private secretary, was helpful and supportive in everything we asked her to do. It was she who prepared both the Foreword and the biographical sketch of the editor which appear at the beginning of this volume.

David Estes, head of Special Collections at Emory University's Robert W. Woodruff Library, generously provided access to newspaper columns, pictures, and other materials which were necessary in evaluating what to include in our book. We remember with especial gratitude the fine and cheerful cooperation of these members of his staff: Linda Matthews, Linda Nodine, Virginia J. H. Cain, and Diane Windham.

We wish to thank our typists, Connie Heider, Sara Ridout, and Barbara Hamilton for their excellent work.

And finally, we thank Martha Strickland for patience and encouragement over a three-year period in which she was a wife to one of us and a constant supporter of all three.

THE COMPILERS

Illustrations

(See Page 210 for Photo Credits)

Frontispiece
Ralph McGill. Portrait by Robert Templeton.

Photographic Section (following Page 151)
McGill and Dr. Martin Luther King.

McGill and others receive honorary degrees.

A farmer's corn captures the writer's attention.

McGill and Carl Sandburg.

The peripatetic columnist impersonates a chef, visits a circus performer, and shoots birds.

McGill and Gen. Lucius Clay in Berlin.

The McGill family with President John F. Kennedy.

Ralph McGill and Robert W. Woodruff.

McGill leaves the White House during World War II.

Vice President and Mrs. Hubert Humphrey and Mayor and Mrs. Ivan Allen, Jr. arrive for Mr. McGill's funeral.

The young Ralph McGill and his mother.

McGill and his first wife and their son at a picnic.

The second Mrs. McGill at a ceremony honoring her husband.

McGill speaks at the Democratic National Convention, 1944.

Ralph McGill beside his desk at *The Atlanta Constitution*.

Text of the "Shining Light Award" Honoring Ralph McGill.

FOREWORD

On a Saturday morning in the fall of 1952 I went to Ralph McGill's office to apply for the job as his secretary. As I finished my "audition" with him and Mr. Jack Tarver, then general manager and vice president of *The Atlanta Constitution* (Atlanta Newspapers, Inc.), the impression came to me that Mr. McGill trusted people: The only question he had asked me was, "Can you make good coffee?" He obviously had taken the word of my friend Kitty Lofton, who had recommended me, that I was qualified.

Ralph McGill saw part of an editor's role to be that of teacher and he devoted his years as newsman, editor and writer to the enlightenment of his readers. All the world was his beat. His keen instinct as a newsman and what he called "luck" placed him on the right scene at the right time. At intervals, mail from around the globe brought his columns to the office, but the South was his home, and it was a source of pride, a joy, an agony, and a burning concern to him.

Wherever he was, on scraps of newspaper, airline tickets, used envelopes, paper napkins, or anything at his fingertips, he made notes of his observations and experiences. Then, sitting at his typewriter in the office typing with his two index fingers, reviewing his myriad notes and drawing on his tremendous store of knowledge, he could write a column in 20 minutes. His typewriter was not his only prop. He carried in his briefcase a legal pad for longhand and, at times, used his knee as a desk. When out of town, unless he was overseas, he frequently dictated by telephone in a fashion he called "off the top of my head." His words on paper could soothe as gently as a mother's hand; they could stir laughter or tears; they could sting and chafe or carry the wallop of a heavy-weight punch.

People marveled at his pace and productivity. Editors have an extraordinary talent for perspepctive and for winnowing out the chaff, so to speak, and going straight to the heart of the matter. Ralph McGill possessed that talent in abundance. In spite of his urgency to utilize precious hours, he had a capacity to make his encounters with individuals seem unhurried, and those whose path crossed his still recall having felt a special, lasting relationship with him after one brief interlude.

The prevailing theme of his writing was man and his right to life with opportunity, justice and dignity regardless of his race or station. He understood the apprehension and distrust toward social change ingrained in the Southerner but, nevertheless, he was fearless in his denouncements of tactics used to thwart full participation by all citizens in the American dream.

Because of his forceful and undaunted stand on issues — which repeatedly subjected him and his family to threats of violence — he had his chivalric adversaries and his haters. Even since his death the haters' mail, sometimes anonymous, sometimes signed, comes forth when his name appears in print. But he had a multitude of supporters and admirers who in various ways let him know of their graditude for what he meant to them, to the South, and to the nation.

A decade since his death, the complexities abide and the image of the new South is not nearly perfect, but minorities are enfranchised and participating, and the region continues advancing.

Ralph McGill trusted young people. The rising generation, black and white, is proof that his faith in "the new breed" was well-placed.

How appropriate that three young men of the South are the first editors since his death to compile a book of his columns!

April 8, 1980   GRACE LUNDY

RALPH McGILL

Ralph McGill's newspaper career began in Nashville, Tennessee, when he was working his way through Vanderbilt University by writing police news and politics for *The Nashville Banner*. After leaving college he worked full-time for the *Banner* and became sports editor in 1923. He left that position in 1929 to be sports editor of *The Atlanta Constitution*. He became executive editor in 1938, editor in 1942, and in 1960 he was named publisher.

He was born at Soddy, Tennessee, February 5, 1898, the only son of four children of Mr. and Mrs. Benjamin F. McGill. In 1929 he married Elizabeth Leonard of McMinnville, Tennessee, who died in 1962. They had one son, Ralph, Jr. Mr. McGill married Dr. Mary Lynn Morgan, a pedodontist, in 1967.

The world was Ralph McGill's beat, starting when he was awarded a Rosenwald Fellowship in 1937 for his farm reporting in Georgia, which sent him to the Scandinavian countries, Germany, France, and England to study farming and farm cooperatives. During that fellowship he was on hand to see and report Hitler's invasion of Austria.

His world travel increased as he received journalistic assignments and invitations from governmental organizations. On a committee of three in 1945, assigned by the American Society of Newspaper Editors, he visited world capitals (a 50,000-mile flight) to talk with leaders in the interest of developing a "free flow of information vital to post-war understanding." In 1946 he covered the Nuremburg trials, and then was back in Germany in 1947 to observe the post-war military government. His travels continued, taking him to Australia, Europe, Asia, Africa, and South and Central America. Some of his most vigorous travel was in the last few years of his life, as he covered Japan, Hong Kong, Formosa, East Africa, Russia, West Africa, the Far East. He paid his own way to spend a few weeks in Vietnam with the armed forces during the U.S. involvement there. In his travels he sent back daily columns describing the people, economic and social conditions, the pathos and the environments. When he was out of town he was in frequent contact with his associate editor and editorial staff by telephone and memos.

Politics of his state and the nation was one of Mr. McGill's favorite subjects, and he attended all presidential conventions of both political parties and traveled with their candidates during their campaigns.

In his role as newspaper man, editor and writer he devoted his career to enlightenment of his readers and in furthering the advancement of American democracy and world brotherhood. After the 1954 Supreme Courrt ruling which nullified segregation, he led Southern editors in a stand for the implementation of law and order and in support of the full realization of civil and human rights and opportunity for all citizens.

Ralph McGill's' wide travels and his knowledge of the South made him a sought-after speaker, even though he disclaimed any gift of oratory. Some of the lectures of note he made were: The Hogate Lecture, DePauw University; the Blazer Lecture, University of Kentucky; the Pulitzer Memorial Address, Columbia University; the Cooper Union Address on Lincoln's Anniversary; the Lovejoy Lecture, Colby College; Harvard Law School Day; Alf Landon Lecture, Kansas State University; Oklahoma University Law Day.

Among the numerous awards received by Mr. McGill were *Atlantic*'s Nonfiction Award, the Presidential Medal of Freedom, Pulitzer Prize for Outstanding Editorial Writing, Missouri School of Journalism Award for Distinguished Service, Lauterbach Award for Distinguished Service in the Field of Civil Liberties, University of Southern California School of Journalism Distinguished Service Award, Medallion of Valor by the Government of Israel, Phi Epsilon Pi National Award, Carney Hospital Centennial Award for Distinguished Service in Editing, National Newspaper Publishers Association's Distinguished Editors Award, Georgia Press Association's Otis Brumby Award, Capital Press Club Journalism Service Award, State of Israel Eleanor Roosevelt Humanities Award, Quill and Scroll, Young Men's Business Club Award of Birmingham, Ala.

Honorary degrees were awarded him by the University of Miami, Colby College, Harvard University, Mercer University, Morehouse College, St. Bernard College, Wayne State University, Atlanta University, Oberlin College, Notre Dame University, Columbia University, Emory University, Brown University, DePaul University, Kenyon College, Tufts University, Ohio Northern University, and Temple University.

For 40 years he wrote a daily column and for the last 20 years of his life it was syndicated in newspapers all over the country. He also wrote features for *The Atlantic Monthly, Harper's, The New Republic, Saturday Evening Post, Reader's Digest, The New York Times Magazine, The Reporter,* and other magazines. His autobiographical book, *The South and the Southerner* won *Atlantic*'s Nonfiction Award and was later translated into Japanese.

He was a communicant at All Saints Episcopal Church in Atlanta; he had been a Marine in World War I; and he was a member of the Society of Newspaper Editors, American Newspaper Publishers Association, the International Press Institute, the Committee for Economic Development, the Advisory Committee of the U.S. Arms Control and Disarmament Agency, and the Board of the Southern Education Foundation. He served during his career on various governmental committees and commissions formed in behalf of world peace and human rights.

After a busy day of work he died while at dinner in the home of a friend on February 3, 1969.

INTRODUCTION

During the 1976 Presidential campaign, candidate Jimmy Carter said on numerous occasions that the 1974 Civil Rights Act was "the best thing that ever happened to the South." Carter stated that "the passage of that legislation served to free the white man as well as the black." To many Northern ears, these were strange words, not entirely understandable.

Ralph McGill would have understood. As editor and publisher of *THE ATLANTA CONSTITUTION* for thirty years, McGill had made the same point over and over. The South trailed the rest of the nation in every respect; in education, in housing, in industrial growth and in political leadership. One factor was the cause. That factor was race.

Racial segregation and discrimination were "the curse of the South," in McGill's words. As long as the white Southerner was preoccupied with keeping the Negro from any kind of advancement or opportunity, it was impossible to enter into the mainstream of American life.

This was not a popular philosophy in Georgia of the 1950s and 1960s, but it was true. Ralph McGill was never afraid of the truth, and because of that he was hated by many: by politicians, by members of the Ku Klux Klan, and by the White Citizens councils. He was loved, however, by an equal number of people. McGill's was not the only voice of reason in those turbulent years, but it was forceful, consistent, and truthful. Many called him the "conscience of the South," and he deserved the honor.

In the world of 1980, it is often hard for young people to understand what the Civil Rights struggle was all about. The issue then was not who gets the job; it was even more basic. The issue was public transportation, public facilities and public accommodations. The struggle was for a seat on the bus, a drink of water, the right to go to a movie and sit wherever one desired, the right to vote. The contest of wills revolved around these basic human rights, the right of over one-third of the people of the South to be full citizens.

The issues of today are more complex, and all of them do not have a right and a wrong side. But none of us, white or black, should forget our heritage, our Southern culture, and history. It is for that reason that this collection of columns is published. The South of the 1980s is changing rapidly — too rapidly for many. In the glow of growth exists the danger of losing the past. Ralph McGill is a part of that past. His wisdom should not be lost.

The South is a mysterious, absorbing region of our country. It has always had definite characteristics of its own. The racial issue was a major part of the South as chronicled by Ralph McGill, but he gave us more than that. He was a journalist for all people. Even his detractors admired his columns on American history, on Southern life, on the political campaigns of his time, on people, places, animals and events. McGill wrote in a manner that touched his readers in a personal way. He had a way of presenting something for everybody. He did not write about bigotry and injustice to the point of boring his audience; rather, he mixed his crucial message between stories of bird hunting, baseball, history and the human drama of everyday living.

Perhaps Ralph McGill had a love-hate relationship with the South. He hated the side that could bomb churches and scream obscenities at small Negro children, but he loved the land, the people and that special quality that few Northerners and not all Southerners could understand.

Both Jimmy Carter and Ralph McGill understood the true meaning of Civil Rights and what it meant to the South. McGill himself best describes it in his own book *The South and the Southerner*:

> As the region loses its fateful uniqueness, based on a subordinate position for a third of its people, the best human qualities of both races can move into the mainstream of American life and the promise of equal opportunity — the American hope and dream in which both Southerners at last may share fully.

Ralph McGill was a major force in Georgia and the South. His work was an important factor in shaping attitudes of people toward the issues of the day. This volume clearly shows why that was so. The preparation of it has been a labor of love on our part — a love for the South and a respect for one of its finest journalists.

MICHAEL STRICKLAND
HARRY DAVIS
JEFF STRICKLAND

April 1, 1980

THE BEST OF
RALPH McGILL

THE SOUTH

Ralph McGill was a man of the South. His reactions, his philosophy, and his conduct were all rooted in that special feeling he had for his native region.

Some of his most memorable columns are about the South. The selections here are representative of his ability to make the rural South come alive.

No collection would be valid without "My Old Mule Is Gone." Also included are columns on barbecue, *Gone With The Wind*, fox hunting, the beauty of nature, and the small town life which to a great extent has disappeared under the bulldozer of progress.

This set of columns reflects one of McGill's' inward struggles. While he wanted the South to move forward in areas of education and economics, he retained a love for those features which gave the South its distinctive regional flavor.

The Small-Town Life

Once upon a time there were small towns —

They had a sameness about them. There were always the two or three ladies "who took in sewing." The whole town knew why they did so. They were widowed or their husbands were "no account," "trifling," and didn't support the family. The good ladies of the town always sought to see that these ladies were given work to do.

There also was the town's "feeble-minded" boy or man. He was the good-natured butt of friendly jokes. If the town had a railroad run through it the town "idiot" (as some were cruel enough to describe him) was always at the train — maybe just grinning foolishly or drooling uncomprehendingly. There were usually one or two others—an old lady or man — who "wasn't quite right." But they were known and understood.

The "town drunk" also was a feature. He was treated with scorn and was also the butt of jokes, some harsh. Often a town would have three or four such characters. Their children were humiliated by their fathers. The long-suffering wives of these men "took in boarders" or "sold cakes," or "helped out" to earn a little cash. The point is — they were known, and their problems were a part of the community.

Other Characteristics There were other characters in everybody's small town.

It was well known that Mr. Smith and Mr. Jones had quick tempers and shouldn't be pushed too far. It was known, too, that Mr. Doe was ticklish and a good goose in his backside would make him leap and yell and maybe drop whatever he had in his hands. The names of the deacons and prominent prohibitionists in the town who liked to take generous doses of "tonic" before dinner — tonic that was about 40 percent alcohol — also were known. There were quiet, knowing smiles about this by the more worldly in the town. Fathers who were unkind to their children and who were "mean" to their wives also were known.

The girls who "went out with drummers," who came periodically to town and occupied the big rockers on the hotel veranda watching the girls go by, were known and regarded as "fast."

If the small town was in the South there would be a "nigger town." It would be separated. The identities, habits and personalities of its inhabitants were known, discussed, catalogued, as were those of the white community. Here, however, was the difference of separation.

3

Human Bonds   There were in these "small towns" what might
be called human bonds — knowledge of one another — an awareness of
persons as individuals. There were divisions of wealth, education, social
status. But they were not absolute gulfs that erased the bonds of awareness. The town banker or mill owner knew the frailties, strengths and
weaknesses of others in the town — and they knew his.

The small town today is gone. It may have the same name. But it
has either grown into a large town, or its old square is dead while the
town has moved to the Interstate. Or it may be simply drying up, its old
store fronts boarded and its people gone — or going.

There is a new environment in life . . . the divisions are deeper; the
knowledge of one another that inspired compassion and understanding
is stifled by today's crowded populations and anonymity of life.

It is less and less possible to treat people as people.

The "nigger towns" of small towns are now ghettos of large cities . . .
and the inhabitants of them remember with bitterness the paternalism.
The terms "boy!" "aunty!" and "Here, you!" are recalled with anger.

There is a vacuum — technology makes life efficient, comfortable,
entertaining, but technology and urbanization stifle humanism, make
human contacts less possible.

There is a new environment.

(July 17, 1968)

Let's Leave
Just One Dirt Road

I am just about convinced that the very best part of the country lies
up some dirt road. The highways are magnificent for travel. But after a
while they come to be lined with signboards, barbecue signs, all spelled
Bar-B-Q, with gas stations and "Eats" shops.

After a while all highways come to look alike.

Yesterday there was a "speak-in" and a program of entertainment
at Tyrone, Ga. Tyrone is in Fayette county. You turn off the highway at
Fairburn and immediately get onto a dirt road. It is a red-clay road and
in wet weather is, I suspect, rather bad. Yesterday it was red and cool
and the tires sounded good on it.

There was not too much travel on it. The houses along the way
looked calm, not hurried. It seemed very odd to have a border of trees
and shrubs and flowers along the road instead of the various imploring
"Bar-B-Q" signs. There were cool looking houses sitting back from the

road under groves of trees. People sat on their front porches and rocked. Cows grazed in the fields. There was a smell of air instead of heat and gasoline. Once off the highway the tempo of life slowed down. Maybe we've made a mistake about all these good roads. I'd like now to insist that at least one old-fashioned dirt road be left in Georgia. That, of course, is a purely selfish idea. The people who live on it likely will send a delegation to the highway department and insist on justice and a hard road. Still, it would be pleasant to have one. Perhaps when every road is paved with concrete and lined with signs and stands and smells of gasoline and hot dogs and barbecue, we shall have to petition the highway department to build us an old-fashioned dirt road along which are to be found magnolia trees and flowers and cool shade and the smell of fields of grain and corn. I remember going to see Sans Souci palace outside of Potsdam, Germany. There the old emperor had built, on top of a hill, a ruin. It was fashionable in those days to look at ruins. The emperor built a modern ruin. He could sit in his window and look at it. I am wondering if the day is coming when we shall build us a dirt road. Just to ride on and let life and the car slow down?

Honored   More than 46 years ago the old Confederates of Fayette county had formed an association. Today their sons and grandchildren carry on.

Mr. Robert Lester, who led the singing at the very first one, 46 years ago, was chairman of the program. He remembered when the old soldiers, several hundred of them, used to line up along the road.

None is left. All Fayette county's veterans are gone. Many of them sleep in the old cemetery near the meeting grounds. Fayette county is 117 years old. It was the resting place of the Confederate troops who had fallen back from Atlanta. There were men there yesterday who had remembered, as boys, hearing the sound of guns at Jonesboro and at Rough and Ready and Atlanta.

There was one old soldier on the platform, "Major Leach," of Tifton, 90 years old and agile enough to dance a jig when the guitar started a tune. He had been at Gettysburg recently for the reunion.

"A great time. Plenty of pretty Yankee women to hug and plenty of whiskey to drink."

"Yes, sir, one of them pretty Yankee women gave me a drink and I told her I was going to hug her for it. Doggone, when I hugged her if she didn't give me another drink. We had a great time."

This was the real America — the America the tourists never see as they drive north and south from Florida and back again. . . . They see the signs and the eating places and the gas stations. They never see the women from the farms, dressed in their Sunday dresses, enjoying a day of fun and "speaking." They never see the little girls with their brown faces and legs; with their Sunday dresses on, starched and clean. They never see the farmers with their families. They never see America or Americans. I am afraid you still have to go up the clay roads to see the best of them.

Any county in Georgia can offer that picture — attractive young girls, women and men with something in their faces — faces that would look well on portraits — faces such as people who have spent generations in the city have in the old daguerreotypes of their forefathers.

I'm going up some more red clay roads.

Dinner on the Grounds   There was dinner on the grounds. This meant tablecloths spread on the ground — platters of fried chicken — platters of stuffed eggs — platters of boiled ham — platters of cooked meats — dishes of pickled peaches — dishes of plums — dishes of preserves — sandwiches — iced tea.

It means standing around and talking and watching the women slice cake and pie. It means homemade apple pie with spices in it. It means chocolate layer cake with heavy icing. It means eating too much. It means a feeling of well-being and wanting to take a nap.

There was the pride of the women and the rivalry in cake-baking and in the golden piles of fried chicken. I wish every short-order cook in the world and every hotel chef who thinks he can fry chicken could visit one of these "dinner on the ground" events. You have to travel up a red clay road to find a real one.

(July 16, 1938)

The Sad Decline In Southern Arts

A lady in Brunswick, Ga., appealed to me by telegraph the other day to settle an argument relating to Brunswick stew. "Should the meat be shredded or ground?" asked Miss May Greer, via Western Union. The controversy was raging.

I was pleased to answer. Any interest in southern cooking, especially the cooking of southern dishes, interests me. It is next to impossible today to obtain real barbecue, fried chicken, Brunswick stew, or even a simple thing like a pine-bark stew. They are heavily advertised as southern, and especially Georgia, dishes and this has been a source of sorrow to me, because our cooking arts have declined. The visitors to our domain come to us with their gastric juices flowing like spring brooks in anticipation. They can hardly wait. They are lured into one of our roadside dens, where the ghosts of murdered meats and vegetables mew in the air, and have a try at what is set before them.

If it is chicken it tastes, nine times out of ten, as if fried in old crankcase oil. The tourist is an unsuspecting soul and if it is barbecue he seeks he is pretty sure to stray into a Bar-B-Q place where some slattern slices off a piece of half-done pork, covers it hastily with a vile, hot sauce, and calls it barbecue. I have never once found it, or anything resembling it, in a place where the sign read "Bar-B-Q" or "Bar-Bee-Cue." Of course, they do not claim to sell barbecue. They are selling Bar-B-Q and it is awful!

Sad Fate As to Brunswick stew, there is a noble dish that has suffered as sad a fate as barbecue. Only here and there may one find it. It usually comes forth as a barely-warm glutinous mess which tastes loudly of canned corn.

I can understand why many tourists go back home and write that southern cooking is barbaric. Much of it is.

Meat for Brunswick stew should be shredded, of course. The stew can be made in a kitchen so that it is almost as good as if made out-of-doors. I would eat unhesitatingly of Miss Greer's Brunswick stew because I can tell from her wire that she has a soul for cooking.

Nevertheless, Brunswick stew should be made in a large iron pot, or cauldron, set on rocks beneath the shade of pine trees. Part of the recipe for Brunswick stew is pine-scented air. Unless that ingredient is in the stew it is not complete. The balm of the pine-perfumed air gets into a stew when it is cooked with loving care in the open air. It must be cooked slowly and across a span of at least 14 hours. Twenty-four are better. It should be cooked with pine wood and the flames should never rage. Just as a pine-bark stew picks up some flavor from the pine bark and cones that burn beneath the iron pot, so does the Brunswick stew take on from air and pine a delicate but necessary flavor.

In these days of hurry there are not enough persons who know how to cook such a stew. And too few of those who know will take the time. The result is that a boiled hen, a few cans of tomatoes and corn too often are served up as Brunswick stew. This sort of stew always contains ground meat.

Do they think that those great pioneer artists who made the first Brunswick stew had neat little kitchen food choppers in their crude but heroic log cabins through which they ran their meat?

The answer is, certainly not. A proper Brunswick stew, especially one made in the open, should contain a number of good fat hens, pork and lamb in the proper amounts. The meat should not be ground. It should be shredded and a few of the bones should be added for flavor. This business of adding a handful of ground hamburger meat to a few cans of vegetables and serving it as Brunswick stew should be prohibited by law. Putting ground meat in Brunswick stew is evidence of decadence; a weakening of the moral fiber of the people; a tear in the fabric of civilization.

Legislation I always have made it a point to stay away from the places of government. I do not suppose in 16 years I have been in the capitol 16 times. I usually try to be present when the legislature meets every two years just to pay my respects. I have never been interested in putting through any one piece of legislation.

Nevertheless, I think I shall spend the autumn months in preparing a bill for the January session. As the legislature sensibly protects the medical profession from the quacks, charletans and others who would be called "doctor" and allowed to practice upon the human body; the law requires pharmacists, lawyers, and others to pass an examination before they may practice. I would require the same of cooks. Any cook would have to pass an examination and receive a certificate before being allowed to cook. Any cook intending to practice on the public would be required to pass a rigid examination in frying chicken, making a chicken pie, barbecuing meat and making a Brunswick stew. It would be illegal to cook barbecue save over a pit. A cook can do more harm to the physical man than a poor doctor.

What's wrong with that bill? So, I think proper a bit of legislation which would restore the noble southern dishes to a proper place of honor and require of a cook that he be a cook, not merely a grease ball.

Also, I think I will have a sleeper in the bill. It would read, "Be it enacted, and same hereby is enacted, that every restaurant providing breakfast shall serve a dish of hominy grits, and that all waiters or waitresses serving same to tables shall inform the strangers within our gates that same shall be eaten with butter, or with chicken or ham gravy. And not with cream and sugar."

(October 4, 1944)

Fox Hounds and An Old Mystery

This was in Ohatchee, Alabama:

It was New Year's Day morning and the sky and air were sharp and clear from a wind-lashed rain which had fallen all night and into the early morning hours.

Before the post office was an old touring car, mud-splashed and bent of fender and body. Its back seat was filled with foxhounds and, looking at it, one could see it had long been used to carry hounds.

Beside it a tall man stood blowing a fox horn. The echoes of it came back from the neighboring hills, but aside from a crowd of those who will always stop to look at hounds, no one else about the square paid any attention.

He was calling up some stray hounds and, pretty soon, they came in, reddish of coat and black of snout, with the mark of the July hounds or the Redbones. They came up with the quizzical look of the hound and were thrown into the back seat, the others whining and quarreling at them until the man with the horn had to reach in and cuff one or two across the head and neck.

There were nine hounds, then, in the back seat, and two boys, prouder then than kings, and a shotgun in the front seat. The man with the horn got in and started the car, calling to another carload of men and boys to come on.

They left the square and hours later I heard, far off down the Coosa River, the blowing of the horns and the faint cry of the hounds riding the winds of the New Year gale.

Ritual   There is something lost, and never found, in the ritual of hunting the fox. It is lost back in the mists of time and legends of the Druids. It is there in the mocking, leering face of the fox. The Irish, who are closer to the secrets of the ancient times than most peoples, know that it is very unwise indeed to trust a woman whose face is shaped like that of the fox. There are men, cold men, who know only to work and never to dream, to whom the sound of a foxhound pack in full cry is just a noise. And such men think unkindly of men who waste their time out in the night, listening to a lot of hounds. But the men who know are closer to one of the great, mysterious secrets, and their ritual is like that of the ancient ritual of a lodge, bound of oath and cause. They know that when they are out on a cold night or morning, and the bugle mouths of the hounds are riding the winds, that they are close to something lost and never to be found, as one can feel something in a great poem or dream. Some lost, atavistic emotion comes back with the mouth of the hounds. It is such as one receives in the smell of wood smoke on a cold day, carrying some lost emotion from the fires of forgotten lodges, or maybe from first fires in the caves of the stone ages when man first began to deal with fear and with fire, and to write his name and scratch his pictures on the walls with charcoal and colored clays.

That is why the fox is hunted by men in overalls and by men in red coats. They cannot tell you why, but they hunt the fox because it brings them close to a lost emotion.

Uncle Alf   The greatest fox hunt I ever saw was one which celebrated the seventy-fifth birthday of Uncle Alf Taylor, who rests now with his kin in the old graveyard in Happy Valley, Tenn.

He was a mighty fox hunter, was Uncle Alf. He could fill the valleys with the mournful bellow of his horn. He could call a hound off a hot scent, and that is something mighty few horn blowers can do.

He had campaigned twice in his old age for Governor of Tennessee, winning once and losing once. And both times he took along his favorite hound, Old Limber. Old Limber would lie by the speaker's table, and look sleepily at the crowd. The last time Uncle Alf ran, Old Limber was like Uncle Alf, old and tired. He had lost most of his teeth, had Old Limber, and he didn't have much heart in the race. He would lie there in the heat and snap at flies and gnats. Even Uncle Alf's oratory didn't stir him as it did in years gone by, when he would stand there on his four feet and question the crowd with his big, solemn eyes. Uncle Alf lost that race.

Hunt   Soon after that race was done, when it looked like Uncle Alf was nearing the end of his, all the fox hunters joined to celebrate his birthday. They barbecued steers and pigs. The watch fires and the barbecue pits glowed all night on Lost Mountain. Had you been there you would have heard 500 fox hounds whining and yapping at the stars. Just at dawn they were all "cast" in the greatest fox hunt of all time, with a thousand men to line on each hound.

They ran down all the fox in East Tennessee and all afternoon the hills were filled with the sounds of horns calling in the hounds.

It was a great day and it wasn't long after that when Uncle Alf retired from his screened front porch, where a man could sit in a big rocking chair and look out across the blue hills that climbed on up into the big Smokies. He took to his bed and pretty soon he and Old Limber went away to the Happy Hunting Ground.

I never see a fox dog I don't think of him and Old Limber and the big day when 500 hounds were loosed in their honor, and 5,000 men cheered them on.

(January 6, 1948)

Dogs
And Grass
And Fields

The handler's whistle shrilled and the two dogs leaped away, running hard and swinging wide . . . a black and white pointer and a white one with tan ticks on her coat.

In a moment they were like graceful shuttles, weaving back and forth in the warp and woof of pine and oak; of dun, frost-bitten grasses and scrub bush.

They moved on, hunting out their terrain, and came to a moving sea of golden seagrass. Into this they went. One could follow them by what looked like an eccentric, invisible finger pushing its way through the tall, golden grasses. The dogs were invisible. But their course was not.

Sea   Our horses moved into it, stepping slowly, and the grasses came up to our stirrups. Ahead of us the dogs bounded from it into the great area of a corn field, the brown and tortured stalks still standing, the ears of corn long ago stripped from the husks.

The horses snatched at some of the husks and the dry, brittle stalks and the shredded blades made whispering sounds as we moved through them, with now and then a crackling sound as a stalk broke.

The black and white pointer worked out a corner of the field and, then, where field and grasses met, froze into a point. The second dog moved in and honored it, both still, but trembling ever so slightly with eagerness.

We galloped our horses through the soft field, the old corn stalks popping and scraping in protest, and pulled up near the dogs.

Point   We got down and pulled gun from scabbard, loaded it, and two of us moved in, right and left of the pointing dog. There is a moment there which may not be described. Somewhere, hidden there in the grasses, are the birds. They may be left or right or dead ahead. They may get up low and to the right or to the left. They may be headed toward one and thus boil up in great banking turns.

But, they are there. And then they get up and you try to fix the gun on one of the brown balls and lead it just enough, and squeeze the trigger. Two birds in each covey is the rule and so, if you miss, there is the added excitement of hunting up singles, scattered far ahead, and trying to be steady on wing shots at single birds.

And then there is the heave back into the saddle and the following of the shuttling dogs, running hard through the bush and grass and field, waiting for the next point.

I like it all, but most of all I like the riding, and the creaking sound of the saddle, the plodding feet of the horse on the earth; the small birds that fly up; the smell of field and tree and earth.

Wonder   And I like to wonder, too, at the great instinct of the hunting dog. Where did he get it, and how? How many centuries ago did this instinct develop and how has it been kept down through the centuries? There is no movement any more beautiful than that of a great hunting dog swinging across a distant hillside, vanishing, reappearing, vanishing, reappearing.

And the point, often with a background of tree or bush or stone, is as beautiful a thing as one may find and see.

So, for three days I, the office earthling, the sitter in airplanes and trains, rode horseback and heaved myself down out of the saddle and back into it again on the many points.

For three days I breathed air which went deep and cold into the lungs, and felt wind and sun and rain, and gloried in them all.

Weary   I was weary at the end of the first day and even a hot bath did not dissolve the soreness from muscles and bones. My whole body, shaken by the gallops, pulled and stretched by many dismountings, and pullings up into the saddle, was gloriously tired. That first night I put my head to pillow and remembered I had forgot to raise the window for fresh air. The next thing I knew it was morning and a new fire, lit with lighter wood, was sputtering its resinous richness in the fireplace.

At the end of the second day I rode hard, galloping through the dusk, hunting a lost dog, and gloried in the feel of the running horse and the wind that beat at my ears. That night I remembered waking once and feeling muscles hurt as I turned.

Third   Before the third day closed, I knew that I was weary to the bone. All of a sudden my arms would not come up with the gun in that necessary coordination of arm and eye and trigger finger. I was utterly and inexpressibly tired; I came off the saddle like a sack of meal. I got back into it with great laboring. I did not ache or hurt anywhere. I was all weariness, close to the edge of exhaustion. That night in the train, coming home, I was almost physically ill from being tired, and I slept fitfully in my berth, cursing the noises; the people who shouted in the stations in the late hours of the night; the freights that rumbled and shrilled by.

And I thought, "Oh, pioneers," how sedentary is man, and how ridiculously he tries to escape from his office and crowd into a few days all the freedom of air and field and the beauty of dog and bird. How juvenile he is, trying to eat all the honey in the gourd of life in one brief time . . . But, it was glorious and one may live on memories of it for a long time.

(January 31, 1948)

Journey In Search Of Spring

Over the weekend I went with friends to a cottage high in the North Georgia mountains. The idea was to talk, to walk, to observe the approach of Spring as already evidenced by blooming flowers and early grass, and perhaps to read a bit and certainly to sleep. Indeed, afternoon naps were specifically on the program.

Friday afternoon was lovely. True, there was a wind with a hint of chill in it. There were white-caps on the lake, and a sweater felt good. But, the skies were clear and as the valleys fell away into the typical dark purple of late afternoon, swallows flew about to their roosts and nature seemed to say, "Be patient until the morrow and I will show you the heart of Spring."

Wind The darkness came and the wind sounded a bit more strong than before. It fingered the cracks and banded a loose awning. It caught at the unhooked screen doors and rattled them. But the night was clear. We sat before the log fire, watching the leaping, flickering tongues of flame; saw the embers glow cherry red and then break into smaller particles of pulsing crimson, cascading down from the logs. Now and then the buffeting wind flung itself down the chimney and made some of the pungent smoke perfume the room with a scent that has made man feel the swift passing of the black wing of loneliness since the first fire was built in the first prehistoric cave.

We had dinner before the fire and then lay back to listen to good poetry read aloud. And so, the night wore on, until about midnight, when we turned in, eager to greet the soft Spring winds of the morrow, and to walk about, perhaps seeing some of the deer in the hills.

Dawn Morning came, but even before the shades were flung up, there seemed to be an unusual whiteness to the light. Also, the house was bitter cold, and while the logs burned bravely, they seemed to conquer only about half the room.

When a shade was pulled aside we looked out on a world which could have been a stage setting for one of those plays in which a lost and unknown world for the first time is portrayed.

The trees hung heavy with ice. Great branches were broken off, their abject smaller branches white with the pale ice, made dark and blue by the blackness of the branches.

The trunks of trees, too, were heavily coated with the frozen rain which still flung itself upon the earth, thickening the coat of icy mail which each tree and tiny shrub and flower wore.

Flowers The half-opened jonquils provided perhaps the smallest bit of beautiful unreality. Each near-to-bursting bud was covered with ice, so that they looked to be crystal bulbs, with flowers imbedded in them; or like amber encased in tear-drop glass.

The forest was mysterious and deep. There were no sounds save the cracking of breaking branches; the ghostly, clacking sound of ice-heavy branches, and the tortured mourning of the trees as the wind blew the heavy branches and sought to tear them loose.

It was a forest through which one could not see. It was like looking into dull silver settings; the trees were like tremendous chandeliers, eccentrically pushed from the earth.

The light wires were torn down. The telephone wires were swept from their moorings, we later were to learn, for a distance of two miles. The worst of a great ice storm had caught us.

Walk We bundled up and took a walk. The rain was freezing as it pelted against coats, hats, and, as we were to find, the hair at the back of our heads not covered by hats. It almost blew us down the slope, and the mile walk back against it found trouser legs soaked from the knees down and freezing to the skin.

Back before our fire, we cooked after a fashion on the coals. We talked mightily, but it was a dark day and there could be no reading. All day and into the night the sleety rain fell.

Sunday dawned foggy, but within three hours the lances of the sun had broken it and before noon the whole mountain was brilliant in a warm sun. The trees rid themselves of their burdens of ice; the limbs straightened; the melting ice filled gullies and made sodden the earth. The jonquils burst into full bloom.

Spring had stood off the last hard assault by Winter. The season we had come to see was at hand.

(March 9, 1948)

"Gone With The Wind"

Beautiful in technicolor, the screen began to unreel:

There was a land of cavaliers and cotton fields called the Old South . . .

It was the last tableau of feudal days, the last ever to be seen of knights and their ladies fair, of master and slave . . .

Look for it only in books, for it is no more than a dream remembered, a civilization gone with the wind.

But is it?

The picture does not defy words. It is a tremendous, emotional picture. When it was done Margaret Mitchell, standing before the premier audience said:

"I am sure most of you have a wet handkerchief, as I have . . ."

Most of them did.

If all of the old south is gone, why do they say of us that we are "different?"

Most of the tangible things of the old south are gone. That is true. The old civilization, as it existed on the plantations, is gone.

Something remains.

It was not all slavery or plantations or banjo tunes or hoop skirts.

The Myth Of The South Just before seeing the picture I had read Josephus Daniels' very excellent book, *Tarheel Editor*, a book all southerners should read. In it there is this paragraph:

The myth that the south had only three types: luxurious slave owners, poor whites and negroes, had little foundation in fact. . . . In the whole south, out of a population in 1850 of 8,000,000, just 340,000 whites owned 3,800,000 slaves. Less than 300 planters in the whole south owned 200 negroes or more; 2,300 owned between 100 and 200; some 20,000 owned up to ten; 77,000 owned one slave each . . .

Only in the deep south, that is to say, the cotton states which really brought on the war, was there a deep gulf between the slave-holding and the non-slave-holding people.

North Carolina, Tennessee, Virginia, Arkansas and Kentucky are southern. The border states are not essentially different in the sense they do not possess the same tradition of the other southern states.

There is something left of that old south. It is a mistake to say it is gone with the wind. It is not to be defined. It is an intangible thing. It is not a matter of saying, "You all" or of slurring the letter "R." It is something in the convolutions of the brain; in the cells; in the blood; in the tissues.

It is not gone with the wind. Perhaps it is best it has not so gone. Perhaps it is best for the nation the south has retained more of the original qualities of America. Having escaped large foreign populations; having been treated by the government of the United States as a colonial possession; something remained.

It is not "Tobacco Roads" or convict camps or the K.K.K. It is something else — something vital. It is a strength. The south has something left from the old days.

Who can say what it is?

The Picture   By all means see the picture. It is, I think, one of Hollywood's best jobs. They followed the book. Indeed, they did a better job than that. They gave emphasis to the features of the book.

Rhett Butler does not just go away. He says, "My dear, I do not give a damn what you do." And walks away.

There is no sugar in the picture.

Vivien Leigh steals the picture. She is Scarlett. Clark Gable is Clark Gable. Vivien Leigh . . . does the greatest job of interpreting a part that has ever been done on the screen.

This English girl, whom a few stupid persons said should not have been selected for the part, plays it as no one else could have played it.

Margaret Mitchell said, after the picture, that Selznick had picked the perfect cast. He shook hands with her, gratefully. He did. It was perfect.

The great jobs, in my opinion, were by Vivien Leigh, by Olivia de Havilland and by two negro women, Hattie McDaniell, as "Mammy" and by [Butterfly McQueen] the girl who played "Prissy." Gable was, of course, superb. He is a very great actor. He was an actor in this picture. The four named were so much the characters they were more than actors.

I saw Bobby Jones, the greatest golfer of all time, after the picture.

"I am worn out," he said. "Nothing has ever taken so much out of me as that picture."

It does that.

It is worth your money. Do not wait until it comes to your neighborhood theater. That is a year away.

See it. Weep over it, as you will. And then come away and think — Has all of the old south "Gone With the Wind?"

It has not. And this picture comes opportunely. It will prevent any possibility of its so going.

(December 17, 1939)

The Delta
Is A State Of Mind

Some years ago, on a journey to Oxford, Miss., to make the commencement address at the state university (Ole Miss), there was time for a pleasant, flawlessly hospitable visit at a large Delta plantation.

There were those on the Delta who said feelingly that God Almighty, Himself, had taken special pains to create the Delta. Certain it is that for more than 100 million years the best soils from the lengthy watershed of the mighty river were deposited there in inexhaustible depth. Whether this was by design of the Creator so that inhabitants of the Delta could grow cotton is debatable. But, nowhere else in the world would cotton grow better.

The late David Cohn, writer of ability and a scion of an old Delta family, was for years its best interpreter. He once wrote that the Mississippi Delta began in the lobby of the Peabody Hotel in Memphis, Tenn., and extended to the mouth of the river. He said this in the years when cotton was king and the Peabody Hotel was where its lords and ladies went for shopping and recreation. He also said, with greater truth, that the Delta was, in reality, a state of mind more than land. It was, and it is. Today, however, this state of mind, like all others which long have assumed that all contrary states of mind were wrong and not worth listening to, is angry and disconcerted to find itself repudiated and condemned.

Educational Interlude The plantation interlude before the commencement address at Ole Miss was educational. The owner was a gentleman of impeccable manners and dress. On the first evening there was a garden party. Japanese lanterns were hung here and there. Fireflies flew about in the soft darkness. House servants, beautifully trained, passed trays of cocktails and juleps. The latter had been stirred with the ritualistic silver spoon (a baser metal disturbed the delicate union of bourbon, sugar and fresh mint). There were some 600 Negroes resident on the plantation, living in well-built tenant cabins. These tenants had their own church and infirmary. Indeed, that evening there was entertainment by a choir from the church, which sang spirituals.

For the visitor, sitting and listening in the glamorously lit gloom, on soil deposited patiently across the many millennia by the Father of Waters, the songs had an unusually moving quality. The spiritual was born out of the hopes and aspirations of slaves for a better land and life in which a kindly Jesus and His Father would take away all care and pain. Jesus, Himself, said so: "Come unto me, all ye that labor and are heavy laden, and I will give you rest." The spiritual looked toward that day.

Serpent Of Change   The conversation went to local subjects. Already the serpent of change had entered into the Eden of the Delta. Some planters already were using flame weeders instead of hundreds of hands with chopping hoes. The cotton picker had come and the tractor had about replaced the mule. One of the saddest of spectacles on the Delta was to see corrals of old mules, with the harness scars on them, waiting patiently to be shipped out to become dog feed, glue, and leather.

Here and there, planters even then had turned to oats or cattle and the host of the evening was a holdout against so much mechanization. He did not really look upon his tenants as just 600 other human beings. They fitted into the old image of a land which God, Himself, had made for cotton planters. He held on to the old paternalistic sense of *noblesse oblige*. He would never buy cotton pickers. No machine, he insisted, could pick cotton as well as two black hands.

The Delta has kept changing since that distant day. It no longer extends to the lobby of the Peabody Hotel, nor down to New Orleans. Today the plantation, which was to use only black hands, has long been mechanized. The cabins that have not been torn down are mostly empty. But the Delta as a state of mind has held on, its ears closed to any story save its own, with its conviction that it has a God-given right to do as it pleases, unshaken by history or events. Oxford reminds us of this.

(October 22, 1962)

A Southerner Remembers

A popular subject for seminars and addresses is "The South In Transition." That it also is not alone in transition but is tied by a stout umbilical cord to the national and world changes is plain.

A Southerner remembers — When did it begin? Was it transition when the boll weevil came about 1919–1920 to paralyze the cotton economy, to break banks, to bankrupt farmers, and to cause multi-thousands of acres of land to be abandoned?

A Southerner remembers seeing the desperate efforts by small farmers to hold on. Down the rows of a patch of cotton he watched many a family go — Grandma in her old dress and her poke bonnet; the mother and father, worn and gaunt; and the stair-step children all strung out armed with a rag-wrapped stick and a bucket or can of poisoned syrup.

The enemy was the weevil. The family would go all day, daubing a touch of the sticky syrup on a leaf of each plant, hoping Mr. Weevil would eat and die. (Usually there was a baby or so on an old quilt pallet at the end of the row.)

Malnutrition A Southerner remembers the hundreds who came to charity hospitals with the scaly red marks of pellagra on their hands, arms, and legs. Many died of it, the malnutrition of rural diets imposed by ignorance and poverty.

A Southerner remembers the research in the 1915–1925 decade that revealed the heavy infestation of hookworm in the rural South and the slums of cities. There were the thin, wan men and women with pale gums and loose teeth.

Was that a South in transition?

The boll weevil wrecked the cotton South. Carl Sandburg used to include a folk ballad written about the boll weevil in his repertoire of songs:

> The farmer put 'im in a pan of ice.
> De boll weevil say, "dat is mighty nice,"
> Just looking for a home,
> Just looking for a home.

There were farms that had produced 2,000 bales of cotton that found themselves harvesting perhaps 200 or less once the boll weevil had come. It was years before machinery and science provided weapons.

Small Farmers By that time those small one-mule farmers and the straggling families with their buckets of poisoned syrup and their sticks with rags wrapped at one end were gone to town — hunting jobs for which they had no skills. The massive out-migration had begun.

Was that a South "in transition?"

The world — and national — depression was dumped on that bankrupt cotton South. When the first Roosevelt election came along the South was desperate for help. It looked at Franklin D. Roosevelt and the song in its mouth was "Put your arms around me, honey, hold me tight."

It is a habit now to sneer at the WPA and the PWA as merely a boondoggle — but have those who sneer asked any whose bread and meat came from those initials?

Who remembers the closed factories, the long lines of unemployed in cities and small towns, lined up to register for WPA jobs?

Who remembers the CCC boys (many of them were rather old for that classification) marching in the second Roosevelt inaugural? It made the throat choke to see them.

Was that a South in transition?

Was the South in transition in the 1940s when labor recruiters came and thousands of our people, largely unskilled, went to the big industrial cities to find "defense jobs?"

Let us not think that now when we have at last come to grips with nearly a century of injustice and of apathy about removing injustice in the discrimination of race, we have just begun "a transition."

It's been a long time on the way — and it is all tied to the past.

(May 26, 1965)

"My Old Mule Is Gone"

On a small farm outside Clinton, N. C., the body of Matt Augustus Usher was recovered from a barn-lot pond near his weather-beaten house.

On a deeply worn path from house to pond neighbors found a scrawled pencil note: "My old mule is gone," it said, "I am drowned in this pond." The rest is silence.

Two days before, Matt Usher's old mule had died. For some 20 years they had made crops together. In the process they had shared the experience of growing old.

There had been a communion between them — as there always has been between those who have borne burdens and shared the secret sorrows of life. Mules and small Southern farmers have been closer partners than man and horse or man and dog. For the small farmer the mule was his one indispensable possession.

The wife and children knew that without the mule there would be no furrows plowed, no seed drilled, no wood and water hauled, no cotton taken to the gin, no way to get to the general store. And they knew that on Sundays there would be no church but for the mule hitched to the buggy or, more often, to the wagon in which the straight kitchen chairs had been placed. This was luxury. The family could ride along the lazy serenity of the dirt roads, with an umbrella raised if the sun was hot, and attend church miles away.

Social Link   The mule was the social link. Without him there could be no visiting on Sundays or the winter days when the crops were laid by. On a small Southern farm the mule was the center of life.

Matt Usher had only the mule. As others before him have done, he learned, in his loneliness, to talk to the mule as they worked together through the long days of plowing, of cultivating, of harvesting. And there was always communion, even though the mule was silent.

There is something of a mystery about the mule. He is a hybrid, "Without pride in ancestry or hope of posterity," but he has sense like a man. The horse is a silly fool which will run back into a burning barn because it is a symbol of safety. A mule will break down a door to get out.

A horse will work until he breaks down. A mule has sense enough to stop when he is tired and refuse to budge until he feels like it. And those whose daily lives have been shared with a mule know that the mule listens and understands. And though the city dwellers will scoff, such men get back an answer from the mule.

So it was in bygone days, before the boll weevil and the machines came, that men sang and talked to their mules in the fields and there were companionship and mutual trust between them.

Machines Came The machines came . . . the wondrous, miraculous machines. And the mules began to go. Even on the rich Mississippi Delta, with its legends of mules and men and cotton, one began to see the grain elelvators on the flat horizon. And here and there were corrals of old mules, with the scars of harness on them, sold to the dog food factories and waiting for death. The machines took over. (We don't know yet whether we shape the machines or they shape us.)

But the little man — the one-gallus farmer, he and his mule held on. They had to. There was nothing else to do. It was a struggle. The economists put their pencils to paper and came up with the conclusion that the mule was obsolete as a unit of energy.

But here and there they hung on — the mules and the obscure Matt Ushers of agriculture in transition. Defeated, lonely, with nothing much ahead of them, they toiled on together.

So when the old mule died, Matt Usher, in his loneliness, thought it over. And having done so he wrote a note, weighted it down with a rock on the path, and walked down to the pond where he so often had taken the mule to drink.

"My old mule is gone, I am drowned in this pond."

(March 22, 1960)

PEOPLE AND AMERICAN LIFE

If Ralph McGill had done nothing else but write about people and customs, his work would be remembered. He had a keen interest in all that was going on in the United States. He didn't always understand what was happening, or why, but he wanted to know. Columns such as "The Bust Up of Joe and Marilyn" evidenced no great insight, but he was drawn to the drama of human events of all kinds, and he was able to produce from them columns that touched his readers.

The columns in this section reflect a number of different moods and concerns. "A Sin Locked in a Room" is a moving piece about social pressure and self-guilt that seems strangely unreal in today's world. "He is the One with Rifle Slung" is a sad tribute to Ira Hayes, an American war hero. "Salute to Man at his Best" is simply that, a salute to Alan Shepard, our first astronaut.

McGill had many friends, but some were special. In reading "Carl Sandburg Turns 88" we can feel the depth of emotion between the two. "An Essay on Separation" reveals

the loss McGill felt when his friend Eugene Patterson left
THE ATLANTA CONSTITUTION.

In the early days, McGill was a sports writer. "Take Me
Out to the Ball Game," "The Derby Merry Go Round," and
"The Georgias and the Techs" are examples of his ability in
the sports world.

Two of Ralph McGill's most beloved pieces, "A Story for
Children" and "To Be Read to a Child" give a special meaning to Christmas. They contain a message for all ages.

Christmas Eve

From the office window I watched Christmas eve come to Atlanta. It came slowly across a cloudy sky. Dusk came creeping down the street; "first dark," as the Negroes call it.

Smoke from the trains billowed up. Lights took on a yellow sheen. The sidewalks were crowded with hurrying people. Old, young, messenger boys, children, all a part of the parade, all going somewhere.

Big buses pulled to the curb, let off passengers, took on passengers. Bicycles went by. The traffic jammed. Police whistles cut the air. Street cars edged their way along.

All arms held bundles. A messenger boy went by, the long neck of a turkey hanging from a sack on his back. It was too high up to see the faces but one knew, watching, they were, with but few exceptions, eager with anticipation.

Up to the windows came the noise of the city; the voice of the city. In it is the noise of trains, of buses, of police whistles, of honking automobile horns, of the sibilant sound of feet on the pavements; in it is train smoke, smoke from the exhausts of buses and cars; smells of food from restaurant doors and hamburger places; in it is the smell of winter and of rain from the cloudy skies; in it is . . . a silent tide of sentiment.

All try to express it. The Negro with the big package and the poor coat; the white man with the package and the ragged coat; the man who reels and whose friend supports him by the arm; the girl in the fur coat with the dainty package tied with ribbons; the fat woman who clutches a bundle — all of them are a part of the voice of the city and of Christmas Eve.

Darkness comes on and blots them a bit, making shadows, showing faces suddenly white and as suddenly gone in the light from a window or the headlights from a car.

That First Christmas The story of the first Christmas is a majestic, tremendous story because of its simplicity and its subject. It, too, was a part of a city.

And Joseph also went up from Galilee, out of the city of Nazareth into Judea, to the city of David, which is called Bethlehem; because he was of the house and family of David, to be enrolled with Mary his espoused wife, who was with child. And it came to pass, that when they were there, her days were accomplished, that she should be delivered. And she brought forth her first-born son, and wrapped him in swaddling clothes, and laid him in a manger; because there was no room in the inn. And there were in the same country shepherds watching, and keeping the night watches over their flock. And behold an angel of the Lord stood by them, and the brightness of God shone round about them, and they feared with a great fear. And the angel said unto them: Fear not, for behold, I bring you good tidings of joy, that shall be to all people; For: This day is born to you a Saviour, who is Christ the Lord, in the city of David. And this shall be a sign unto you: You shall find the infant wrapped in swaddling clothes, and laid in a manger. And suddenly there was with the angel a multitude of the heavenly army, praising God and saying; Glory to God in the highest; and on earth peace to men of good will.

That, too, had its accompanying voices. There were the narrow streets, the crowded city, the soft sound of the feet of camels and donkeys, the smell of spices and the odors from the shops and houses.

And there was Herod, plotting and preparing to go out and slay cruelly and wantonly. There are those, cruel and harsh, who seek by terror to build strength. They will be forgot or remembered with curses as is Herod. The story of the first Christmas will be remembered when all their names are dust.

Last Christmas   I will never forget Christmas of a year ago. We were in Copenhagen, Denmark. The man who reels and whose friend supports him by the arm; these remained. All others had gone home.

We awakened early that morning in a silent house. Outside there was snow falling and over the quiet city there came the sound of the great cathedral bells.

It was a lonely, solemn sort of morning. The Danes take Christmas at home. In the city there were no restaurants open, no clubs, no entertainment. . . . There were only a few lonely visitors to attend them.

The year has gone very fast. It is good to spend this one at home and to wish for you all a very merry Christmas and to say, with Tiny Tim, "God bless us every one."

(December 25, 1938)

Take Me Out To The Ball Game

I was nine years old before I saw my first professional baseball game. Back in the country we had played a little. I still remember the old yarn balls we used to roll up out of raveled-out woolen stockings. I remember, too, the rich warm smell of the first "real" outfielder's glove I ever saw. I coveted it mightily. We used to borrow it and put it on and pound a fist into it. It was something from out of another world.

My collection of baseball and stage stars (taken, I think, from Sweet Caporal cigarets, although at the moment I am not sure) was one of the best. We used to swap those things and buy them with marbles and "agates."

I recall, too, the first real baseball I ever had. I wanted to be a great pitcher in those days. Long, long hours I spent pitching to Jim Kelly who lived two blocks away. He, too, wanted to be a pitcher and that complicated things. We alternated. Many is the hour I worked trying to develop Mathewson's "fade-away" and the "drop."

I had my own glove by then, and a catcher's mitt too. We learned to take out the padding so the ball would "spat" into the glove, stinging the hand.

I can recall the smell of the old gloves as we kneaded oil into them, rubbing and rubbing it in, trying to give it the professional look. The smooth feel of the bats, the hot smell of the grass and dust, the sweat, the eagerness at bat . . . it was a long time ago in time and time has been flowing on faster and faster . . . but I'll always like baseball.

Something Out Of Life Baseball is the American game for a very good reason. It is something out of life. There is something in it that answers the American tempo.

Every moment something is happening in baseball. It is a drama played on a handsome stage of emerald green and black earth.

The pitcher winds up — it will be a strike or a ball — the batter will hit it or miss — it will be fair or foul — it will be caught or missed.

Baseball offers the drama of success or failure, not once in an evening, but every time a man comes up to bat.

Two men work on the batter. This early in the season they will be guessing on the new men, recalling old weaknesses on the old ones.

This one will be likely to swing at one close in toward his hands. Another cannot resist one just a little better than shoulder high, the kind that are hit down into the ground or popped up. They are just high enough so that the batter cannot get any real power into his swing. Another one may be a sucker for curve ball just at his knees.

The wise old catchers know. They sit back there in that crouch that does things to the long muscles of the leg, and they signal to the pitcher. The signals flash from coach to coach — a cap is adjusted, an ear is pulled, hands are cupped to the mouth . . . the infielders shift just a little.

They all are plotting against the hitter. He stands there, watching, hands loose, but ready to tense. He, too, is guessing. "Will he throw me a fast one or will he work the corners? Will it be a curve or will he try to throw this one by me? I think maybe that shortstop is pulled over too far. If he throws me one just right I think I can put it between that shortstop and third . . ."

He stands there, an actor in the drama — eyes half shut, watching the pitcher wind up and throw — keeping his eye on the ball.

The cries of the coaches echo across the diamond — always the same old cries — "You can do it kid . . . hang in there . . . this is it! . . ."

Always something is happening . . . and when it happens the next unfolding of the play is stepping up to the plate.

The batter is the center of it. He has but a split second or so to judge the pitch and make up his mind to swing or let it pass.

The others wait on him and his success or failure.

Southern Association   Play in the Southern Association begins this week. The association is more than half a century old. This year it goes on, properly refusing to give up because of the war. Its players are in all branches of the service. It plays with some 4-F's, some youngsters and a few players from Cuba.

It was a war that took baseball to Cuba. Our soldiers and sailors played baseball there after Cuba was freed from Spain and the game has caught on until it is Cuba's national game, as it is our own. The Cubans will, I think, be popular.

Professional baseball offers more skill and entertainment than any other sport and for less money. The caliber of baseball will be off because of the absence of so many players. But all things are relative.

Go see the games. They can take you away from the war and worry. Our old friends the umpires are with us, as usual. Theirs is a curious profession, and a lonely one. But umpries have friends and they, too, like the game. That's why they are in it.

So, I'll be seeing you. Along the first-base line.

(April 27, 1944)

Tutankhamen
Was A Good Little Guy

Cairo, Egypt — *(By Mail)* — I can do a great many things which seem dumb to me at the time, but can never escape them. I had this feeling coming out of the museum at Cairo. I was feeling genuinely and rather deeply sorry for a youngster who died some 3,000 years ago.

I went there, as I go to all the museums, because I am a tourist at heart, I guess, and therefore a sucker for museums. I went especially to see the treasures which came from the tomb of Tutankhamen. And when I came out it was this young king for whom I felt a real sorrow. Somehow, I felt as if I had known him somewhere in the past. I came out thinking more of him than of the vast treasure which they stacked about him in his tomb when they sealed him up and hid his tomb from the robbers of the centuries.

I think it was one tiny little object or so which got me. He was a wistful-looking youngster, was Tutankhamen, and his wistfulness shows through all the statues they made of him, especially in the gold mask of him they put about his face wrapped in the many windings of the mummy.

But it was not this. It was a small toy of his sister's and a small paint box she had used that had been put into his tomb with him. There, in all the fantastic magnificence of tremendous wealth and regal glory, were these two little toys. He had been such a good brother that his sister put them in there with all the gold and jewels, and there they are today, after 3,000 years.

He was a small lithe kid such as you may see playing halfback on a high school team where kids still play. I mean one which has not gone in for the professional high school game.

I think it was that which got me and made me feel a sort of personal friendship for this youngster dead 3,000 years there in the darkness of the great tomb in the Valley of the Kings at Luxor on the Nile.

Gold Everywhere I recalled the many newspaper stories of 1923 and the pictures and the description of the gold and jewels. I remember some pictures of the objects. So, I was curious as I walked up a short flight of steps here at the museum to see the objects which occupy a whole floor of the museum. I was curious, but nothing had prepared me for the sheer shock of so much, so lavish a display. The first impression of this treasure is something impossible to convey to one who has not seen it.

Color photographs cannot convey it. The skill of artists, of goldsmiths, silversmiths, the workers in wood, alabaster and ivory who lived more than 3,000 years ago in Egypt had gone into the making of that treasure. It has never been surpassed.

The first impression is of gold. Gold shining, gold gleaming, gold burning red, gold rose-red, gold dull, gold in masses, gold in paper sheets, gold hammered, woven, inlaid — as far as one could see down the great hall there was the sheen and shimmer of gold.

There were the great golden beds with the snarling heads of dogs done in gold and ivory; there were golden vessels, golden chariots, ornaments, rooms of the temple all coated with hammered gold.

It was the little things that got me. There were woven gloves there, every thread perfect. I saw a little loaf of bread, baked 3,000 years ago, and bouquets of flowers picked 3,000 years ago to cast on the coffin of the young king.

A Sad and Lonely Face   The gold mask found over his face, beneath the wrappings of linen, is truly magnificent. The face is of burnished gold, and the striped headdress is of alternate bars of dark blue glass and gold. Upon the forehead are the two emblems of the kingdom, the vulture and the cobra of Upper and Lower Egypt, both of solid gold. It is one of the great works of antiquity. There is something ineffably sad and lonely about the face. He has gazed with his golden eyes for 30 centuries into the darkness of his vault and for a few years into the light of the museum room. He lives as a human being, the only one to do so in that great museum. And he was not a happy one.

I came out feeling sorry for him and I came out, too, thinking how true was the prophet when he said: "We have brought nothing into this world and it is certain we can take nothing out." Had the tomb not been found it would have been there yet in the darkness, waiting, waiting, waiting.

Those who know say that the young king was not a wealthy king, as was Kheops, who built the great pyramid at Giza. Nor was he as rich as the kings who built the others. No one will ever know what was found in them when the thieves of antiquity broke into them and robbed them of their vast treasure which even the imagination cannot picture.

They believed in immortality 30 centuries ago and they believed the soul would come back someday. Therefore, it must have something to which it might return, a mummy or a mask or a name carved on a tomb. There must be something of the owner. For the kings there was a great massing of material wealth. We know what some of it was by looking at what was left for the poor young king known as Tutankhamen. All of it avails nothing. But I think Tutankhamen has the best chance. Those small things his sister put there with the great treasures of gold, silver, and alabaster and ivory may carry him across the great unknown and bring him to immortality. I believe he was a good little guy.

(April 3, 1945)

The Leprechauns
Look After Left-Handers

"Dear Sir: I realize newspapers get many queer requests. I dislike sending you another, but I am desperate. My five-month-old son seems to use his left hand almost to the exclusion of his right. I cannot bear the thought of him growing up with the nickname of 'Lefty.' The doctors say they cannot help me. Do you know anything that can be done to prevent him from developing into a left-hander?"

Indeed, madam, let me hasten with advice before it is too late.

Get down on your knees and pray that he turns out to be a natural left-hander.

Left-handers are protected by special fates. Leprechauns accompany them everywhere and give them aid and comfort.

Even the Bible carefully lets it be known that for ordinary tasks, calling for no special skill, any hand will do. Most of the events of the Bible are detailed without any mention of left or right hand. But in the really tough spots the scribes were careful to remark that it was the left-handed who did the job.

It is in the book of *Judges* you will find that left-handers occupy a very special place in the world, being created for great things. If you will get down the family Bible and turn to *Judges* 3:15–22, you will find how a left-hander was selected to free the children of Israel from bondage.

They had turned away from the Lord and were worshipping material things and frolicking around in the groves, and so the Lord sold them into the hand of the Mesopotamians, where they languished eight years.

Being rescued, they sinned again and King Eglon, of Moab, went over and smote them and took them into captivity.

After 18 years — but, this you may read in Judges:

> But, when the children of Israel cried unto the Lord, the Lord raised them up a deliverer, Ehud, the son of Gera, a Benjamite, a man left-handed and by him sent a present unto Eglon, the king of Moab.
>
> But Ehud made him a dagger which had two edges, of a cubic length . . .
>
> And he brought the present unto Eglon . . . who was a very fat man.
>
> . . . and he said, "I have a secret errand unto thee, O King, who said, "Keep silent," and all that stood by him went out from him.
>
> . . . and Ehud said, "I have a message from God unto thee," and he rose from his seat.

> And Ehud put forth his left hand and took the dagger . . . and thrust it
> into his belly: and the haft went in after the blade and the fat closed over
> the blade so he could not draw a dagger out . . .

Thus was the Hitler of his time removed. It was a left-hander who did it.

700 Left Handers   It is a scientific fact that left-handers are lucky. The Bible, too, sustains this.

In *Judges* 20 one may read about a terrific battle between Israel and the Benjamites. It was not a nice war, being one somewhat akin to the great wars of Troy, growing out of a quarrel about a woman.

Nevertheless it was a war and a lot of persons got killed in it.

But not the left-handers.

In *Judges* 20:15–16, you may read about how the Benjamites assembled an army of 26,000 men, and how:

> Among this people there were 700 chosen men, left-handed; every one
> could sling stones at an hair-breadth, and not miss.

On the first two days the Benjamites slaughtered the children of Israel, but on the last day of fighting the Lord helped out and every man of the Banjamites who drew the sword were killed.

But, the left-handers, being slingshot men, and not swordsmen, escaped.

There is an old superstition, fostered by an eccentic character in Texas named John King, who hated left-handers in baseball because they were lucky, that exactly 9,999 left-handers went into battle with the American Army in the first World War and not a one was scratched. The statistics of the second war have not yet been made available by Mr. King.

He was an old baseball umpire. His phobia against left-handers was so great that one day after putting a quarter in the cup of a blind fiddling beggar on the streets of Dallas, he went hurrying back and snatched the quarter out of the cup. In gratitude the fiddler had picked up his fiddle and started to play. John King saw he was a left-handed fiddle player.

In later years John King struck oil on his land and became calmer about left-handers.

It was a left-handed oil driller that struck the oil.

In football, of course, a left-handed passer is a gift from the gods.

In baseball most of the really great have been left-handers. The greatest home-run hitter of all time, Babe Ruth, was left-handed. The two greatest outfielders of history were Tris Speaker and Ty Cobb. Speaker was left-handed, and Cobb, best all-round hitter in baseball's annals, batted left-handed.

So, encourage your son in his left-handedness.

Glorify in your southpaw.

The leprechauns will watch over him.

(September 11, 1945)

Waiting At The Mine's Mouth

There isn't anything worse than a coal mine disaster. I have never been to Pineville, Ky., where 30 to 50 men are trapped by explosion and fire, but I know what it looks like.

There are the women, gathered about back from the entrance to the mine, behind the roped-off area. Many of them holding whimpering babies in their arms. Their eyes are red with tears and lack of sleep. Their winter coats are plain and somewhat threadbare and shabby. Now and then one of the women will faint and fall to the ground.

All eyes will be glued on the mine-opening. They will follow the rescue workers going in with their oxygen tanks and masks. When anyone comes out of the mine there will be a straining forward of bodies, leaning against the roped-off area about the mine. There will be coffee handed about, and sandwiches. There will be small groups praying. There will be an occasional outburst of hysterics. Small children will play about, or stand holding to their mothers' coats or dresses, not really comprehending, but knowing something deep and awful has happened.

There will be rumors sweeping in the mine area. There will be one that they have reached the bodies and that all are dead. There will be rumors that sounds of knocking have been heard. But, finally, an official will come up and say that nothing is known for sure, but the probabilities are that all are dead. Then the rumors will start all over again.

That crowd will be there, night and day, until it is all over. Some will go back to their houses that look all alike and cook for other members of the family. Others will take their places.

Of all the waiting, I don't know any worse than that.

Scream In 20 years of newspaper work you collect a lot of sharply etched memories. Most of them are more or less trivial, but for some curious reason the acid of emotion cuts them deep in the plates of recollection.

One of the things that comes to my mind often is the memory of a woman and a scream. Some 30 miners had been trapped at a mine in the east Tennessee mountains. They finally had sealed up the opening to put out the fire, knowing that all were dead. But that sealing was a finality. After that there really was no hope.

I had left the mine and was walking back to the hotel to write a story. Word of the sealing had gone ahead of me. It was just dawn, the first false dawn that comes on in which the birds wake and begin to move and chirp. I still can smell the coal-smoke, cindery smell of that shabby, dismal street. Suddenly, just ahead of me, a woman ran from one of the small, dreary houses. She was screaming. It was one long, high scream in which she drew no breath.

It lasted until she got to me. She ran at me, her hair disheveled, her eyes staring, and caught me by the arm.

Suddenly the scream ended. She drew a deep breath and said, quietly:

"It ain't so?"

I nodded, knowing what she meant.

"Oh, my Jesus, my Jesus," she said, and walked back through the open gate. Halfway to the house she crumpled up. I picked her up and carried her to the porch. Neighbors reached there as I did. She was opening her eyes as I put her down.

I can see every small detail of it: the unpaved, cindery streets, the old picket fences, the drab houses from which the paint was peeled; the poor patches of discouraged grass, the geraniums in old cans and pots, the outhouse behind each house, the whole vista of a coal mining town. I can smell the cinders and the dust and the coal smoke as plainly as if it happened an hour ago.

Later on I went back to the mine. They still were there. They were there two days later when they opened the mine and went in. I recall the bodies as they brought them out, faces blackened and swollen. I can see them yet in their cheap coffins in the small parlors of the houses along the row, the mourners weeping, the children whining.

Pathos I went back into that mine, later, while rescue crews cracked open a way to the last bodies. They lay in a "room" which they had attempted to seal off with lumps of coal and mud. They had fashioned a crude wooden fan which they had turned to try and stir the air and prevent the "black damp" from coming in with its concentrated but invisible fog of death. They had left a few messages. But the black damp had got them at last and there they lay, black of faces from suffocation. They had died before the mine was sealed.

I have been to other mine disasters and I know how they are — they are all alike. Safety measures are better today. Laws, all of them opposed by operators, are a protection. But it still is a hazardous occupation and I never quite understood why men liked it. But they do.

It also explains why, when coal miners are out [on strike], I may be very genuinely and utterly at outs with [their union leader] John L. Lewis, but my heart is always on the side of the miners. I think their lot has been the very worst in all our industrial history and I don't think it is very good today. If you think so, then go stand about the mouth of the mine up there at Pineville, Ky.

(December 28, 1945)

The Plucked Peacocks of Nazidom

Nuernberg, Germany. — *(By Mail)* —

As I stepped toward the door to enter the trial room of the Nazi war criminals I had in mind their entry into Vienna in 1938 at the start of their plan.

I recalled Hitler, now dead, whom the more bitter Germans now say did not have the courage to live and face defeat. I remembered, too, the bulk of Goering with his medals. In my mind, too, was the picture of Hess and of Rosenberg and of Seyss-Inquatt, von Papen and others. They were peacocks in those days, gilded and gaudy and arrogant.

As I looked at them, walking to my seat in the third row, I shook my head and into my mind came the trite old phrase, "Lo, how the mighty have fallen."

They sit in a box which is like one of our jury boxes, except this one holds almost 24 men, not 12. Behind each of these in the rear row stands an American soldier. By each end of the box where the criminals sit, stand two more.

But the men themselves are the show. They look like almost any jury one might get together in any city court. There is no sign of former greatness about them. Their suits are commonplace. Their features are not noble or handsome. Only one, Gen. Keitel, looks at all distinguished. After all, they were never distinguished by learning, education, character, or any of the attributes one associates with greatness. They were cunning and, in some instances, very able. They were cruel and merciless. They were liars, and they were corrupt in their private and public lives. They look so, sitting there while the witnesses and the documents steadily, inexorably, reveal their guilt.

Hermann Goering   After one sweeping look at the plucked peacocks of Nazidom's fairest garden, my eyes fastened on Hermann Goering, once named by the Fuehrer as the man he wished to succeed him should anything happen to remove the Fuehrer from earth's mortal travail . . . but, in the last will and testament he denounced him as a traitor.

Goering is daily well-groomed, as are they all. But he persists in wearing a scarf around his neck, though the courtroom is warm. He wears, too, a uniform. It is, or was, a sort of robin's egg blue. About his neck is the scarf of red. It is a mystery scarf. Reportedly it was given him by someone for whom he has a great affection. It is said he believes it to be lucky.

The man makes copious notes. More than any other of the defendants, he listens with great intentness to the proceedings. The others at times show evidences of weariness. Not Goering. He bends forward, he stares, he gets an inspiration and writes a note which is handed to one of the attorneys for the defense, he confers with those about him.

Rudolf Hess, who flew to England to give us one of the early bits of good news when that item was so scarce, sits next to Goering. The two talk often, but most of the time Hess stares ahead, wrapped in his own thoughts. He it was who startled the court by rising to protest that his lawyer, who was arguing insanity, was wrong. He was not, said Hess, insane. Even now his attorney works away despite a warning from Hess that he wants no defense.

Gen. Keitel, too, makes frequent notes. The others mostly sit and listen through their earphones.

Van Papen, who was in trouble in America in the first World War; who helped make Hitler; who married the daughter of a Wiesbaden champagne manufacturer and became rich; who was the sinister agent for most of Hitler's moves in diplomacy, rarely listens. When the proof of terrible cruelty and atrocity comes on, he refuses to listen. For the most part, he sits with head in hands, thinking.

What Are Their Thoughts?   One would give a lot to know what he thinks, as, indeed, one would give a lot to know what is in the minds of others about him and in the heads of those Germans who go about the street. What do they think of it now? A lot of men in high places would like the answer to that. What does the farmer one sees out in his field think about things? That would be an interesting thing to know, too.

The prisoners live in the usual jail cells. They have a chair, too frail to hold the weight of a man. Outside each cell is a guard whose orders are that every 30 seconds he must look into the cell. The chair is taken out at night. The men eat the usual Army fare. No more.

Despite precautions, two have committed suicide. They could not endure the strain of it, the facts of it, and their Lucifer-like fall from glory. That must plague them all; must at times drive them to the edge of madness. They were once so strong and powerful; armies marched for them; planes roared for them; they heard not the prayers of the thousands who groaned and died miserably in prison camps. They flourished like the green bay tree and were cut down.

Now they sit with the label "criminal" upon them — and the evidence mounts.

(February 26, 1946)

Maggots Eat In Cadavers And Minds

They are dead now, over in Nuernberg. Ten died on the gallows. One took poison and died. He always was theatrical, was Hermann Goering. But just how theatrical it is to die in a prison cell of poison is difficult to say.

But, at any rate, they are dead. They will not mouth again their foolish words or strut to the swelling chant of "Sieg Heil," their faces lit, their eyes glowing with an awareness of the power that was theirs.

The grass will cover them. Maggots will eat them.

But the wind that blows through the grass will play a tune and the words of it will read:

> *All this has changed nothing.*
> *Everything is as it was before.*
> *Hate still lives. And prejudice.*
> *Men still rant about a super race*
> *And pogroms erupt in Poland.*
> *Lynchers still go with rope and gun.*
> *Maggots eat the bodies.*
> *But ideas are maggots, too.*
> *They eat in the brains of the living.*
> *Which is richer fare than cadavers.*
> *Oh, Death, where is thy sting?*
> *Oh, Grave, thy victory?*

This, the song will say. And as the maggots uncover the skulls it will not be surprising if the skulls are grinning in the way skulls have.

And if, years later, someone sees the skeletons dancing in the night, it will not be surprising. But very grisly and most sad.

Maggots We knew long before the weary trial dragged to an end that the verdicts were of secondary importance.

The dreary, second-rate men sitting in the prisoners' box were but the instruments of an idea.

The maggots had writhed and turned in their brains and they had gone forth to so mistreat human beings that death came to be a gift greatly to be desired.

Children and old people, sick people and crippled, were gassed to death. And that was merciful, if cynical.

Young girls, carefully selected, were cruelly tatooed with the initials setting them apart as prostitutes for officers or for the "Wehrmacht." Men and women starved and degraded to the status of animals. Men and women beaten, tortured into bloody masses and left to moan out their few remaining minutes of life.

Always their cries were drowned out, because these men walked with their heads above the clouds of their own making. And always there was the sound of marching feet, and rumbling guns and the whine of planes in the air. And always the shouting "Sieg Heil."

Ideas Also they knew that in other countries the maggots of their idea and philosophy were at work. They knew it in the early 1930s, when they heard Americans and other peoples saying:

> You know, that fellow Hitler has got something. A little crude, maybe. And, of course, he is an impossible person, a clown. But still, he has got something . . .

And they licked their lips and their eyes shone as the maggots of hate and prejudice moved in their brains.

Even they were honest enough to say, after Munich, that when Neville Chamberlain had gone they looked at one another in disbelief and then broke into shouts of joy and exultation.

They had no idea the maggots had eaten so deeply.

But they had. Very deeply.

Fear Fear came. The craven were for opening the gates. But opened instead were the furnace gates of war. Misery came to all the world.

> The tongueless caverns of the
> craggy hills

Cried "Misery!" then; the hollow
    Heavens replied
"Misery!" And the ocean's purple
    waves,
Climbing the land, howled to
    the lashing winds,
And the pale nations heard it,
    "Misery!"

It was a long agony. And somehow, we believed in things then. We did not grow red in the face if we had no steak. We looked across old barriers and castes and lived for a time as men and women created by God.

And now — there is not much that is Godlike in us or about us. The Nazi maggots are at work in too many brains. And while men who richly deserved death are in their graves in Germany, their ideas live on, leaving us to answer, finally, whether these graves are to symbolize defeat or victory.

(October 17, 1946)

This Was Tom Wolfe's Town

Asheville, N. C. — This was Tom Wolfe's town.

And it was of Tom Wolfe I thought when I reached it today, thronged though it is with the Southern forces of the American Federation of Labor in Southern convention. Before I could put my mind to them and their convention, I had to go through a ritual I long had planned for the first time I reached Asheville; a ritual for the tall, gargantuan young man with the torrent of majestic words and phrases who died eight years ago. Time has walked fast since then.

This was his town. This was "Altamont" of *Look Homeward, Angel*, the novel that sent Asheville into tantrums of invective — the same Asheville that welcomed him back with receptions and Chamber of Commerce praises a year later when the world had acclaimed the novel.

This was the town in *Of Time and the River*. This was "Old Catawba" in *The Web and the Rock*. This was "Libya Hill" in *You Can't Go Home Again*.

I will match the satire and the skin-flaying writing of the early chapter, "Hidden Terror," in that last book with anything that has been written. The conversation in the Pullman car in the train rushing home to Libya Hill — with the blind, corrupt old Judge Bland discussing the town's great men, many of whom were in the car, is writing of a sort that Sinclair Lewis attempted and never reached. He never came close, as a matter of fact. His little satires were brittle and artificial when compared with the vital, brutal strength of Wolfe.

For writing with a feeling for America; for writing that makes poetry of her rivers and mountains and their Indian names; for writing which probes so deeply into emotions that one feels almost afraid to lower the mind into the torrent and be carried away with it — for some of the greatest writing that will ever be done in America, you must come to Wolfe.

This was his town. It was here he lived as a boy. It was here he was a newsboy delivering the morning paper, remembering always the cut of the heavy bag's strap on his shoulder; the smells of the early morning hours; the reek of the alleys in Asheville's "nigger town"; the smell of the ink on the papers . . .

This was his town. It was here they brought him to be buried after illness had struck swiftly, cutting down his huge frame that he had abused with so much labor and relaxation, driving it as if subconsciously he knew he was not long for this world.

Writers   What makes writers — real writers? God only knows. Tom Wolfe was born of a stonecutter whose stock in trade was tombstones, and a mother who kept a boarding house. She was a great woman. The father was a frustrated man who did not have it in him to be a success at anything. He drank to escape the reality of himself. There were brothers and sisters. You will never find anywhere more sorrow in words than those telling of the life and death of "Ben," a brother.

He went to the University of North Carolina. He was on the school paper. So many are. He taught for a while at New York University. He went to Harvard to be a playwright and failed. He went hungry, ragged, and endured humiliation because there burned within him the flood of words he could find no way to release.

He worked hard. No writer has ever worked more. He wrote with pencil in ledger books. The words come so fast he could never keep within the limits of a novel. Once they sent him a novel all trimmed down for proof corrections. He wrote in 50,000 words correcting proof. When he died and editors worked getting out his last two novels, they had almost a million words left over. He never lacked for words or phrases. There was a vein of poetry in him almost as pure as that of the Old Testament poets. He had some of their feeling for the color and life of words. He never knew what made him a writer. He had a great contempt for the false and the smug. He was really one of the few worthy to be called an artist.

And this was his town — a town that he loved and hated — his town which never really knew him — but his town which is known primarily because it was Tom Wolfe's town.

(May 11, 1946)

"Tiger, Tiger, Burning Bright"

He came in and talked, and while I had never known him, we each knew people from bygone years. "You knew about Bob?" he asked.

"Yes," I said, "I heard, but I know nothing, really. All I know is that after a long struggle with drink he took his own life."

"Yes," he said, "it was very sad. We never knew why he drank. He had everything he wanted, and he hated and feared drinking and yet the bouts with it came closer and closer until, one night, he counted life so little worth the struggle that he quit it . . . I was one of the pallbearers."

I remember college and a room — laughter and fun — words called in the darkness from bed to bed in a fraternity house room.

Sea   It is a curious thing how some go down in the sea of life and, while they struggle up for air, they go down again and cannot swim in it. They cannot swim though there be those who try to buoy them up and thrust hands under them in their struggling or blow up waterwings of hope and love and trust and tie about them. It comes, finally, down to the fact that there is within them something of which they are afraid and which they feel until it grows into a tiger which must be met and slain, or which will devour them.

I think I know what was his tiger, and it was in the beginning so small and so absurd a thing . . .

He was kind and gentle and a great friend, but somehow in his childhood years he had become afraid to lean on himself . . .

I remember so many things.

Daring   He always admired daring of deed or word. I recall his running laughter and his adjectives as he shook his head in our college room over the exploits of two of us who shared the room with him. They were sophomoric exploits of putting beer kegs on the Chancellor's front porch, or of locking the campus policeman in a closet, or entering the Professor's rooms in the dormitory wing and changing the furniture from one room to another.

In the occasional college drinking bouts, which prohibition brought, with the thrill of driving into the country and finding one of those dirty men who sold the stuff, he would become boisterous and difficult to control as the inhibitions melted and the false assurance made him do and dare.

Remorse sat heavily upon him afterwards and guilt roweled him with its spurs.

Hidden   There was no one to dig into the shadows of his mind and find the fear and drag it forth into the light and say, "It isn't real."

There was none to probe into his feeling of uncertainty about himself and say, "You have a fine mind that will carry you far." He made fine grades and was a brilliant student, but when he went into the law he was not good before a jury, but could find the law and prepare the case . . . but hate himself and curse himself for his fear to stand before a court and fight. There was none to look into his mind and find the key to unlock that door for him.

And so, to remove that croaking raven of black doubt which sat always before the door of his inner self, he turned to drinking so deeply that he was for days blacked out. Then his family would find him and straighten him out and he would try again, but by now his feeling of guilt and his fear were a dragon and it was not in him to face it and slay it.

He was good and fine and gentle — yet it would have been better had he never lived.

They are not cowards by design or plan . . . yet they put the burden on their families and those who love them most.

Finally, if they will not themselves find the way out of their own maze, or if one cannot find it for them, there is nothing left to do but be cruel and cut them off before they drag all others near them down. In the end they will lie and deceive and lose the dignity that is a person's best asset, a mouse in the paws of the tiger.

The answer is not in law, but in self . . . And looking back across the years, remembering young laughter and careless, carefree days, I do not know how man and God's plan for man so often grow apart so that neither love nor prayer nor force may call them back.

(June 12, 1948)

A Sin
Locked In A Room

For a long time I have had a letter in my desk. There was no way I could answer it. I kept it, thinking that some day the tortured person who wrote it would communicate again. But there has been only silence.

I was reminded of it by another story of torture, mental and physical. In Boston, Mass., an almost Tobacco Road story broke before the eyes of a dismayed people. A woman had kept her 14-year-old illegitimate son in a 6 by 9 room for nine consecutive years. The boy, who must have a fine mind, learned to talk by keeping an ear against the door and listening to conversations on the other side where his mother and her legitimate brood lived.

The boy knew only vaguely of God, had never seen a movie, had never tasted ice cream. He hated his mother.

Sin   The mother had hidden the boy because she thereby hid her sin. She was ashamed. Her sin drove her to do much church work. Her reputation in the neighborhood was that of "always doing good deeds."

There is a fine moral there which I will not seek to draw. I could apply it, even, to regions, to cities and States. They, like persons, often try to keep their sins locked in some room and cry out to the nation "look how many good deeds I do."

This boy is in a home. He will have a full life. But he will not forget. And the "sin" of his mother now has come down about her head and destroyed her little world which depended always on the lock on the fearful door where the living evidence of her "sin" was kept.

Incidentally, for those who always say, when confronted with some of our own unhappy stories, that only the Southern stories get front pages (an erroneous idea), let me point out that this one hit all the front pages in the nation. It was from Boston, hard by Harvard.

Letter   Now to my own letter. It was the letter of a tortured woman who would not cease punishing herself. She, too, had mothered a child out of wedlock. She did not say what had happened to it. Where the child was hidden was not even suggested.

But, it was, nevertheless, in some "room," and she lived in fear and in agony and remorse. Obviously she was not a bad nor a sinful person. But she would not let herself rest.

She said that she was a college graduate, a Phi Beta Kappa, and therefore her "sin" was the greater because she had had advantages. She said she had planned to take her life and had come close to doing so, but could not. She told of going sleepless, weeping, of wanting to die, until she had found, she said, the answer. "Tell them to pray without ceasing," she said. "Prayer, constant prayer and appeals to the mercy of God are the only answers."

Prayer   I am sorry for her because she has no more found the answer than had the woman who tried to keep her sin in a 6 x 9 room. Prayer for forgiveness is fine and being convinced of its balm is good.

But this woman is throwing away her life. I doubt if she really is a sinner. I doubt if a merciful God has any special punishment marked out for her. One could only judge she had placed the child in a good home or had managed to keep it as her own. To keep on flogging herself with the whips of her conscience, to kneel always with uplifted hands, is more of a sin than that of having the child. A wasted life is the greatest sin. And forgiveness points the way to a useful one. I hope the tortured writer of that letter has at last ceased to accuse herself and has obeyed Him upon Whom she called, and is using her life well and living it normally. I would like to forget about her letter.

(March 19, 1949)

The Last Joke On John Lynn

In the midst of all the great news stories clattering in on the teletype keys from the great and troubled continents, the seven seas, and the islands in them, I cannot get John Wallace Lynn, 53, native of Mitchell, Ind., out of my mind.

He was hastily dug from a grave at Boone, N. C., the other day, where he had found rest and a place to sleep, and routed out, as he had been many times in many a flop house and jail. It had been found he was not Frank Shore, who was alive and kicking in Mullins, W. Va.

On the night of May 15 he had knocked at the door of the jail in Calhoun, Ga., and asked to be allowed to spend the night. He was a meek and mild little man, harmless looking, and the jailer let him. And that night, in the long, lonely darkness of the jail, with only the snores of a drunk or two as a requiem, he died.

This caused a lot of trouble, as of course, some effort had to be made to identify him. Relatives of a missing man came from the Tarheel state and looked at the body taken from the Calhoun jail. The corpse was a bit pathetic. The hair was thin and graying. There was a deep scar from the upper part of one eye to the hairline. But the relatives said it looked a lot like the missing Shore and, though some doubt was expressed, the body was claimed, and transported to Boone.

Rest   And there occurred perhaps the nicest thing that had happened to the dead man in a long, long time. Likely it was the kindest thing that had happened to him since he was a baby and his mama bathed him and loved him.

There was a service. He was preached over and kind words were said. People wept tears for him. And then they put him away in the family plot, the homeles, friendless man, in the kindly unrebuking earth, and placed flowers on his grave and left him there in what likely was the first peace and ease he had known in a long span of harshly exacting years.

And, for a while, there was peace.

But, then Frank Shore was found alive and well in Mullins, West Virginia.

So, they went back and dug up the poor battered body and looked at it once more. There he was again, homeless and friendless and on the bum as before.

FBI   They took the prints from the tips of his dead fingers, rolling them in the black ink, and putting them on the forms, and sent them to Mr. J. Edgar Hoover, in the big FBI office in Washington. When no one knows the old bums who are fished out of rivers, or found dead in cheap hotel rooms; when there is no identity on the bodies discovered in hidden graves, in frowsy, bed-buggy flop houses, and in the jail cells where the vagrants are held; they ask Mr. Hoover.

He just says, "Young man, will you look at these prints and let me know what you find?"

And they look. And they find.

Mr. Hoover was the only fellow in the whole wide world who knew him. He sent back the name and life story of John Wallace Lynn.

It was pretty sketchy. But, at least, they knew who he was. He was born in Mitchell, Ind., 53 years ago. They knew that from the police records at places where he had been "detained" — Charleston, S. C., Minneapolis, Minn., Dothan, Ala., Houston, Texas, Indianapolis, etc. Once, when he was in Cincinnati, John Lynn registered for the draft. He listed no relatives. He was, from the record, just a bum stumbling toward Calhoun, Ga., and the final of life's jokes.

And after years of sleeping in jails and flop houses, the fate which had used him so badly put upon him the last cruel jest. They let him be wept over and buried in a family plot. But, then they dug him up and asked Mr. Hoover who he was and buried him in a potter's field where all the homeless bums, male and female, sleep, and where few tears are shed and no mourners go.

(June 6, 1953)

The Bust-Up
Of Joe And Marilyn

For the life of me I couldn't exactly say why, but it was sad to see the Joe DiMaggio–Marilyn Monroe marriage break up.

I never knew either of them. Once I met Joe DiMaggio in one of those cocktail crowds where the little pieces of dead fish on toast are passed around; where the trays of drinks catch the light and the little suns glow in the Martinis, the Manhattans and the highballs; and where the smoke and the conversation are thick and faces stare at you and bodies push by. He must have shaken a hundred hands — and properly remembered none.

I saw him play a few times. He was one of those effortless ones, who see, think, and act all in one graceful, fast smooth motion.

As for Marilyn Monroe I never even saw her, on or off the screen.

Symbols There isn't any reason why the marriage breakup made me sad, but it did. Maybe it was because they were symbols. Both had come up from the "other" side of the tracks. Both had known it rough. Each had beat the game and had gone to the top in the two professions which create the American idols — baseball and the movies.

After all, it is something for a man to become the greatest outfielder and hitter in his time. And through it all DiMaggio kept his head. He walked with kings, as they say, and he had a lot of adulation and pawing and fawning around him. But he stood tall all the time and was his own man.

Marilyn Monroe had it rougher. The cinema business demands a lot of phoniness because the American people, in turn, expect it. "Box office" is a phrase which means that when a movie girl sits down she has to have her skirts up high for a cheescake shot. She must be in the gossip and movie columns. She must be interviewed for this and that and photographed with as little on as possible on beaches and by swimming pools. That's part of "box office."

We make idols of our baseball stars and our movie stars . . . we gawk and stare and crowd and push . . . we get signed baseballs and auto-graphed photographs . . . we crowd about the players' gate and studio gate.

And Joe DiMaggio, the son of Italian immigrants in San Francisco and Marilyn Monroe, the kid who was lonely in an orphanage and who was in 11 different "homes" before she was 15 years old — these two got to the top in our idol factories.

Monroe Both had had an early marriage which failed. The kid who'd had 11 sets of foster parents, who had married a seaman at 16, who had worked in a parachute factory during the war, and who had taken a job posing for cheesecake pictures for a Hollywood studio — she got to be a star with millions drooling over her and fighting to see her in person.

You see a lot of big-time executives, with good families behind them, and college and clubs, who slip and fall when they get to the top and start trying to handle all the power that money and adulation provide. A lot of them do a lot worse than Marilyn and Joe. Many who had better chances make even worse marriage and provide much less honest separations.

Money doesn't help you in a spot like that even if you were born to wealth, luxury and had all the best of it.

Nor does birth or position or a stick of type in *Who's Who*.

Maybe I am a soft-hearted touch, but somehow I got the feeling they both were pretty honest and lonely and didn't know what to do with a marriage that was doomed from the start. The fellow who was the greatest centerfielder in the game can't sit around all day while his wife works and answers all the demands of "box office."

Somehow the news made me sad.

(October 9, 1954)

Homecoming Games And Pain

This is the period during the melancholy days of autumn when universities and colleges schedule what they call "Homecoming Day." They seek thereby to lure the old grad back to the old scenes.

The football opponent on homecoming is, of course, selected with the view that said opponent will have little more chance than did a Christian when thrown to one of the emperor's lions. It is true, of course, the uncertainties of life being what they are, that as now and then the Christian killed the lion, home-coming days have been ruined by a visiting team.

Even with all possible precaution, home-comings are usually rather cruel and sad, and only the perpetually ebullient and the continually optimistic are made happy by them.

More often than not, as the Old Grad wanders along the old paths, his memory of happy days when he strolled one of the paths with a co-ed beside him becomes an ache and a pain. He can smell again the perfume she wore and recall the lilting sound of laughter, and can smell again the aroma of autumn-fallen leaves, the wine of cool air, and the nostalgia of wood-smoke which blows through all the winds of fall.

Pain It is at precisely such moments that he encounters a couple of undergraduates, faces alight, holding hands and talking happily as they come along, oblivious of him, or throwing him the most fleeting and casual of glances, such as they would give a tethered goat. Usually, they titter loudly after they have passed by.

His dream goes. He feels, suddenly, the weight of the fat that is on him. His bridgework or his plates feel loose and monstrous. His bifocals blur. His legs suddenly feel heavy and unaccountably weary, as if he had walked for miles, instead of strolling a few hundred yards along the old campus paths. Bitterness comes over him and the taste of time is like unripe persimmons in his mouth.

It is not much better if he meets with old classmates. Too often, unless he hails them, they pass him by. He recalls with a wry smile the wit who said, on returning from a homecoming reunion, that he would never go again because all his class had changed so much they didn't even recognize him.

Disenchantment   If they do meet and recognize one another, slap backs and embrace, the moment soon is done. After all, when one has asked what ever became of old Joe and Charlie . . . when one has inquired who it was Sue Brown married and where it is they now live . . . when questions are asked and answered about families and children, and old professors . . . when the fame and its probable outcome has been exhausted . . . that does it.

By then one begins to notice the middle-age spread; the gray hairs, the eyeglasses, bodies that are too thin or too heavy; the fading signs of old beauty; the athlete of bygone years who wears a size 46 suit and puffs when he has finished a sentence of any length . . . then it it time to break it up and move on.

It is, if anything, worse on the old player . . .

He sits in the stands and doesn't like that. Enough of his life was spent there on the field for him never to like watching the game as a spectator in the crowd. He always feels lonely. A team feels something. On a team a man feels he is a part of it and akin to the men next to him. In the stands he is lonely and lost, no matter how many are about him.

He sits there, remembering the tense moment before the ball was snapped; the churning of straining feet, the rasp of the canvas pants; the smell and feel of hot, wet woolen sleeves against his face. He remembers the desperate, panting breath; the long runs on the kick-offs; the hard jolting tackles; the breakthrough; the desperate agony of goal line stands. All this he feels there in the stands, and so, he squirms with each play, remembering his youth.

But it is no use. It is gone.

No matter how often a man goes back to the scenes of his youth and strength they can never be recaptured again.

(October 23, 1954)

He Is The One
With Rifle Slung

It was bitter cold on Iwo Jima in February and March of 1945.

And it was cold a few nights ago in the Arizona desert when Ira Hayes, Pima Indian, started home. He was pretty drunk and sleepy. It was below freezing. After a while it seemed a good idea to lie down and sleep for a while. So, he did. After an hour or so the blood slowed down. The overworked heart began to pump irregularly. Maybe it seemed to the Indian, dying there from overexposure, that he was back on the cold sands of Iwo. No one will ever know on earth. He was dead when the dawn broke and the early rising ones found him on their way to their fields.

Suribachi On the morning they found him dead the tourist cars were pulling up in Arlington, Va., and the visitors were climbing out to stand there, weeping, some of them, before one of the great war memorials of all time . . . a massive statue of the group of United States Marines raising their flag on the summit of Mt. Suribachi on the fourth day of the fearful agony of Iwo Jima. They were members of a 40-man patrol. A photographer took a picture of the intent and close-grouped men, struggling against the wind to raise the flag which was large enough for all the ships at sea to recognize.

The statue was made from that picture — faithfully catching all the concentrated intensity and feeling of it.

In the massed, struggling group there is one Marine, second from the left, who has his rifle slung over his shoulder. That one was Ira Hayes, the Pima Indian who died of exposure, futility and of being lonely and lost and never found, on the Sacaton reservation two days ago.

He was present, neat and well-attired, when they unveiled that mighty statue before which men and women stand and weep, or bow their heads in prayer, or look in awed silence. (That day, they said he seemed lost in thought, his eyes troubled.) There was none to weep when he died on the desert. But, as long as the nation remembers its dead and Iwo Jima there will be some among those who come every day to weep over Ira Hayes and those who, maybe, luckier than he, died in the desperate, bloody assault which took the most heavily defended terrain in all military history.

"We hit the beach at Iwo with 250 men in my company," Ira Hayes said once, in an interview, "and left with 27 a month later . . . I still think of those things all the time."

Some companies had it worse, being wiped out.

Landing   The Marines landed February 19, 1945. They bogged in the deep, quicksand-like volcanic ash — and the thousands of machineguns, mortars, rockets and heavy artillery, zeroed for every yard of the area, waited an hour before opening up on the congested beach. The cruel fire chewed them up, but they kept coming. Four days later Hayes and his patrol reached the summit and raised their flag.

In the light of the dawn of March 26, the last defenders were killed.

Of the Marines, 5,324 died; 16,090 were wounded.

Some of their folks come now to sob before the statue which has on its base a listing of the Marine Corps' battles around the world. (They were fighting for the republic before its birth.)

"Uncommon valor was a common virtue," a line says of their deeds.

And in the statue the second from the left, with rifle slung, is Ira Hayes. Why did he fail himself when he never failed his country? He didn't know. Some who knew him said he was a hero to everyone but himself. It's a good line. But not enough. It was tough for an Indian in a white man's world, he said. But, also, he said, he had plenty of good chances and fouled them up with whisky. What did he want to forget? What couldn't he face — with everyone wanting to help? The tragedy is no one can help. But a merciful God won't be hard on any man who was at Iwo Jima.

(January 27, 1955)

The Derby Merry-Go-Round

Late this afternoon at Churchill Downs they will spring the gate and the gay and gaudy carousel will spin. It runs only once a year, does this merry-go-round, and the brass ring is worth many thousands of dollars.

Men and women who contribute 50 cents a week to their church budgets will crowd into lines at the $2 windows, waving fresh money, crying "take mine." Persons who subscribe $5 to the Community Fund will be thick as bees at sorghum time around the $10 windows betting across the board.

You get very giddy riding the whirl of this merry-go-round.

It's full of history, juleps, romance and rubbish. It's wet with the tears of maudlin drunks who weep every year when the bored attendant puts the sad and slow-playing "Weep No More, My Lady" record on the machine which plays into the amplifying system.

But, for all of that, when the starting gate springs the horses surge into a gallop, the quickening drumbeat of steel-shod hooves begins to echo down the track, and the bunched entries come by the stands with the tiny, silken-clad figures crouched over the bobbing, silken necks of the magnificent animals they ride ... the heart constricts. It is a moment when life's familiar pattern is shattered. For a little more than 60 seconds existence is on a high, pulsing plateau filled with shrieks and shouts, punctuated by the fading, recurring thud of hooves ... as if the brass-shod, riderless horses of the Apocalypse themselves were riding down the skies.

Memory   The best Derby story I ever got was in 1933. That was the year Col. E. R. Bradley, last of the traditional and legendary gentleman gamblers, won the Derby with his dark horse Broker's Tip, with Don Meade up.

The favorite was Head Play.

They came down the stretch together — those two.

The jockeys were swinging bats at each other between licks at the rumps of their laboring mounts. There was a pull or so at saddle blankets. But at the wire, Broker's Tip had his head there before Head Play, with Jockey Herb Fisher aboard.

By arrangement with Mr. William McGregor Keefe, of the New Orleans *Times-Picayune*, I departed when the race was run to interview the winning jockey.

So, it came about I was one of two or three men who saw the drama of the Lilliputian jockeys.

The winner is delayed by the ceremony of the roses.

So it was that when I presented my credentials and got into the dressing quarters, there was Herb Fisher, naked as the day he was born, standing by his locker and filling the room with curses. His face was streaked with hysterical tears. It was contorted, too, with ill-controlled sobs. Wild maledictions were heaped upon the still absent head of jockey Don Meade.

On adjoining chairs jockeys dressed for the next race. They understood how a jockey felt who had just lost a Derby purse.

Suddenly the door opened. There was a sound of excited talk. In came the grim-faced Meade, his silks dust-stained, his face grimy. He had brought his horse from behind.

Fight   Fisher went for him as the arrow is released from the bow.

For a few seconds they clinched and flailed there, the small, naked man sobbing and crying out his choked, angry wrath, and the calm, hard-faced little man in his gay, silken shirt, white riding pants and boots.

It was an odd sight, full of sound and fury.

It soon was over. Men separated them. Fisher was led away to a shower.

Meade slowly took off his clothes. He had won 10 per cent of the purse and perhaps a bonus. After all, he had brought a long shot home. It was the second year in succession the Bradley stable had done just that. The year before an unknown Burgoo King had come home first.

"What happened, Don?"

"Well," said the still calm little man, "he tried to do it to me and I did it to him."

And he had, too.

It's a spectacle all right — the big annual gambling merry-go-round.

(May 7, 1955)

"America, I Love You"

The place: A small mountain college town in the Blue Ridge of the Appalachians — Young Harris.

The time: Commencement weekend.

There are two scenes. The first is the annual champion debate, held on the evening before commencement, across a span of almost 70 years. The small college has no football team. In the years when the school was all but isolated in its mountain depths by lack of roads to the outside, the debates often ended in fights, or refusal to accept the decision. Through the years the debates have become more formalized as to ritual. There are no dark threats against judges. The participants wear rented dinner suits, in the manner of commencement participants everywhere. But, the champion debate at Young Harris remains the Yale–Harvard game, the Ohio State–Michigan contest, or the meeting between Tech and Georgia.

Debate, which was one of the great traditions of college and university life in the early years of the Republic, has suffered somewhat the fate of the buffalo and the whooping crane. Of all the debating societies of yore, only a few remain. Most of them make but a pretense of debate. But, here and there the strain has bred true to old breed, who prepared well and spake with fire and strength.

Scene One   The chapel was crowded with townspeople, alumni, students, fond parents, and relatives. Judges, imported from a distance, sat separated, unidentified in the audience.

A team of three represented each society.

The subject was, *Resolved: that the non-agricultural industries of the United States should guarantee their employees an annual wage.*

Keyed up, yet under control, they came forward and argued their case. Arguments gave off sparks. The second affirmative speaker, Fred Shockley, was blind, though none would have known it had he not been led to the old pulpit, his braille notes in hand. Jimmy Winn, Fred Shockley, John Kay, for the affirmative. Ray Cox, James Pleasants, Harold Jennings for the negative. The former seemed to have an edge in oratory, the latter in argument. But then came Jimmy Winn with a smashing rebuttal which turned the tide to a two-to-one vote for the affirmative.

There was then a rush for the stage. Dinner dresses, of brilliant hue and of white, swirled like some technicolored dream. Male students came yelling and vaulted to the stage, pulling girls up after them. The winning team was hugged and kissed. The losers were consoled. It was something like students greeting a winning football team, yet there was more substance in it, and more of a feeling of values.

Scene Two In the morning there was the second scene — the cap-and-gown procession to the gymnasium. There, on the basketball seats, the families and friends sat. Young alumni, with their first babies, were there. Some of these infants fretted, some carried on a happy, unintelligible prattle. But none minded. The choir sang. The valedictorian spoke wisely. The commencement speaker was properly sage. The diplomas were handed out, with here and there a mother or father blinking back tears.

And then they stood and sang their alma mater. In the crowd in the basketball bleachers the young parents, and old, joined in, as did graying oldsters. And then the processional marched out to the music of piano-quick-march.

Outside in the sun there were embraces, tearful promises never to forget one another, to write, to visit. Here and there a girl in her cap and gown went to a proud father, put her arms about him and thanked him. Here and there a capped and gowned boy or girl would throw arms about a mother and thank her for her sacrifices.

It was a scene repeated many times in America, at small colleges and large. It was an authentic bit of Americana, a look at the real heart of a people.

America, I love you.

(June 4, 1956)

A Story For Children

Birds are perhaps the favorites of God's many creations. The pleasure of having a bird feeder about the house is one of the purer enjoyments of life. They are beautiful without exception. There are no ugly birds. They have many foibles shared by humans, but their beauty causes us to overlook these, or to be amused. It is not at all a coincidence that birds are the center of some of the most pleasing and happy stories about the great events of the Bible in the folklore legends of the ancient countries where the bearded prophets, the Apostles and Christ lived and had their being.

One of these concerns the nightingale, which Keats immortalized in "Ode to a Nightingale":

> *Thou wast not born for death,*
> *   immortal bird!*
> *No hungry generations tread thee*
> *   down;*
> *The voice I hear this passing*
> *   night was heard*
> *In ancient days by emperor and*
> *   clown;*
> *Perhaps the selfsame song that*
> *   found a path*
> *Through the sad heart of Ruth,*
> *   when sick for home,*
> *She stood in tears amid the*
> *   alien corn . . .*

Bethlehem   Jesus was born, as we all know, in one of several caves or stalls cut into the side of a hill at Bethlehem. It was one of the stalls of a caravanserai. You may see them even today in parts of the Holy Land, in India and in Arabia.

They are picturesque places, where the camel, donkey or horse caravans come. Their attendants sleep in the stalls or on piles of straw and blankets in the open by their animals. The area about the stalls will be filled with dogs, people coming and going, and with cooking fires. The air will be heavy in late afternoon with the smell of mutton or goat meat cooking and of tea being brewed. All about will be vendors of the flat, round Arab bread and of sweetmeats and tobacco. I, myself, have seen these in Iran and India. They are not too greatly changed from the time of Christ.

Wherever there are horses and camels, there is grain. And wherever there is grain, there are birds.

Now, legend has it that in the stall where Jesus was born there was a little brown bird which had its nest high in the top of the stall on the ledge of rock. It is a most inconspicuous bird. It could not sing a note. He lived a very dull life, and he was shy and sad because he could not sing like the other birds.

One night, as the lonely and little bird slept on his nest, he was awakened by a great white light in his cave-like stall. He could hear the angels singing. And one of them said:

"Sing with us, little bird."

"Alas," he said, "I cannot sing."

"Try," said the angel.

Nightingale And the little bird did try and found that he really could sing the joyous songs the angels were singing. He was so happy he sang with them, song for song. And that is why, even today, the poets and everyone else agree the nightingale sings like an angel.

Indeed, the reason all children like animals is because children are closer to the Kingdom of God than anyone else. Jesus said that. And that is the very reason why children especially like chickens, donkeys, cows, oxen, birds and lambs — they were all in and about the stalls when Jesus was born a long time ago. In fact, ever since then the rooster has greeted each morning with that triumphant crow of his his — which isn't "cock-a-doodle-doo," as some ignorant persons would have you believe. He is crying out "Jesus Christ is born."

And the warblers ask, "When? When?"

And the crow answers, "Now! Now!"

And the cow moos, "Where? Where?"

And the sheep says, "In Bethlehem."

If you awake and live on a farm, maybe you can hear them all.

(December 23, 1957)

To Be Read To A Child

Early Christians had stories for their children. They were legends which grew with the years and in the years following Constantine's acceptance of Christianity. Being closer to the simple origins of it, they associated all things of life more close to their religion. In their stories Christ touched the lives, not only of men but of birds and animals.

There was one about how the robin got his red breast:

The bird called the robin had lived in the East long before Jesus was born. He was an undistinguished bird of olive-gray color, but good-natured, and of a good heart.

On the night that Jesus was born a robin was asleep in a tree near the stall.

Joseph and his relatives had built a fire not far from the mouth of the cave and they were sleeping on goat's-hair blankets placed on straw. The women were with Mary. All of a sudden a great light came from the mouth of the cave and awakened the gray bird and the men, who ran to the cave.

The bird watched all this from his tree. All at once he saw that the fire which Joseph and his family had left was about to go out. So, he flew down and began to fan it with his wings. The flames grew into bright red ones, and he kept fanning until the fire was good and hot. And because it was a holy occasion, everywhere the reflection of the flames touched the helpful bird, his feathers turned the bright red color of the fire and have remained so to this day. That is why the bird came to be called "Robin," which means "bright with flame."

And that is why it is wicked and wrong to kill a robin. All children like to see robins hopping about. Indeed, children are especially fond of the animals present at Christ's birth, — the cow, the ox and the donkey. There is an old English carol which has the donkey proudly say, "I carried His mother to Bethlehem," and the cow to boast, "I gave him my milk to drink."

Perhaps the most charming legend is . . . of how the lightning bug got its light. The story is:

Once upon a time they were just ordinary long, black bugs with wings. They flew in the daytime because they couldn't see at night.

One night almost two thousand years ago one of these bugs was asleep in a cave near Bethlehem. It was one of several such caves used as stalls and was really the first motel. Just as we have motels for travelers in automobiles, there were places for caravans in ancient times. There were no beds, nor rooms, and those traveling with the caravans had to sleep on the straw or blankets in front of the stalls.

It was in one of these stalls that the little black bug was asleep.

All of a sudden he was awakened by people coming into the stall. This didn't bother him and despite the noise he went back to sleep. All of a sudden, though, he was awakened by a wonderful, soft white light which filled the cave. He looked down and he saw a beautiful young woman with a baby in her arms and all about was the beautiful light. Then the angels came into the cave and began to sing.

The little bug was looking on, his eyes big with excitement. Suddenly one of the angels took a bright, green jewel from her crown and laid it up on the small ledge of rock where the bug was. She put it down right on the bug.

"Ouch," he said.

But the angel didn't hear him. And after she had rearranged her crown she picked up the jewel and put it back in place.

It was then that the bug noticed that the back part of his body was lighted up with a light, just like the color of the jewel. After the angels left, so the mother and child could sleep, and it was dark again, he could still see because of his own light.

So he flew out of the cave and went about to tell all the other night bugs of the wondrous event in the cave. And ever after that he and all his children's children have had a light to carry with them at night because he was lucky enough to have been in the cave where Jesus was born.

(December 24, 1957)

Byron Reece — "As I Lie Down"

When one looked at Byron Herbert Reece one thought of the young Lincoln. There was the same lanky thinness; the lean, craggy face, the unruly hair, the deep-set eyes with pain and brooding sorrow in them which laughter temporarily could remove.

Byron Herbert Reece was a poet — one of our major ones. He also was a novelist, articulate and skilled. But, most of all, he was a poet. One of New York's larger publishing firms published all he sent them.

He was mountain bred and born. The Appalachians which thrust into South Carolina and Georgia saw his forebears before the Cherokees were gone. He was born in a log cabin in north Georgia which in its building had been guarded against Indian attack.

The mountains were in his poetry and ballads. They, and the Bible, which had come into the mountains in the saddle bags of horseback riders or in the old trunks in the oxen-pulled wagons, colored all his poems. The skies, the clouds, the cold lakes, the tumbling rivers, the forests, the cold, keen nights when the stars looked green as ice, the winds of summer and winter, the wild flowers, the corn and cattle — all these were in his poems as were the prophets and peoples of the Old and New Testaments.

> *Now in the heart there is*
> *A sound, as if of song;*
> *Strange, muted melodies*

> *I hear all summer long.*
> *When Summer's emerald wings*
> *Feathers of silver show*
> *Something there is that sings*
> *Of hills beyond the snow.*

Tuberculosis   There was tuberculosis in the cabin — a scourge of many mountain homes in days gone by. Byron Herbert Reece almost died of it as a young boy. Later he was to know hospitals and weary days of illness, pain and despair. He had the mountain man's reticence, pride and an independence sometimes almost unreasonable in its assertion. It would come to him, suddenly, living in a hospital where he was doing well and his illness was being arrested, that he couldn't stand it any more. So, he would take his thin, wasted body off the bed, put on his clothes and go home.

He never knew much of joy or pleasure — but there was some. How great the measure of it was to him none will ever know. Not much money comes to poets. But honors had come, and were coming. The University of California had enjoyed having him teach in summer. The Guggenheim Foundation had discovered him. His own college, Young Harris, had him teach. And he kept a mountain farm going in one of the valleys. He had many close friends who knew and loved him.

Now, at 40, he is dead by his own hand. Illness had come swiftly for a month. His thin, sick body was racked with a nervous disorder. And so, with a favorite record playing in his ears, he went quietly to the God in whom he believed . . . a God of mercy and understanding.

His Mountains   He sleeps now in his mountains. He had written . . . years before:

> *I give my love to earth,*
> *   where I*
> *A longer, deeper sleep will take*
> *Than woken from when night is by,*
> *As I lie down to wake.*
> *To earth I give my love, my love;*
> *I give my love to earth to keep*
> *Against the time, with earth above,*
> *When I lie down to sleep.*

And from an unpublished poem sent in a letter:

Whatever season fawns or frowns
As I go lonely in the woods,
Or through the streets of stranger
*   towns,*
A ghost engages all my moods.
The ghost, that's strange to see
*   by day,*
A look half love, half cold as
*   frost,*
Ventures before it turns away.
A ghost is always something lost.

Now, the tall, thin man with the fine face and pained eyes is in the earth he loved, and understanding sadness sits in the hearts of all those who knew and loved him.

(June 7, 1958)

The "Drunk" Legends

It seems to me that it might be a good project for the Columbia School of Journalism to find one of the almost extinct species of newspaper drunks and arrange to have him stuffed and put on display when he has, as they say, written "30" to his last copy. The relatives likely would offer no great objection. And certainly, the young journalists of today and tomorrow would find the old character interesting, gracing their museum or, perhaps, standing silently in the waiting room of President Ed Barrett.

The search would not be easy. Most have died. Of the living, the worst addicted, after many jobs, have sobered up and are working at public relations, on weeklies or trade journals, and doing a good job, since most of them were extremely competent. They usually are bitter, somewhat vindictive men who tend to think that today's journalism is somehow soft. The most venomous of these came to sobriety on doctor's orders. Those whose path was A.A. have a philosophy which makes them attractive associates or friends.

Near Retirement   Here and there, however, in some corner of a city room one may find the old-time newspaper drunk, graying and full of reminiscences. He is near retirement. Management keeps him on because he was a good reporter and was maybe the hero of a great story or so. But there are not many of these.

They have added much to the legends of newspapering and are an inherent part of the laughter and the recollections of old days and of bizarre events. Somehow, one never thought much of their families. There must not have been much amusement there.

The movies helped augment and gild two false newspaper legends. One is of the reporter . . . who wrote better drunk than sober. The other is of the drunk who got the big story hours after being fired "for the last time."

There never was a drunk who wrote well drunk. The legend grew because the byline appeared over a sound story when the man was seen, or known to be, in a far-gone state of alcoholic haze. The big story came through; the football game, trial, or convention was covered. But the job was done by a friendly rival or associate who was sober.

Old Story   One of the oldest of newspaper stories is that of the news editor who began to receive story after story of a distant event. They were each different, each well-done, and each signed by his reporter's name. After the fourth, the news editor wired back, "Send no more. The fourth one can't be beat."

As for the second legend, it is almost as false as the other. There are, however, certain striking exceptions. Years ago a reporter, sleeping off a binge on the long padded seat in the patrol wagon parked beside the station, was carried directly to the body of a murdered girl when police answered a call early on Sunday morning. His paper got the exclusive on what was one of the great newspaper stories of that era.

Once, in Europe during the war, I knew a correspondent who attained temporary fame and a big bonus because he was sleeping off a drunk when a big story broke. He came to and learned it hours after all his competitors had filed their copy with the censor. He morosely re-wrote it and filed his own. The censor put it on top of the pile. When an over-worked security censorship crew reached them later they took the one on top first and it was cleared and cabled ahead of the others. The congratulations and the bonus set him off again, but his luck didn't repeat. He was soon called home.

This was when America was a hard-drinking country. It was especially so in its pioneer days and well into the 20th century. But today, America is drinking less and less, per capita. And newspapers aren't any happier about people coming to work drunk than banks or businesses. If Columbia likes the idea it will be necessary to move fast. "Time's a-wasting."

(October 3, 1958)

Bobby Jones; Ben Franklin

Certain notes on reading that Bobby Jones had been given "The Freedom of St. Andrews," the first American to receive this honor since Benjamin Franklin more than 200 years ago:

In the Year of our Lord 1930, when Robert Tyre Jones, called Bobby, systematically was destroying his opposition in the British Open, a despairing writer began his story with one of the great image-making leads of golf reporting:

"They wound up the mechanical man of golf today," he wrote, "and set him clicking about the course with never a falter in his magnificent precision."

It was a lead which sticks in the mind like a Scottish bur on tweeds but Jones was not a mechanical man. He suffered and bled. He often was so keyed up that he went to the clubhouse at the conclusion of a tough round and lost the contents of his stomach in the privacy of the men's room. He made errors and recovered from them heroically. He was an artist, not a craftsman.

But as the affection shown him in St. Andrews so eloquently illustrates, he was more than just a champion. He was very much the gentleman and the man. He was one of the great ones of sports' "Golden Age" . . . the twenties.

No Flaw   But of all the great champions of that gay and gaudy time, Jones was the only one without a single flaw of character or personality . . . the lone one without so much as a touch of clay in his feet. There was no phony touch about Jones, the champion, as there has been none about Jones, the man. He had no facade, no artificial smile or facial mask. He was never a Cafe Society man. His values were sound. He was never Puritan or prude, but always himself.

This was why the Scots liked him. They had seen golfers come and go across a great many centuries. They had their own pantheon of golfing gods. And when Jones appeared they knew him for what he was and placed him prominently in his own niche.

Once he appeared at St. Andrews with some duffer-friends, including Robert W. Woodruff of Coca-Cola. It intrigued Woodruff that within a half hour of their unannounced arrival several thousand enthusiastic Scots, their usual reserve broken by smiles, were following Bob Jones. For years Woodruff pestered all Jones' friends, and Jones himself, to put into words what quality it was that Jones possessed which made the Scots regard him with such spontaneous affection. It wasn't something one could put into words. But it was there . . . and is there yet . . . as events of the week have shown.

A Good Thing It is a good thing, in a way, that Bob Jones received the "Freedom of St. Andrews" now and not at the time when he was clicking his way about the course with such perfection.

"Freedom of St. Andrews" gives the right to hang one's wash on the land or to hunt rabbits about the course — a right granted to the owners and heirs from which the land was taken centuries ago to be made into a golf course. Had the honor been done in the old days, St. Andrews, without question, would have seen some of Bob Jones' linen hung on a line and rabbits would have been chased on foot through the bunkers and the rough.

Until Bob Jones was given the "Freedom of St. Andrews" no American save Ben Franklin had been so honored.

It was in February, 1759, that the University of St. Andrews conferred on Franklin, whose electrical experiments had made him famous, the degree of doctor of laws — the only title he ever had. The city, too, gave him its "freedom." The man who was to be the greatest civilian personality of the American Revolution had his closest friends in Scotland. Edinburgh made him honorary burgess and guild brother.

One has the strong feeling that Ben Franklin would approve this latest American to be given the "Freedom of St. Andrews".

(October 11, 1958)

Did You See Churchill Plain?

In the years ahead, among those who read history and think on the great names on its pages, there will be asked of the more aged, "And did you see [Sir Winston] Churchill plain?"

His American visit reminds us that this may well be his last. His step falters. The bugles are gone from his voice. His wit remains keen and his convictions are unshaken. But he is 84 and in the nature of things he will hardly pass this way again.

It will always be among my great joys that I saw him plain. Among them were two great moments of history, and another of great personal and emotional satisfaction to him.

I recall him first in 1938. That was the time of the Chamberlain government and appeasement. Britain had suffered a lot of dry rot in the years of Stanley Baldwin's premiership. And the waiter in Destiny's cafe was approaching with the bill.

Whenever there was news of debate I would go to the old, shabby, yet glorious House of Commons to hear Churchill speak. He was like a prophet of old.

He would stand and condemn the government for its neutral course in Spain. With visionlike clarity he said that this was a rehearsal for war, that new weapons and aircraft were being tested in new and daring tactics.

Jeering Laughter That was 1938. Yet I can hear as plainly as if it were an hour ago, the jeering laughter which ran through the benches. And especially do I recall the moments when Neville Chamberlain, that caricature of an Englishman, would arise, and reply. He would taunt Churchill in a light, immature and supercilious manner. It was smugness almost unendurable. Yet, the opposition benches would laugh and jeer, and cry, "Hear! Hear!" with voices dripping with irony and satiric emptiness.

I went many days. And I will never forget that Churchill, so soon to be vindicated by catasrophic events. I was quite prepared for the wartime Churchill.

I heard him in the House of Lords. A Nazi bomb, dropped by a bomber trained in Spain, had wrecked the House of Commons.

He was, of course, magnificent. It was almost as if the free men of the world hung on his words. Until we were brought in by the Japanese attack on us and Franklin Roosevelt began to speak with inspiring eloquence, Churchill's voice was the only one to defy the Hitler lie.

Full Story Not many know the full story of Sir Winston's great speech of defiance in the face of imminent invasion. He spoke over BBC and he said to the Nazis that the British would fight on the beaches and in the streets. It lifted hearts around the world. It has in it all the emotions of the Alamo, of Thermopylae and of all the great trumpet sounds of brave hearts in history.

But a man who was there said that when the speech was done Churchill turned wearily and said, "I don't know with what we will fight — our hands, I guess." His head drooped, but lifted. "But we will fight!" he said.

In 1954 I saw the gracious young Queen Elizabeth come home from her journey around the world. The next day, from a gallery in the House of Commons, I saw Churchill enter. He came in slowly. Yet the squat, square figure with the pink round face looked older than I recalled it. But then, I knew years had passed.

When it came his turn to speak he pulled himself up. But then he came alive. The old resonance was in his voice. It was the expected Churchill symphonic arrangement, with now and then a trumpet solo. His words purred. They rolled like summer thunder. They caught the ears, the mind, the imagination.

He extolled the young Queen, whom he loves as a daughter and reveres as a sovereign. He spoke of her as symbolizing constitutional government and freedom — and the sort of family life which British people most respect. He offered a resolution of loyalty and affection. It was a great, warming moment.

There were other sights of Churchill. But in these I saw him plain.

(May 10, 1959)

Did You Ever Dip A Tiger?

With Gov. Earl Long in and out of mental institutions and the Long political dynasty reportedly shaken by internal eruptions and ambitions, the name of Huey Pierce Long bounds back into the news.

Huey was much more entertaining and had arrogance and drama where brother Earl, always vulgar, is now merely pathetically amusing and frightening. There are many stories about Huey but the one I like best is about him and the Ringling circus, the LSU football team and the Louisiana tick law.

Huey took a great interest in the football team at Baton Rouge. He referred to it as "my team." He liked to put on a sweater and sit on the bench on Saturday afternoons, running up and down and showing off.

The Story The story is one told to me by Red Heard, then athletic director at LSU.

"One afternoon early the week before the game with Rice Institute," said Red, "Sen. Long came into my office."

"'Red,' he said, 'what sort of a crowd will we have Friday night?'

"Oh, we'll have a good crowd, Senator," I said, "but, of course, the circus will hurt us some."

"The circus?"

"Yes, sir. The Ringling circus is playing here Friday night."

"Who owns that circus? John Ringling, isn't it?"

"I think so, Senator."

The Senator stood there for a moment. He then picked up the phone. When the switchboard answered he said, "This is Senator Long. Get me John Ringling in Sarasota, Florida."

"Mr. Ringling," he said, "this is Huey Long. They call me the Kingfish of Louisiana and I guess you are the kingfish of the circus world."

Heard said the Senator laughed heartily and he assumed Mr. Ringling did, too. But that was the last time.

"Mr. Ringling," said Huey, "we've got a mighty nice little football team here at LSU and they play a game Friday night with Rice. Now your circus plays here that night. I'm going to ask you if you won't transfer it to the next night or the night before. We'll be happy to have you."

Mr. Ringling Red Heard said that Mr. Ringling apparently explained, patiently, that he really had nothing to do with the circus management, because Huey replied sharply:

"You own it don't you?"

John Ringling then explained that the circus itinerary was made out a year in advance involving railroad schedules, feed contracts, and so on. He would like to oblige Senator Long but, regrettably, it couldn't be done.

There was a pause, and Huey Long said:

"Mr. Ringling, have you ever heard of the Louisiana tick law?"

Mr. Ringling had not.

"Well, Mr. Ringling, that law requires that every animal entering the state of Louisiana be dipped in a vat and quarantined for two weeks. HAVE YOU EVER DIPPED A TIGER, MR. RINGLING?"

Mr. Ringling said he would call back. He talked with his lawyers. They told him that Kingfish Huey Long would surely enforce the law, making it necessary to dip all the elephants, tigers, lions, giraffes and hippos. The date was cancelled at considerable loss.

For years, the punch line was a classic. "Have you ever dipped a tiger?"

It was, to be sure, a funny story and people laughed about it. But when you examine into it, it isn't really humorous. A man with great power used it capriciously and pettily, at great cost to another citizen's property, just to gratify his own vanity and have his own way about a football crowd.

He was to use that power as ruthlessly in many other ways until, one night, a young man, whose family had been viciously slandered and abused by Huey, shot him down.

But Huey was in character all the way. "I wonder why he shot me?" he asked, just before he lapsed into a coma to await the coming of the old man with scythe and the hourglass.

(June 26, 1959)

The Georgias
And The Techs

History to the contrary notwithstanding, all roads today will lead to Athens, not Rome, as the Techs and the Georgias have a go at one another in their annual football Iliad of Achilles and Agamemnon.

It will be a day of wassail and wreckage, of screeching and screaming, of banshees and banalities, of gloating and groaning, of hurrahing and hemlock, of push coming to shove, of welkins ringing, of hills echoing, of going from the sublime to the ridiculous, of sorrowing and rejoicing.

It will be a day when gleeful pneumonia germs and vivacious virus strains will crowd into the stadium, seeking out the drunks who shed coats, thinking it isn't very cold, after all; creeping into the bodies of those who dress for show instead of warmth; settling happily upon those who didn't feel well enough to go to the game but went anyhow.

It will be a day when operators of automobile wrecking companies rub their hands like so many Uriah Heeps and smugly promise the little woman that, maybe after all, she can have that Christmas fur coat.

It will be a day when surgeons sharpen their knives; when operating room nurses put in extra supplies of ether, bandages and thread; when ambulance drivers check their gas and tires; when undertakers make sure the coffin stock is not too depleted.

It will be a day of toil for the State Patrol.

In short, it is the day when the Techs and the Georgias meet in the concrete mixing bowl on the ancient campus of the state university.

The Coaches   It will be rewarding now and then if the interested spectator, who can't follow the belly plays and the pitchouts very well anyhow, will give a little attention to the two coaches.

Mr. Robert Lee Dodd, the tall Tennessean, with the lean, expressionless face of an Andrew Jackson, is not quite as rewarding as is Mr. James Wallace Butts. The headmaster of the Techs walks about, wearing his battered "lucky" hat, and rarely permits any expression of pain or joy to move the muscles of his face. But, in moments of stress, he is worth a look. He looks fraught. He is somewhat reminiscent of a lonely crane wading in the dismal swamps looking for a scarce frog, as he walks up and down in the bog of despair, looking for a break.

Mr. Butts, on the other hand, is almost the Barrymore of the sidelines. His face reflects joy or despair. His muscles leap. If he sits, his legs jerk and flip as if some invisible physician were tapping him on the knee with an unseen rubber hammer, testing his reflexes. If he squats he plucks bits of dead grass and chews them. If he walks he is often humped like Atlas, bearing the world on his back. Now and then he may be moved to snatch his hat from his head and slam it to earth. He gives body English on end runs. He spirals with passes.

The Result   The summoning of substitutes; the whispered instructions; the suffering and joy of the players on the bench — all these are interesting to watch. And, in these days of faking, of pitchouts, the "keep" plays, and the various, fascinating tangents of the abdomen option, one seldom sees the ball anyhow.

As to the outcome of the game, the soothsayers, the able gentlemen with a crystal ball typewriter, have looked into its murky mists and seen the Georgias as winners of the game.

The records, of course, sustain them. And it is folly not to follow the form sheets.

Still, and all, footballs bounce.

And men get hurt.

The Techs, in one respect, are close to the edge of adversity. They do not have a passer to match the magic of a Tarkenton and his passes. The Georgias have the better balance in offense. But the Techs have Williams, Graning, *et al*, and all is not lost before the whistle blows.

Injuries and a capriciously careening football often make mock of form sheets. We shall see what we shall see.

(November 26, 1960)

Salute To Man At His Best

There is a line in Carl Sandburg's "The Family of Man" which says, "There is only one man in the world and his name is all men." And this is philosophically true.

But, for a few minutes after the historic blast-off of the Redstone rocket at Cape Canaveral there was, in so far as 180 million Americans were aware, but one man in the world and his name was Alan B. Shepard.

He left the world and returned to it. And that portion of it to which he came back was better because of him. He had not re-made it. He had solved none of its pressing international problems. But, he had transformed its spirit.

For a time he had been where the winds blow between the planets. When he had returned, it seemed, somehow, as if the rushing speed of these winds had blown away a miasma of failure, disappointment, frustration and doubt. His swift flight out of this world and his re-entry into it lifted up hearts and minds.

For a time on that day, the blood ran faster in all of us. For minutes in that hour there were no small or unworthy thoughts. There is nothing more noble than man at his best, and for awhile that morning, all that yearns within us to be useful and worthy of life was riding with the calm and prepared young man in the marvelously complex capsule machine which some men had conceived in their minds and others had wrought with tools.

"God has made man a little lower than the angels," the Psalmist sang, and when Commander [Alan] Shepard left the earth and returned to it again, we understood better the meaning of that sentence and something within us gave answer.

Let us salute, therefore, man at his best. He often is. But, rarely do we see him so magnificently presented with sky and space as a backdrop and all the hearts of his countrymen as his stage.

And let us salute, too, the Russian, Yuri Gagarin. Let us forget for the moment his politics and the cause he serves. Let us greet him, too, as a man who played well that role. Alan Shepard and he as individuals make us proud and enable us to understand there are many wonderful things in the scheme of God's creation, but the most wonderful of all is man.

Commander Shepard controlled his space craft. He, himself, used his brain and his training to explode the critical retarding rockets. He, too, had time to note that earth of land and sea and sun is beautiful. He also reported from space to earthlings far below that all was well, that the myriad of dials, valves, wires, pumps, compressors, batteries, and dozens of recording devices were functioning together in the manner of a vast mechanical symphony.

Preparedness   Alan Shepard was a prepared man, inwardly as well as outwardly. He knew what to do with each of the many controls before him. But this alone was not enough. Outside him was space. For a time he was free of earth's mysterious pull. He was weightless. God alone knew what was outside. The invisible forces which physicists and mathematicians chart were pounding at his capsule. Friction was heating its outer skin to a burning temperature.

Down on earth men and women were praying for him. It is a tremendous thing to leave the known things of earth and enter into unknown space, but there was no panic in him and no doubt.

And so it was that man and the mechanism made by man jointly left the earth and jointly returned to it for doctors and scientists to examine, and learn what they can for future and greater ventures into space.

There is a kind of healing in what Alan Shepard has done. We can hold up our heads again. He has cured the fevers of frustration. He has lifted up our hearts.

At such moments we can comprehend that man is an earthly man, but worthy of heaven.

(May 6, 1961)

Hemingway: Our Best!

Ernest Hemingway is dead in Idaho —

In early January 1945 I came into the dimness of the Scribe Hotel in Paris. The desk and the lobby were lighted by acetylene lamps, which hissed and flared, and made shadows in the corners.

The lift door opened at last but I did not get into it because Mary Welsh, whom I had not seen in a long time, came out. She looked very small and smart in a war correspondent's uniform.

"Come on down and see Papa," she said, "he is waiting down in the bar."

Ernest Hemingway, his beard, grown during the months he had been with the French Maquis, neatly trimmed, was waiting in a booth.

I said I was glad to see Mary, whom I had not seen in a year and a half.

"I am glad I do not have to wait that long," he said simply, and with no note of jest.

We talked a long time, about the war and what was going to happen to the world when it was done. The Battle of the Bulge was just then being cleaned up, and Hemingway was full of ideas about it. He was excited, too, about the underground troops with whom he had been fighting and observing. Later, I met one of his friends from that group and he told me, "He fights well, and shoots well. He is a brave one. We had our doubts when he came. But he is a brave one. He was never a burden to us, but a help."

It is this memory of Hemingway which I like best — in the unheated bar of the old Scribe — with the war still going on — and him talking of fighting, of brave men, and of being in love with Mary.

Violence Hemingway's death was violent. A 12-guage shotgun is not a minor weapon. But, it is not true that his life was violent. His preoccupation was with hunting, sports, bull fighting, and the fact that always, as man lives, he moves inevitably towards death. But he was, in a very real sense, a shy man. He did not suffer fools gladly.

It can be argued that contemporary American fiction begins with

Hemingway. There will always be controversy about him. He angered some because he did not write about ideologies or some other aspect of life other than, as they said, death and danger. But, he did write about much else, and if one looks for a drawing of morals, Hemingway drew more than almost anyone else, if one is willing to look for them. Some did not like it because his style, which was lean and pure, exasperated them. He did not follow all the rules.

In a letter of a few years ago, he said, in answer to a query, that when he began to write he only knew how to handle the first person. "I learned the third person over the long route," he said. "You'd think a teacher of English could figure that out . . ."

The Best   But, of all our contemporary novelists, he was the best. Certainly he inspired more imitators and caused the critics to get busy themselves with more pro and con essays than has any other of our novelists. Those who disliked him did so with such intensity they revealed their own spite. They would seize on some small bone of error or alleged weakness and gnaw at it for a dozen pages.

They could not do much to tear down the short stories or the novels, *The Sun Also Rises* and *For Whom the Bell Tolls*. But, when they got to *Across the River and Into the Trees* the hostile critics had a fine time. Perhaps it was not a great novel, but, it was a true one.

The Old Man and the Sea silenced even these critics.

Hemingway began to emerge in 1923. Even then he had that marvelous mastery of his form.

The world of books is much emptier without him and, one suspects, will remain so for a long, long time.

(July 3, 1961)

Grissom And The Fire Gods

It was the fire that held the eye . . .

A voice at Cape Canaveral finished a count and spoke the word ignition. Billowing smoke replaced the casual vapors. Fire appeared.

This took the eye.

Before that spoken word the mind had thought how like a graceful minaret the rocket looked, with the capsule atop it. How strange it would be, the imagination said, wandering uncontrolled in those uneasy, anxious, waiting moments, if a robed muezzin suddenly were to appear from one of the sealed apertures and begin to call the faithful of Islam to prayer. . . .

Slender, beautiful of line, it waited for the word and purifying fire.

Grissom was high above, strapped like a sacrificial offering to a ceremonial altar. The fire gods could consume him if they wished. In one roaring inferno of released flame they could have obliterated every vestige of him.

Everything depended on the fire. So, we watched. Here was Prometheus defying the gods and stealing fire from the sun. Here was the Zoroastrian god Ahura Mazda, the cosmic power whose symbol is the purifying flame that burns away the dross of life. Here was the fire of ambition, the fire of spirit, the fire of belief, the fire of life.

The Minaret It burned. The minaret lifted. Then one could hear the clean exulting voice of the consuming flame, singing its hymn to its kinsman, the sun. Prometheus was unbound, and in possession of the sacred fire. One felt almost like a pagan. For the moment it was necessary to believe in the power of fire.

So, we watched, like Parsees at a sacred ceremony. We looked on like Hindus feeding grain and butter to a sandalwood fire greeting a new life. We were the Greeks or the Romans looking on the eternal in the temple of great Zeus or Jupiter. We were a Christian community of the early church during passion week, seeing the symbolic new fire created from flint and steel.

"Burn fire, burn," the mind and emotions shouted. "Burn! Burn!"

The flame was the last thing the human eye could see. The sacrifice, strapped to the altar of the fire god, was living. Prometheus had stolen fire from Zeus in a hollow reed. Now Grissom was riding atop the symbol of that reed. Great Zeus' fire had lifted him out of sight. He was somewhere out in space.

Mind Runs We wait. The mind runs on. Somewhere on Siberian steppes, or deep behind the Urals, the Russians work with such weapons. In Red China, men toil to create them. Around the world ambitious men, greedy for power and conquest, yearn to possess them.

Aeschylus said it in 458 B.C., in the closing lines of "Prometheus Bound."

> Lo, in grim earnest the world
> Is shaken, the roar of thunders
> Reverberates, gleams the red levin,
> And whirlwinds lick the dust.
> All the blasts of the winds leap out
> And meet in tumultuous conflict,
> Confounding the seas and heavens . . .

We fire worshipers think of this. But, the voice of Gus Grissom, the grinning, confident man, speaks from the invisible distance which only three of the millions of earthlings have seen, and says the earth and sky are beautiful. Only Yuri Gagarin, Alan Shepard and Virgil Grissom have seen that beauty. It is somehow odd, and hopeful, that the mysterious wonder of earth and sky was what most impressed them.

If we could somehow inject their personalities and their joy of life, their ability to see beauty, into the politics of this world it would be, one believes, a better world.

One thinks this as Grissom, his fiery reed abandoned, comes back from sun to sea, and symbolically, moves to earth.

(July 22, 1961)

Virgil I. Grissom and two other astronauts were killed in a fire which destroyed their spacecraft on the ground, Jan. 27, 1967.

What Is The "Will Of God"?

Weary and worn ministers and priests, talking after their many visits to the families of the 106 [Atlanta] Art Association tour members killed in the flaming crash of their chartered jet which could not lift off the runway at Paris, reported that a heavy majority asked variations of one question: "Why does God allow such things to happen?"

Secondly, they said, many persons controlled their emotions, and said, helplessly through their tears and grief: "I know it is the will of God and so I accept it. But it is a hard thing to do."

Theologians are used to both the question and the despair behind the resignation to tragic accidents as being, somehow, the will of God.

Contradiction   Save for the fundamentalists, and certain of the more fervent evangelical sects, very few ministers and priests believe that God "Lets such things happen," or that they are a part of a divine plan, or, as the expression goes, "God's will." These attitudes, however sincere, reflect a contradiction which is inherent in the early "predestination" theory. This teaching insisted that everything is fore-ordained, and that man, in a sense, simply waits for what is sure to happen. The ancient Greeks gave to this seemingly inescapable aspect of man's fate the word "tragedy." We speak today of a Greek tragedy as being a situation in which man struggles against troubles and forces which are bound to prevail — no matter what he does.

The word tragedy means, literally, "The song (or cry) of the goat." It derives from the piteous bleating of the goat which is brought, bound, to be offered as a sacrificial prize. In some of the early dramas of tragedy, the central figure, fated to meet death no matter how skillfully or courageously he struggled against his destiny, wore a goatskin to identify, and symbolize, his role. Today, we employ the word tragedy rather loosely.

The old pagan philosophy carried over into the concept of pre-destination.

This is a contradiction in Christianity.

Man is born as a person of free will. He lives in a world in which there are natural laws. His life is lived in association with these laws. If a child loses its balance, gravity will cause it to fall. The child may be hurt, or killed in such a fall. If an aircraft is so heavily loaded it cannot use the laws of nature, it will crash. If the driver of a car employs all the horses in his engine and drives into curves at terrific speed, or surges into heavy traffic, he is sure to be hurt or killed and is likely to injure or slay others.

Are these events the will of God — or are they the willfull abuse of natural laws? Does God create man with free will and then deny him the expression, or use of that will, by foreordaining every act, small and large?

Free To Decide This is hardly a Christian concept. If man knew God's' will, man, being free to decide, would seek to make use of such knowledge and thereby subvert and destroy.

Man's journey through the maze of natural laws and his own acts, many of which are in hopeless opposition to natural law, is one in which he daily meets many so-called "turning points." He may be quite un-aware of most of them. Most of the time this journey turns out fairly well. At times there is disaster. Because of this we speak of "providence" or "Luck."

But the central "plot" of life's drama remains a mystery.

Accident does not depend on the presence of choice, or the existence of alternatives. An aircraft meets a storm which is produced by winds, heat, cold, and certain meteorological conditions. The plane has been taken up by a student pilot. He is unable to cope with the violent turbulence and is dashed to death. God's will? Hardly. Man is free to make decisions. God does not tie man to His apron strings.

The best theology maintains that if man has faith he will better steer his life. Man believes in a destiny chartered by God . . . but he and his daily acts are not predestined.

(June 5, 1962)

A Small Boy's Hurt Feelings?

Washington Notes: A psychiatrist who watched Richard M. Nixon's incoherent, confused and compulsive farewell and rebuke to the press, has said that it revealed one of the most commonly encountered disturbances of the psyche — the small boy yearning to be liked — and the feeling always of rejection.

Mr. Nixon, who is being treated most unkindly by California Republicans as they proceed to create a state organization which will exclude him, also is being subjected to analysis by the press of California. He chose to attack it. This was an almost incredible performance, since 100 per cent of the larger newspapers were for him, as was about 80 per cent of the others. Indeed, Mr. Nixon long has been the darling of about that same percentage of the nation's press. Most of the country's newspapers are Republican on their editorial pages. Yet, this somehow was not enough. Mr. Nixon apparently felt reporters did not take good care of him. They did not correct his errors and make him say what he meant to say.

The psychiatrist, commenting on this, said: "Here is another interesting revelation, akin to the first. Mr. Nixon seemed to be saying that he thought he should have had the best of it — that newsmen should have been kinder because, somehow, he wanted people to be kind to him, to like him; and their unwillingness to do so was wicked and wrong."

Volunteer Workers "In this connection," said the psychiatrist, "it is interesting to note Mr. Nixon also criticized his volunteer workers. The barb for them seemed almost an afterthought, he saying they had failed to get out the vote in important precincts. Here again, we had what many would call a revealing psychology of feeling rejected, let-down, or neglected. There was never any awareness of having failed himself. It is likely Mr. Nixon already rues his compulsive decision. Meanwhile, it has explained many things not heretofore understood about this unusually complex man."

Whatever the psychological reasons for the curious, almost frantic performance, it is odd he should have had a good word for television. It was television which really destroyed him. It was the television debates with President Kennedy which cut away the fat of the then-huge advantage which Mr. Nixon possessed at the outset of the 1960 campaign. Candidate Kennedy was very much the underdog. Television is, in a sense, a merciless instrument. If it does not tell quite all about the person on the screen, it comes near to so doing. The inadequate, pretentious, glib men who lack substance — all these are pitilessly presented. Richard M. Nixon never recovered from the very first of the TV debates with John F. Kennedy.

Error Compounded Mr. Nixon compounded the error by debating the incumbent Gov. Edmund (Pat) Brown. Mr. Nixon was the more polished, the more articulate. Gov. Brown was, in contrast, bumbling and groping for the right words. But according to the polls, the public sympathized with the governor because he seemed more the human being, and less the smoothly articulate, professional debater.

Mr. Nixon will remain perhaps the major post-mortem case of the election in which the Democratic party had such astonishing success. It is an examination which will go on for years to come . . . but the last picture is almost certain to be that of the final press conference . . .

(November 12, 1962)

Having convinced a majority of Americans that there was a "new Nixon" (see page 192), the subject of this column was elected President in 1968 and re-elected four years later. On Aug. 9, 1974, however, he resigned his high office in disgrace after his own secretly-recorded conversations clearly revealed that he had lied to the American people about his role in the unsavory "Watergate" scandal. Then, as earlier, there was no intimation that he was aware of personal failure.

They Still
Write About
Mrs. FDR

Washington Notes: Days of tensions and decisions have passed since all that was mortal of Mrs. Eleanor Roosevelt was buried . . . at Hyde Park. But it almost seems that the very fact of her moving from life into the mysterious silence of eternity has made the presence of her personality and life more real.

She was a very great lady. The measure of the affection held for her has astonished even those who knew it was substantial. In the hours after she had "slept away," (to use the words she cabled her sons when FDR died in April 1945), the first messages were from the heads of governments, from Queen Elizabeth, from Nikita Khrushchev, from ambassadors, governors, and the many who had come to know her and had vast affection and respect for her.

Other Messages   These messages were all but inundated in the flood that followed. The people who do not wire or cable, but who sit down and try to put their feelings on paper took over. They still are writing. Letters are coming in a steady stream from all over America — from all over the world. Some are semi-illiterate. Some are scribbled with pencil on cheap tablet paper. Others are in foreign languages or in the awkward phrases of writers who know little English. But each is trying to say what Eleanor Roosevelt meant to the writer.

Eleanor Roosevelt was a believing woman. She had faith. She was resolute. She had known sorrow, grief and loneliness. She had been the awkward, not-pretty young girl. She had married young Franklin Roosevelt. She had mother-in-law trouble. As a young wife with [five] children she was confronted, one day, with a paralyzed husband. She was to have other griefs and testings. She never broke.

Somewhere along the way she had learned that one must go forward and grapple with life — but one must expect to do so on life's terms — not one's own. Writing about her philosophy in her autobiography, *This I Remember*, Eleanor Roosevelt said of the need for facing life on its terms after the death of her husband:

> It is hard for me to understand now, but at the time I had an almost impersonal feeling about everything that was happening. The only explanation I have is that during the years of the war I had schooled myself to believe that some or all of my sons might be killed and I had long faced the fact that Franklin might be killed or die at any time. This was not consciously phrased; it simply underlay all my thoughts and merged what might happen to me with what was happening to all the suffering people of the world. That does not entirely account for my feelings, however. Perhaps it was that much further back I had had to face certain difficulties until I decided to accept the fact that a man must be what he is, life must be lived as it is, circumstances force your children away from you, and you cannot live at all if you do not learn to adapt yourself to your life as it happens to be.

The key sentence is: "This was not consciously phrased; it simply underlay all my thoughts and merged what might happen to me with what was happening to all the suffering people of the world."

The strength of this remarkable woman — as one better understands from the tributes paid her — is that she honestly lived the Second Great Commandment "Thou shalt love thy neighbor as thyself."

She took no special talents into battle. She did not speak well. But to people weary of perfunctory speakers, of glib bringers of "messages," and of bores and phonies in general, she was a person welcomed and acclaimed. She did go to see the misery of the South's sharecroppers and tenants in the depression years. She did speak strongly against the now generally admitted evils and abuses in a system of social segregation. Wherever injustice and people in trouble were, there she was also.

(November 15, 1962)

"Free Country, Ain't It?"

One of the attitudes which foreign persons notice about every American is a sort of built-in cockiness.

That's because he is free . . . and always has been.

As a child he grew up being told he was an American, a free-born American, able to look the whole world in the face and tell it where to get off. His papa and mama might cuff him around for being fresh, and later he had to be careful where the boss was concerned, but otherwise he could speak his mind — get it off his chest . . . make his beef . . . cuss the President . . . damn the courts . . . denounce the mayor . . . give the Bronx cheer to the chief of police . . . he was an American.

We are that way because of the Bill of Rights . . . the first 10 amendments to the Constitution. Not one in five Americans has read them.

"Me? I'm an American, see. Don't try to tell me where to get off. It's a free country, ain't it?

Much Harm The late Joe McCarthy and his ideological Birch-group heirs have done us a lot of harm.* They persuaded a great many persons that the way to remain free was to abandon the rights so carefully written by Jefferson, Mason and others — the rights which go with a trial by jury, the many rights of a defendant to be regarded as innocent until proved guilty. The miasma of fear and hysteria made us afraid of one another. We allowed this to happen because we weren't sure of ourselves. And there was a very real menace . . . communism.

Sen. Joseph R. McCarthy (R.-Wisc.) was condemned by vote of his colleagues in 1954 for contempt and abuse of, and for insults to, the Senate during investigation of his unsubstantiated charges of Communist infiltration into nearly every sector of American life.

Now we know we can't afford to be afraid of it. We must know it for an ever-present danger and we must oppose it with vigilance and courage. But it must now be plain that we can't win the fight with communism, which allows no individual rights, by giving up our rights. We can't win by becoming like any of the totalitarian states. We must make the idea of America — the American dream of freedom and liberty for the individual — come true.

The Constitution of 1787 did not contain a Bill of Rights.

It wasn't overlooked. A lot of persons wanted it in there.

But the framers of it said the rights had to come later. There was a good reason. Until the Constitution was adopted there wasn't any republic . . . So, the first thing to do was to ratify the Constitution which created a country, or republic.

Then they began to prepare the amendments.

They had something to go on.

Amendments   George Mason of Virginia some years before had written a Bill of Rights for his state. Mason's bill was not too different from the amendments finally adopted.

At first they thought they might simply rewrite the Constitution and weave the rights into it. But it was pointed out this would take forever. So they got the states to suggest what they wanted included.

These men had known what it was to live under tyranny.

They knew that men were arrested on trumped-up charges and that revengeful people often perjured themselves. So, they made sure a man, if arrested, had a right to know all about the beginnings of the accusation against him. They wrote in all the other protections of freedom of worship, speech and assembly. And, for that matter, of conscience. They guaranteed the right of a press to print the news and comment on it. They made secure the rights of a family in their home. They went to great lengths to protect the individual.

When they wrote that all men were created equal they didn't, of course mean they were equal in ability or knowledge or mentality. They did mean that in the United States citizens should be equal in opportunity and liberty.

A good idea would be for every family to get the Constitution and read the first 10 amendments out loud.

That will enable us better to understand some of the Supreme Court decisions. They gall us at times, but they remind us we do have rights which to lose is to destroy ourselves.

(April 11, 1963)

"Now I Know About The Guy"

It was 5:30 p.m., and the freeway traffic crawled. "You know what," said the taxi driver. "I found out what kind of a fellow the President is."

"You mean President Kennedy?"

"Yea, Him."

"Well, what do you think?"

"A good guy. I learned that from a newspaper picture."

"How was that?"

"It was that picture of him and the little girl, Caroline, ain't it, going to see the mother after her baby died. You see it?"

"There were several pictures."

"The one I mean was the President and the little girl walking to the hospital. She had a bunch of flowers in one hand. Her hair was done in a pony tail. With her right hand she was holding on to the President's left hand. The President, he was looking dead ahead. It looked like he was in a dream or something. And the kid, you know what she was doing? . . . she was kissing his hand. Wait a minute . . . I got it here."

A Clipping He reached in an envelope on the seat beside him that contained trip records and took out a folded newspaper clipping.

"This is it," he said, handing it back, "I cut it out of the paper." (The picture is a moving one. The President, tall and slender, is looking straight ahead, his face solemn and grief showing in it. The little girl, aged five, wearing a plain, simple dress and rubber-soled sneakers, was kissing her father's hand in a wordless communication of her love for him and of her child's inability to express herself in words. The picture almost certainly will win some of the major photograpphic awards for the news service man who made it. It caught, in the eloquence of clean simplicity, a scene which deeply touches the heart.)

"It's a fine picture. You going to keep it?"

"I look at it now and then. I got a kid about the age of this Caroline. I show it to some of my fares. You know, I'd often wondered about what sort of a fellow the President is. You see him and hear him in television. He speaks this New England talk and he is always so serious. Maybe this is because he has serious things to talk about. But, you wondered. Now I know. A fellow whose kid walks along with him at a time of sorrow and is kissing her father's hand — well, that lets me know the guy is all right. A kid don't feel that way about her father if he ain't all right. You can't fool a kid."

The Kennedys "I get fares in here and some of them open up on the Kennedys. They tell dirty jokes. And they cuss him and his wife. The well-to-do, they cuss him, about taxes. The ones that hate the nigra people, they cuss him, too. My old man is for him. He tells me they used to do that to Franklin Roosevelt. The rich ones seem to be mad because they ain't getting to keep it all and the others are mad about nigras. My old man told me just to keep in mind the guy is president of everybody. He takes an oath about that. Anyhow, I know, and I am just a driver, that he didn't start all this segregation thing. That's been around a long time. But, I'll tell you the truth. I had questions about him. He talks so proper. But that kid of his told me all I need to know."

"It's a great picture and it does tell you something about both of them — the President and the girl."

"Yeah. You got any little girls in your family?"

"No."

"You miss a lot."

"I guess that's right."

"You read where one day they took the dog to see the mother?"

"Yes, I read it."

"I liked that. I wish they'd had a picture. I didn't know about taking dogs. But this was an Air Force hospital and the rules ain't the same as other hospitals . . .

"The Chinese have a saying that one picture can tell more than ten thousand words."

"Yeah. That's good. That's what this picture did for me. It told me."

(August 23, 1963)

A Salute To 40 Years

Forty years ago a somewhat frustrated board of directors, of a then not-so-well-known soft drink company, hired the sales manager of a truck company to be president of The Coca-Cola Company, and it turned out to be the best thing they ever did. Today, representatives of foreign countries that quite literally represent all the world (save the Communist countries) are in Atlanta to salute Robert W. Woodruff, whose dream of 40 years ago they have helped come true.

Woodruff, himself, has become, for all his reticence, as much of a legend as the story of his company. He personally has given to hospital and public health work in Georgia and the City of Atlanta a great many millions of dollars as he and the company came along together.

It is largely due to him that Atlanta has become a medical research center in which a U. S. Communicable Disease complex is the heart. The

Emory Medical School and Grady Hospital are what they are chiefly because of his interest, generosity and indefatigable determination to see to it that his friends also were generous. Just how many young persons he had educated in colleges, universities, and art and music schools is not known, but the number is large.

Malaria A Killer   It is inconceivable to today's Georgians, for example, that just 30 years ago malaria was a killer and a scourge of south Georgia and neighboring states. It was a Woodruff idea and Woodruff backing that established [near] Newton [in Baker] County a joint Emory Medical School–U. S. Public Health research station in malaria. Within a few years malaria ceased to be a medical problem in Georgia and the South.

The truck salesman who came to sell soft drinks has been a valuable citizen in all areas of the city's development. Not much of his giving becomes public property. But it is safe to say his interest in the total development of Atlanta will endure. He once said, in a conversation many years ago, that it was difficult to give away money wisely. That he has managed to do it, and to accomplish it so that relatively few people in the city know about it, is a further tribute to his sagacity.

Robert Woodruff genuinely dislikes publicity, but one must be honest and say there also are practical reasons for it. Every time word of his philanthropy gets publicized he soon has to take to the tall timber to escape the flood of requests for unwise bequests.

Atlanta Native   Coca-Cola's Woodruff is, like his product, native to Atlanta.* Coca-Cola was invented and sold in Atlanta in May 1886. Only 25 gallons of syrup were sold that year. In 1919, an Atlanta syndicate purchased the company from the late Asa G. Candler. Today, there are operations in 125 countries and territories around the world. The largest bottling plant is in Buenos Aires. The second largest is in New York and the third in Mexico City.

As representatives of companies around the world join those of this country and continent to celebrate the 40 Woodruff years, the man being honored retains a sharp interest — but he leaves it to the organization he has created. At 73 he still tries to think about the day after tomorrow, instead of yesterday, and he believes the future belongs to the discontented.

Atlanta continues to be his home — and he will be around for a good long time yet, doing what he can to make it a better place.

(October 22, 1963)

*An Atlanta resident since 1893, Mr. Woodruff actually was born in Columbus, Ga.

Carl Sandburg Turns 88

On Carl Sandburg's 85th birthday his last book of poems, *Honey and Salt*, was formally "published" at a dinner given him in New York. John Steinbeck, but recently returned from receiving the Nobel Prize for literature, was one of those attending, and speaking. The bearded writer whose books are read "round the world" was brief:

"Carl," he said, "all of us could have learned from you and, thank God some of us have. Thank you for living."

Carl Sandburg has this month entered into his 89th year, and it is possible to say one can go on learning from him, and from Paula, his quiet, strong wife who is as wonderful as is he. In a way, Sandburg is a warm and human symbol of what we mean when we speak of the American dream, or of the particular genius of our invention — the pluralistic society.

Poor Background   Carl himself grew up poor. He shined shoes in a hotel barbershop and did the associated jobs of cleaning and polishing the spittoons and of sweeping floors. He was a hobo and a college student. He read ominiverously. He was slow to seize opportunity by the forelock. But he did graduate. He did give himself a sort of postgraduate study in bumming about the country, in writing, in observing, and in thinking. A broad streak of compassion and an awareness of pain, poverty, grief, and loneliness prevented him from even contemplating entering into the "establishment."

Once in 1951, we walked about Glassy Mountain, outside Flat Rock, North Carolina. The house in which the Sandburgs have lived for 20 years was built on the slope of that mountain about 1843 by Christopher G. Meminger, Charleston lawyer and later treasurer of the Confederacy. Meminger broke his heart and health trying to manage the worthless Confederate currency. We sat on the outcropping of a large shelf of stone and talked.

"I often walk here to be alone," said Carl. "Loneliness is an essential part of man's life and sometimes he must seek it out. I sit here and I look at the silent hills and I say, 'Who are you, Carl? Where are you going? What about yourself, Carl?' . . .

Loneliness   "You know," he continued, "one of the big jobs a person has is to learn how to live with loneliness. Too many persons allow loneliness to take them over. It is necessary to have within one's self the ability to use loneliness. Time is the coin of your life. You spend it. Do not allow others to spend it for you . . ."

Another time we sat on his front porch, which looked out on the tumbled foldings of the Appalachians. After a while, he recalled a story about Julia Peterkin, the South Carolina novelist. "Once she sat looking out a window of her room at the vista of the countryside. An old Negro woman came in. 'What are you doin', Miss Julia?' 'Writing . . . tryin' to write.' The old woman motioned to the scene outside. 'There's writin',' she said." Carl motioned toward the endless peaks and ridges, which were growing a deeper blue as the afternoon waned. "'There's writin'," he said.

His poems, and his six books on Lincoln, total some 30 volumes. One year, when he was at work on his one-volume Lincoln biography, he talked of Lincoln's education. "Salem," he said, "was Lincoln's university. There was a Dartmouth graduate there teaching school. He had books. There were a handful of Europeans there. They were educated men. Salem, for all its smallness, was a good university — better than any formal schooling that existed on the frontier. Salem was where the Lincoln mind was stirred and motivated."

Carl has stirred many Americans. Steinbeck was right to say that some of us have learned from him.

(January 10, 1966)

Honey And Salt

When Carl Sandburg was 85 his publishers, Harcourt, Brace and World, published what was the last book of poems to come from that wonderfully gifted and prolific man. It was titled *Honey and Salt*. These two are perhaps the most satisfying essences of life. There was a small dinner in New York to mark the occasion. His family, old friends, John Steinbeck and other writers, a Justice of the U. S. Supreme Court, and a variety of persons were there to do him honor.

His bearded brother-in-law Edward Steichen, whose photographs are admired around the world, and which still frustrate cameramen with modern marvels of lenses, light meters and filters, talked briefly.

He recalled a day in 1908 when his young sister, Lillian, told the family that the next day a young man was coming to call on her. His name was Carl and, said Lillian, he had told her he was a poet. She had taken his word for it, said Steichen. Nothing had been published. The mother was excited, the father glum. "I could hear him thinking," said Steichen, "My God, another long-hair. He will never be any good around the farm." It was decided between his sister and the mother, said Steichen, that poets were always hungry and underfed. So chicken was vetoed. A turkey was selected. The daughter drove a horse and buggy to the railroad station and fetched Carl home. A few months later there was a wedding.

Death   Lillian Paula Sandburg, almost 60 years his wife, was with Carl Sandburg when, after long months of illness, the weary heart stopped. News of his passing brought back memories of the man and his writings. One of his early poems is called "The Junk Man." Sandburg wrote that God saw Death and gave Death a job of taking care of all who are tired of living.

> When all the wheels in a clock are worn and slow and the connections loose,
> And the clock goes on ticking and telling the wrong time from hour to hour.
> And the people around the house joke about what a bum clock it is.
> How glad the clock is when the big Junk Man drives his wagon
> Up to the house and puts his arms around the clock and says: "You don't belong here."

At Connemara farm, on Glass Mountain, out of Flat Rock, North Carolina, Carl wanted the family to be happy when the Big Junk Man came to get an old worn-out clock and say to it, "You don't belong here."

There are so many memories:

The late Ed Murrow liked to tell how, shortly after the conclusion of his broadcasts, the phone would ring. There was always an identical message in the deep, organ-like voice:

"Ed, this is Carl. Whatever there is wrong with the world you ain't it. Goodbye."

In the summer of 1959 Steichen's majestic views of humanity, "The Family of Man," was one of the featured showings at the American exhibition near Moscow . . .

Volunteer   Near the Steichen pictures, for which Carl Sandburg had written the captions, was a small, quietly beautiful grove of aspens. There were a few benches there and some statuary. Late one afternoon it was my good fortune to sit resting and talking there with the two of them. Russians who could speak no English would see Sandburg and Steichen and come slowly across to shake hands, to smile and beam their pleasure. We talked of man's hopes and of home and the old place called Connemara.

"Mr. Steichen," I said, "I want you to know that I love your sister."

"You will have to take that up with Carl," he said.

Carl patted my knee. "It's all right," he said. "I've been in love with her since 1908."

Sandburg was very proud of having been a member of Company C, Sixth Infantry Regiment of Illinois Volunteers in the Spanish-American War. In 1963, when he stepped forward to receive the Presidential Medal of Freedom from President Johnson in a White House ceremony, he threw a snappy salute, and said, "Private Sandburg, of the 6th Illinois Volunteers reporting, sir."

One day . . . he said . . . "One of the most important things a man can learn is how to be alone . . . Man must have hooks inside himself on which to hang things he can take down and use when he is lonely . . . the knowledge, philosophy and escape from self found in books, in music, in the ability to see landscapes, trees, the sky. Man need never be afraid of being alone . . ."

Sandburg liked simple things . . . wheaten bread, goats' milk cheese, a deep, redripe tomato, a glass of wine, conversation, the talk of books, people, and life simply and faithfully lived.

(July 24, 1967)

Man For All The World

FLAT ROCK, N. C. — As the family cars left the two-story white clapboard house where Carl Sandburg had lived since 1945, on the way to the church . . . where the last rites for the internationally loved poet and biographer were to be said, the front car halted. Edward Steichen, brother-in-law of Sandburg, whose photographs have been shown in more than a hundred nations around the world, climbed laboriously from the car. He walked to a nearby pine tree and cut from it a large twig and then returned to the car.

The procession moved on down the long winding road, built in 1843 when Christopher Gustavus Meminger came from South Carolina along with family and friends to establish a community where they might live in summer and escape the miasmas which they then thought produced the dreaded yellow fever. Pine trees, firs, and great poplars and oaks grow thickly along the way. Through them could be seen the ocasional juttings of some of the huge stones of the Appalachian chain, which thrust into North Carolina and adjoining states.

We came at last to the church of St. John in the Wilderness. It, too, was surrounded by the huge trees with plantings of dogwood, rhododendron, and boxwood adding further to the beauty of its surroundings. The parish is an old one. It was established in 1836.

It was a family funeral, with only a few friends added. As we entered the church, Steichen left the group and walked forward to where the coffin stood covered with the cloth pall of the church. He placed the twig of Connemara pine atop the pall and then walked regally back to his seat in the pew between Mrs. Steichen and Mrs. Sandburg. The Episcopal diocese had lent the church to the Sandburg family for the service.

The service was conducted by the Rev. George Tolleson, a Unitarian clergyman from Columbia, S. C., who is spending the summer near Flat Rock. The service was non-sectarian, and all present regarded it as most solemn and fitting. There was an occasional smile as we remembered Sandburg, his simplicity, and his feeling for humanity. The readings from the pulpit were from Sandburg's poems and from Whitman. In one of Sandburg's brief poems, called "Finish," he had written:

> *Death comes once, let it be*
> *easy . . .*
> *Sing one song if I die.*
> *Sing John Brown's Body or Shout*
> *all Over God's Heaven. Or sing*
> *nothing at all, better yet.*

Low Singing So after the reading of this poem the organist played "John Brown's Body" and some few of us joined in a low singing of the old song which Sandburg thought one of the most rousing tunes in American history. There were more readings. There was one which concludes, "There is only one Maker and all of His children are God's children." The minister looked toward the organist and she played a few bars of "Shout all Over God's Heaven."

There was no eulogy, but the poems were eulogy enough. The minister read them well and those in the ancient church sat enchanted with a feeling of happiness and assurance that all was well with Carl Sandburg.

After the service Carl Sandburg's body was sent along to a distant city to be cremated. The ashes later will be buried or scattered in Galesburg, Ill., where Sandburg was born in 1878. A public memorial service will be arranged and held some time in the fall in Chicago. Sandburg's first published poems were his famous ones dealing largely with Chicago and the great prairie country. He was a man for all the world, and so it seemed here today in the quiet little church tucked away among the trees and flowering shrubs of western North Carolina.

(July 25, 1967)

Scarlet Letters Out-Of-Date

Aspen Institute for Humanistic Studies — A tentative assumption about the American society of the future is that it will be one in which the moral emphasis will shift from activistic striving for more power and possessions toward what we ambiguously refer to as the life of being. This would mean a shift from a culture of acquisitiveness toward a culture in which there will be a better balance and satisfaction growing out of creative development in all dimensions of life.

Participants here in a seminar discussion on morals and ethics think that this will come about because the population grows more young with each year. By next year, it is expected that 50 per cent of all Americans will be 30 years old or younger, and by 1972, 50 per cent will be perhaps 25 years and younger. Such a change will, if it comes about as anticipated, create conflicts between technology and the market place on one hand and the orientation of a younger American society toward the "traditional seeking of man for a better life" on the other.

Moral Concepts   There is a growing belief, for example, that perhaps Americans are not as immoral or as lost in sin and materialism as the Jeremiahs would have us believe. Moral concepts, the group values of what is wrong and right, come to us out of the most ancient times. The sources have been varied. Tribal chiefs, patriarchs, prophets, high priests, the Greeks, and others handed down concepts of ethical and moral systems.

The Victorian era is the one which Western civilization looks to as having formulated and applied precedents of morality and ethics which still persist in the minds of many in this country and Europe. Yet, there is general recognition that enforcement of these standards was largely by fear and the most severe religious austerity. Fear of hell, fear of the loss of one's soul, fear of burning fires — these and other fears were a part of the great evangelical developments in the 80s, 90s and the early part of the present century.

These fears are replete in the history of the times and in the diaries and writings of individuals. Gossip in a small town was, for example, a great influence on restraining the lives of the inhabitants. Fear of what the neighbors thought was a powerful force.

Big City Growth   The present growth of big cities in which man is anonymous if he chooses to be is but one of the several factors which have reduced many of the old values to absurdities.

Hester Prynne, the historical character in *The Scarlet Letter*, was exposed and convicted by neighborhood gossip. She was branded with the letter "A," which she was forced to wear embroidered on the bosom of her dress. Gossip continues to brand some young ladies in small towns with this symbolic letter, but in our larger cities one rarely sees young ladies branded with an "A."

The diaries of Michelangelo are replete with his expressed fears of going to a fiery hell. Diaries of individuals in the American frontier and the 1890s also express these fears. All of them reveal there is a vast difference between being careful and being good.

It was about 40 years ago that the South was described as the Bible belt. Participants here from Southern universities report that up to about 10 or 15 years ago a basic influence in the enforcement of moral values current at the time among students was the church and religion. They now say this is no longer true. Students seem to be trending more toward humanistic Christianity and humanistic values than ever before. They will have a large part in the revolutionary social changes ahead.

(July 26, 1966)

Linda Refused Guilt Burden

In Phoenix, Arizona, a father and mother have been charged with involuntary manslaughter in connection with the suicide death of their 21-year-old daughter, Linda.

Linda's death surely is a new and challenging exhibit in today's multitudinous cacophony of comment by religious dogmatists about morals, sin, parental discipline, reponsibility of parents, influence of the home, love, generation gap, and so on.

Linda, 21 years of age and divorced, went to a dance. She spent what remained of the evening following the dance with an Air Force officer. On her return home she informed her parents where she had been.

The father is the one who comes most clearly through in the relatively meager reports. It was he who telephoned the officer after his daughter's frank statement and demanded that he marry the daughter. The officer, unhappily for such a suggestion, was already married.

What followed was, in many respects, right out of a psychiatrist's or psychologist's textbook. Daddy was determined his daughter must feel guilty about something. Since she was not remorseful about having spent an evening with a married man, daddy had to find some way to make her put on the hairshirt of guilt. (He was quoted as being determined to make her "sorrowful.")

Daddy's Idea   So, daddy had an idea.

Linda loved her dog. (Maybe it was the only thing she had met who gave back the gift of love.) Daddy's decision was to "make" Linda kill her dog. She would then feel guilty about that! He got his pistol. He required Linda to come with her dog to a site a hundred yards from the house. He thereupon handed Linda the pistol and ordered her to shoot the dog she loved.

Linda took a look at the dog and at daddy and immediately shot herself in the head. She was dead minutes later.

She had escaped one grief at any rate — and had left daddy with the responsibility and burden of taking on guilt.

One puts down an impulsive reaction that Linda was well off out of reach of her loving moralist father, who was determined that his daughter had sinned and, come hell or high water, must feel guilty about it. Psychologists, amateur and professional, will wonder if there is not a somewhat obvious explanation why Linda, at 21, was a divorced woman. The psychologist would wish to know if she took one of the first young men who asked her just to get away from home. Was not Linda, at 21, with the grief of an impossible marriage, entitled to live her own life?

No Answers   There are no answers to these speculations — and will not be. Daddy was arrested on a charge which may or may not hold up. What the mother thought was not reported in the wire service stories. Daddy was, apparently, the "deus ex machina" who, in the manner of gods in the ancient dramas, intervened in the second act of Linda's life.

Linda, aged 21, divorced and unhappy, is dead. She did not think she had "sinned." She refused to be "sorrowful." There had been one chance to live her own life and it was halted by divorce. Standing there with the gun in her hand, her dog tied before her, and daddy nearby, she apparently thought there would never be a second chance.

If there are those who insist on "sin," then who was the greatest sinner — daddy or Linda?

Who was the more immoral — in the broad meaning of that word rather than the narrow interpretation daddy had put on it? Will Linda "go to hell" or is there a deity of compassion and mercy who regards someone else responsible for Linda's divorce and night out?

Who will explain the stern and overly self-righteous who would impose on all persons a sense and burden of guilt?

(February 14, 1968)

The Kennedys:
Style and Guts

When Senator Edward Kennedy, aged 36, strode to the pulpit in the hushed sanctuary of St. Patrick's Cathedral to begin the service of his murdered brother [Sen. Robert Kennedy], the solemn silence, with the aroma of burning candles in it, seemed to deepen.

His words reached clearly to the great exit doors:

> The answer is to rely on youth, not a time of life but a state of mind, a temper of will, a quality of imagination, a predominance of courage over timidity, of the appetite for adventure over the love of ease . . . My brother said many times, "Some men see things as they are and say why. I dream things that never were and say, why not."

The silence was broken here and there by muffled sobs and whispered words. One of the mourners said to a friend seated by him:

> By God, you will live a long time and not see anything to match that. There may not have been more in his mind than his tribute. But do not fail to see what else it was.

A Reminder Ted Kennedy was reminding us that the Kennedys have the guts and they have the style. And he was saying, too, that the Kennedys are still here and that more are coming on. There is young Joe—just 15. He acted like a Kennedy when he helped take his father's casket off the plane from California—and here as a pallbearer. There is no mystique about the Kennedys as some of the critics keep saying. They just have the style to say what they believe, and the guts to die for it if they must.

Until there is a Kennedy decision, speculation as to the future of Edward Kennedy, youngest and last of four young brothers, will not be silenced.

Certainly he would be a dramatic addition to create a Humphrey-Kennedy ticket. It almost certainly would win in November.

The somber mood of some of the old Irish Mafia — those who started with young Jack Kennedy — want Ted Kennedy to go for broke — to plunge in now and try for the Democratic nomination sought by his brother. He will hardly do that.

There is yet another force — some of it coming from close friends and the ranks of his church's clergy — who love the Kennedys. They want him to retire from politics and to head up the family.

Still others hope, he will remain on as Senator — an office likely his as long as he wishes to offer for it.

Another Possibility   The writer recalls a visit to Senator Edward Kennedy when he lay with a broken back in a Boston hospital following a plane crash.

[He] had books on finance, taxes and Senate tax bills on a bedside table. The visitor knew the Massachusetts Senator Kennedy had been interested in foreign relations. He asked about the new study.

"Well," said Senator Ted Kennedy, "You know my brother's major interest is foreign affairs. So I am going on the finance committee."

"But," replied the visitor, facetiously, "you are senior to him in the Senate. Pull your rank on him."

The younger senator brother smiled and said, "I suppose I could. But in our family we always give way to the elders."

Political realism requires thinking about the vice presidential nomination for Senator Kennedy. Certainly President Jonson, the Vice President and others in the party's closest councils have thought about it.

But whatever it is, nothing changes the fact that when young Edward Kennedy stood there in old St. Patrick's Cathedral, his eulogy to his brother was also a reminder that the Kennedy breed, with its style and guts, is by no means extinct.

(June 18, 1968)

An Essay on "Separation"

On the morrow Eugene Patterson, for almost a decade editor of *The [Atlanta] Constitution*, will assume new duties as managing editor of the *Washington Post*. John (Reg) Murphy, as previously announced, will succeed him.

One of the more comforting and reassuring endorsements of the individuals and papers involved came from Georgia's Governor Maddox. The governor said, somewhat sadly but confidently, that he was sure Mr. Murphy would carry out the same liberal policies as those of the publishers and Patterson. We do very much hope, in expressing appreciation, that the governor, in affirming this belief, was tuned in to his oft-advertised source. None of us would wish him to be in error.

One hesitates to write of separation from a person one has long held in affection and respect lest the result appear too much like an obituary. That this should be a problem is not surprising since, psychologically at least, any separation is something of a death. But Gene is not really going away. He still is in the craft of newspapering. He had been thinking, and talking, for some time, out of the restlessness that was in him, of one day going on to some other job in search of what might be called fulfillment.

Fulfillment   Some writer has said that life is a patchwork quilt that can never reach fulfillment, and there is truth in that sentence. But, it is in man to keep trying, or wishing, for fulfillment of what he conceives to be his abilities and reach. This, I think, is a more powerful urge for many men when they reach their mid-forties and, in their reflecton of the years that are gone, are often spurred to hasten with the business of lengthening the patchwork quilt of life. Gene has gone to one of the nation's great papers and Murphy, we feel, has come back to one. Each can be made better and that is a part of man's wish to fulfill himself.

Gene and I, despite the gap of years between us, had the rare gift of being able to talk with one another in the full meaning of that word. We could talk philosophy, ethics, morality, books, poetry, history, men and meanings. This was true before the time he came to the paper as editor at the time I was given the title of publisher. We both were thrilled with the long history which the newspaper now has extended into its second century. The staff, too, thinks of this history, its traditions and policies. The old pictures, the old stories, and the old papers add a sentimental leavening to life and work.

Beginnings   He and I often would talk about ourselves and how we had put our feet in paths that brought us together in person and also in the intangible but important values of life, attitudes, and so on. He was born on a small farm in South Georgia near the progressive small town of Adel. I was born on a farm hard by the Tennessee river some 8 or 10 miles "out from" Soddy, Tennessee . . . not too many miles from the Georgia line. (A saying of old Soddy boys and girls, in answer to an inquiry as to where Soddy might be, is that it is a mere three miles from Daisy.)

Each of us had had a struggle to acquire what education we possessed. We each had held student jobs, had little spending monies, rarely owned more than one suit of clothes at a time, and so on. He had come out of the army of the second world war, in which he was a decorated commander of tanks under George Patton, and had sought out a newspaper for a job. I had gone back to school after the first world war and taken an afternoon copyboy job on a paper in Nashville, where I was in Vanderbilt university. Despite these widely separated paths, life had brought us together in affection and mutual respect. We enjoyed this. Sometimes we wondered about it as we worked as we said, to keep the light burning in editorial windows so that all wandering sinners might return and the Philistines be more able to see.

So, though Gene has gone on to Washington, we count him still with us in faith and spirit. We shall watch his career with confidence and admiration and feel no "separation."

(September 29, 1968)

Testimony Of The Old Days

Let us have a preamble:

On November 22, 1968, an old woman died in the Central State Hospital, Milledgeville, Ga. She was 90 years of age. In an old ledger, its pages yellowed with the slow passing of years, was this entry. "Lunatic, from Bibb County. Age 19. Baptist, Violent toward mother . . ."

So, Annie Lee W., young "lunatic" who was hostile toward her mother, entered the lunatic asylum, as the institution was then called.

She was just 19 . . . a country girl from a rural county. She and her mother did not get along. The yellowed pages do not say why. There is only the entry in the old ledger. It was easy then — a bit easier then than now — to railroad a troublesome person into the lunatic house. How hostile was Annie Lee? What sort of person was Mama? Did she try? Did she deserve to be honored by her child? We don't know.

Annie Lee's mother got even — that we know.

In all the years she was there — young girl, young woman, middle-aged, and old — not one person ever came to see her. Not once was there an inquiry about her. No visitor came — no mother, no father, no relatives. They put Annie Lee W. away. She had been hostile toward her mother. So, they got even.

A Record Annie Lee set a record. She was in the lunatic house for 71 years — with not one visitor. When she was an old woman, doctors said she was schizophrenic and beyond help.

But, as an afterthought and guess, the doctor said that even in the years when she was committed, had family kindness been shown, her "chances would have been better." But in October, 1897, nothing was known about schizophrenia. If a child was hostile to her parents, that was meanness showing and such a person must be crazy — not to love mama. The Bible, commands it . . . "Honor thy father and thy mother . . ."

And if they don't, beat 'em 'til their nose bleeds — kick some sense into them, or put them in the crazy house. In nearly all lunatic houses — or crazy houses, as they were called in the good old days — directors will tell you, are many persons who are there because they are unwanted. There are old people who are in the way and expensive. And there are others who are maybe alcoholics or schizophrenics who had available no out-patient health clinic care.

Sense of Guilt   Somehow, Annie Lee W., dead at 90, with not a single visitor in almost three quarters of a century, makes one rage against those who treated her so and then confessed their sense of guilt by never going to see her.

"The good old days" had fewer people and fewer cities. But they had no more morality than the crowded world of our time.

Nor did they have more parental love or kindness than now. There was a harshness to life in the good old days that evolved from a lack of knowledge of health, sanitation, medical skill and a total absence of any conception of mental health.

The mistreatment of mental prisoners in the early years of our civilization, in this country and Europe, is too horrible to delineate. Many lunatic asylums were open on Sunday to visitors who could walk through and laugh at the antics of the crazy ones. Chaining the more disturbed persons was commonplace.

A reporter asked of Annie Lee — "Could she have been saved by better treatment?"

"We will never know," said the doctor, honestly.

Annie Lee may have been a schizophrenic at age 19. But she may have been a sensitive child in a home where mother was the one who was really the "lunatic." We will never know.

One confession remains. Those who put Annie Lee there never came to see her.

What about mental health programs in your community?

(December 3, 1968)

CIVIL RIGHTS

Ralph McGill was in London when he received news of the 1954 Supreme Court Decision *Brown vs. Board of Education*. He knew instantly that the South was about to enter a new era. He knew it would mean facing up to a legacy of neglect. In a column printed in 1953, "One Day It will Be Monday," he had correctly predicted the ultimate outcome of the historic case being considered by the court at that time.

Throughout the effort to give black Americans an equal chance at the American dream, Ralph McGill was on the front line, with reason, with calmness and with strong statements of moral truth.

In the 1940s, he portrayed hate mongers and rabble in "Men Who Shame our State and Flag" and "The Yellow Rats of Unadilla."

In the 1950s, while he tried to guide public opinion along a productive course, he could become outraged at

95

callous acts of lawlessness. This is evident in "A Church, A School" written in 1958, which won him a Pulitizer Prize.

Throughout the rest of his life, Mr. McGill continued to write of man's obligation to man. The columns here selected provide a moving journey through thirty years of struggle.

The Criticisms Coming To South

WASHINGTON — Those Southerners who resent what generally is termed "outside" interference," and I often think some of it is harmful and stupid, might just as well prepare to make the most of it. Or best of it.

We with our lynchings and our politics are a national story. We will continue to be. It is not at all a question of whether we are right or wrong or what traditions we advance as unassailable. The fact remains that about all the others States regard us as a news story.

They are going to continue to examine us critically. I am all for that. It will make us think and it will cause us to examine with our own criticism those institutions, customs and traditions against which most of the "outside" criticism is directed. Self-examination always is helpful.

There will be some fools, sensationalists and unwholesome propagandists among those who come and there will be those with sincerity and intelligence. It will be [the former] who attract the most attention and it will be they who will muddy the waters of fact because always their charges are shoddy and lacking in factual support. They usually are vulnerable and at best half truths, easily refuted. The resentment they arouse is so proper and so inevitable that it makes it difficult for the sincere critic to make a point. But, they are coming. . . .

There is murder and violence in other sections, including gang warfare, but it never quite takes the turn of our lynchings which, for downright brutality and barbarism, matches anything evil ever designed in the mind of debased people. . . .

In the rural sections . . . the people know what it means to have lawless bands on the loose. Burned barns, houses, and ambush killings accompany lawlessness. The people don't want it and won't have it.

But, that doesn't remove national horror and curiosity. We are a story, whether we like it or not. And, while the rest of the nation has its share of crime, ours is different and it too often is un-American.

So the critics are coming. I don't like it either. I will resent the fools who come with their silly questions and their weak articles and comments.

The sincere, intelligent critic we should welcome.

Morality   We in the South cannot cry "let us alone." What we must do is busy ourselves lest we allow our resentment at being a news story [to] throw the moral weight and indignation of the nation and world against us.

We did that with slavery 85 years ago. No matter who started the trade in human beings, the fact remained that a few states ended up with them and opposed every measure to end slavery by federal payments to owners.

We resented outside interference and we formed a new nation and stubbornly made slavery the keystone of our arch of government.

From that moment on the moral weight of the nation and the world was against us. The workers in the British spinning mills were willing to go unemployed and hungry rather than spin the cotton brought through the blockade. There was a revulsion of feeling against us which quite overshadowed every just measure we proposed or sought.

It is evil and it is fundamentally wicked and wrong to fly in the face of humanity and of divine laws and preachments. We cannnot afford to do it. We cannot make intolerance and murder the keystone of our society without destroying it.

So, with more than 40 of the nation's 48 states looking at us with fear and wondering, with our deeds recited to the nations of the world who join in condemning them, we cannot expect not to have outside curiosity and interference.

We have said to let us alone and we would do the job.

We have not done that job. Shall we have the moral courage to do it or not? A lot of Americans want to know.

(August 3, 1946)

A Tradition Is Badly Treated

In a way you can feel a certain pity for the Kiwanis Club of Ahoskie, N. C.

It was engaged in an illegal enterprise, to wit, a lottery. The lottery was to raise money for a welfare fund and the prize money was a big green Cadillac.

Tickets were sowed down pretty thickly, in drugstores, grocery stores and any other place where a chance taker might appear with a loose dollar with which to take a chance.

The tickets plainly said, "You do not have to be present."

The tickets were all sold. The money was in hand. The big dance was on. A pretty girl, vocalist with the orchestra, was blindfolded and drew out the ticket.

So far all was merry as a wedding feast.

But who held the winning ticket? He was not present.

The search was made.

Shabby From then on the story becomes a shabby one. I don't think what subsequently happened would have happened anywhere else, in Mississippi or Georgia, even, where the record is not too good.

They found that a Negro tenant farmer, a veteran of the war, held the ticket. Other tickets had been sold to Negroes, since the club was out to sell as many tickets as possible. And — they wouldn't give him the car.

They took back his ticket and gave him his dollar, and asked all the others of his race who had bought tickets publicly offered for sale to come and get back the money the club was so eager to get.

It was just a shabby, unfair deal and you can feel a little sorry for the Kiwanians of Ahoskie, because they know in their hearts it was a shabby, unfair deal. The nation knows about them now, as having done a litttle and mean act. Before it is finished the Ahoskie Kiwanians will wish they had given the winner the car and filled it up with gas for him. They probably are very good people who now are sorry, but who will go on defending a mistake.

I imagine the Kiwanis International headquarters will feel like taking away the charter of the club. And there must be thousands of Kiwanians who will resent their club being advertised so adversely by men who were so thoughtless and so lacking in a sense of fairness to their own community.

Effect In one sense, the effect of this is considerably worse than a lynching in its net result for the South.

Almost everywhere there is a realization that lynchings grow out of violence and are done by a lawless element.

But one may be sure that the Russians, the British, the French and all the peoples of the earth who hear radios and read newspapers will learn that the leaders of one community in the South, themselves engaged in lawlessness, were not good sports enough to let the winner of their lottery win on a legitimately purchased ticket, simply because he was a Negro. The Russians will make much hay with it and there isn't any answer.

They will learn, too, that he served in the Army of his country, and they will simply not be able to understand the action of the region that produced the act.

Tradition There can be no claim of violating traditions. The holder of the ticket didn't have to be present. It was so stated on the ticket itself. The winner was at home in bed when the Sheriff — and that was a bad touch, too, to take the Sheriff along — awakened him. The

Sheriff, had he been doing his full duty, would have been locking up the lottery operators. There wasn't any reason for the Sheriff except the guilty consciences of the lottery operators. The only tradition was the tradition of fair play.

No Excuse   The South just hasn't got an excuse for this one. And there isn't one that can be dreamed up. Even the worst of the anti-Negro set won't go along with Ahoskie people on this one.

Mr. Rupert Massey's statement, as head of the club, that "We've tried to be fair," is amusing, or would be, if it were not obvious he really is trying to sell himself on the idea that he was fair.

This is something the South itself can't explain or understand.

It will get an airing all over the world and the net result will be bad. It is so senseless and so unnecessary, in addition to being in bad taste and in poor sportsmanship.

The damnyankees and the "outsiders" didn't have any part of this. This was something the South did all on its own.

It makes every fair-minded, honest person ashamed.

I wish Southerners would quit knocking themselves out and leaving the gate open for the critics to drive in.

We asked for this one — as we so often do.

(Editor's Note: Late Wednesday, hours after the writing of this column, the word came that acting under a stinging rebuke from Kiwanis International offices, the Ahoskie club had voted to give the poor tenant farmer veteran a car, but didn't know how it would get the money or the car. The damage was done by the original stupid decison.)

(July 17, 1947)

At Midnight
There Was A Call

It was just after midnight. I had finished packing and was lying down in my hotel room at St. Paul, Minn., wishing sleep would hurry up and come because I was to be called at 5:30 to get an early aircraft from St. Paul to Chicago, and thence to Atlanta.

The telephone rang. It was a St. Paul reporter.

"This is going to be embarrassing to you," he said, "coming as it does on the heels of your speech. But we want to ask you about the Ku Klux Klan forcing the presidents of the Negro institutions in Georgia to leave a university meeting."

Well, there I was, lying there a long way from home and I had to give answers to something about which I had just learned.

A few hours before I had asked the indulgence of a large audience of several hundred, including the Secretary of the Treasury, and had said I wanted to depart from my text to talk a little bit about the South.

South   I told them I was proud of the South and of my State. I told them of the fine people who shared every good wish and desire for good will Americans in all other regions had. I told them the people of the South were for civil rights, even though we disagreed with the methods proposed by the Messrs. Truman, Dewey and Wallace. I had talked of our progress and our desire to have our farmers make incomes as high as those of Minnesota and Iowa and the other great states of the Middle West. I told of our determination that our children, one day, should have as much an opportunity in school as theirs. But, most of all, I asked them to believe that despite occasional evidence to the contrary the people of the South were not willfully mean and violent, but were as eager to make a great America as they.

And then, two hours later, there I was with a query about the Ku Klux Klan at Milledgeville, Ga.

Shame   I told him I knew he had an edition to make, and asked him to say that the people of Georgia were ashamed of it and repudiated it, as they had other similar events. I told him that those who engaged in the stupid affront to decency and the name of the State, were the usual assortment of mentally-arrested, natural-born jerks and oafs to be found in any community, St. Paul included. I explained that the three Negroes were much more valuable Georgians than the whole membership of the group, which had made jackasses of themselves, their city and State. I said that if all the membership of the Ku Klux Klan would leave Georgia the moral and intellectual level of the State would be raised considerably. I told him the Klan membership was of a level which had very good reason to worry about social equality, when no one else did, because there was grave doubt if many of its members could take off their masks and honestly qualify as fit to be in the company of honest, Christian people, white or colored. You've got some of the same kind, I said. "Down our way they join the Klan. Up here they take other tactics."

Another   I got a later call from Minneapolis, across the river, and I tried to explain to them that what had happened didn't change what I had said — I am still proud of the real South — of its earnest, decent people, white and colored, who are honestly striving to be good citizens; who are working and saving and trying to give their children a better chance than they had; who are not full of hate and fear, but who have confidence in themselves.

The next morning I bought papers there and in Chicago, and the story was there. What happened at Millegeville was so stupid; so obviously a product of dim-witted, infantile evil little minds, that people in states where nothing like that ever happens can't understand it. They simply can't comprehend that sort of stupidity. And I must confess I find it difficult, too.

Symbolic Anyhow, following hard on the shooting of a Negro in Montgomery County for voting, according to the Sheriff, comes this act of interference with a meeting of the Board of Regents. And again the nation shakes its head and wonders why one State seems to have so great a share of that sort of people. It was symbolic, in a way, [that] the Klan should have interfered with an educational meeting. Because the philosophy of Ku Kluxism stands for spiritual and mental darkness.

We will simply have to weather a period in which stupidity and lawlessness will from time to time appear. The Dixiecrats agitate it; the Truman and Dewey proposals are objectionable to many who know what they mean. To many more they are accepted in a distorted manner. Henry Wallace has been cleverly used by the Communists to create trouble.

The Kluxers fall for the Communist tricks. Right now no one is working harder to help the Wallace ticket than the Kluxers. The Milledgeville boobs made a lot of Wallace votes. We learn as we progress — slowly.

But, I am still proud of the real Georgia and the real South and proud, too, to say so.

(September 20, 1948)

There Are Times When A Man —

Hodding Carter, the able Mississippi editor, has come along with a definition of a Southern liberal which I think sums up such a person very accurately indeed, as follows:

> The Southern liberal fits into no mold. He is rarely a theorist. He is not bound to an ideology that excludes the dissenter, nor does he recite a manifesto as if it were a prayer. He is as often condemned by the distant left as by the nearby right. He has a deep-rooted, provincial love for his homeland. His objectives are usually what are termed limited ones, and he

may differ even from his fellows in his proposals for attaining them. But he shares a common determination to make democracy work and thrive through individual and concerted effort on the battle line itself and not from a distant ivory tower.

You don't hear too much about him. He is an educator, an editor, a churchman, a representative of organized labor, a writer, a political leader, a business or professional man, a farmer. Usually he would be embarrassed if you praised him for his courage, or labeled him a liberal. Even when he organizes, his organization is loosely knit, and he may be unaware that his neighbor shares his own convictions.

As Harry Ashmore, the brilliant young editor of the *Arkansas Gazette*, puts it: "I figure there are thousands in the region, men of good will, who are really getting the job done where it counts, and the hell of it is that [we] so-called experts on the South don't even know who they are."

That's very true. It explains the Southern liberal's position better than I have ever been able to do in many forums where the question was asked.

Love   This business of loving one's country and one's region is a curious thing anyhow. Certainly I love the South. I fancy I can detect the beginning of its fields and the colors of its soils high up from an airplane when flying home from a distant region. They seem to call out to me, saying, "You're back home." One always has a sentiment for one's own people and one's own land. I long ago came to the conclusion that all of us ought to think first of ourselves as Americans, and secondly as residents of our region. I try conscientiously to do that because all our future is tied up with our country's future, not that of any particular region. We must work to make a better North, South, West or New England, because in so doing we make a better America.

The global outlook as a viewpoint for organizations or individuals devoted to improvement is unfortunate if global remedies be the objective viewpoint. The job always to be done is the one at home. Any state which advances means a stronger, better United States. To create a better South we must begin at home. As the small and large communities improve their government and their public attitudes, as they assume their responsibilities as citizens, we will obtain better counties and, finally, superior states which educate their children, depend on their law-enforcement bodies and courts; vigorously condemn and prosecute those responsible for violence, and otherwise present to the nation the gift of true citizenship. Organizations looking for ways to improve their counties, their states, their regions, must understand the place to begin is at home — with local attitudes of politics and responsibilities of citizenship.

Region It seems to me the Southerner who loves his region must love it enough to fight for it. He most love it enough vigorously to denounce and oppose all those who seek to say the American dream of justice and opportunity for all Americans is not a Southern dream, too. The person who really loves the South must love it enough to refuse to see it exploited by those who seek to say that lynchings and mob violence are a part of the South. They must love it enough to say the Negro may have full justice and economic opportunity without any harm to the South's true traditions.

Paradox So, it is perfectly true that the left-wing radicals speak of the objectives of the Southern liberal as "limited" and as a "Jim Crow liberalism." It also is true the extreme right in the South at the same time condemns him as too advanced, as "pink" and as fouling his own nest. It is a paradox which is often frustrating.

But the real Southerner, who loves his region, must first of all be an American determined his region shall be second to no other region in the meaning of America. The South must have education as good as other regions; must have opportunity and justice and jobs; must have happiness and good will. Those who love it will not be afraid to fight for the South and its future as an effective part of a great nation. This means eating the bitter bread of frustration, disappointment and abuse, but these can be digested and the effort is worth while, because a man's region loves him back and there are times when he can feel it and know it.

(July 7, 1949)

MEN WHO SHAME
OUR STATE AND FLAG

Two persons from Bainbridge came to see me. They were solemn and sad, worried and a little bit afraid.

They had a right to be.

This was their story. A short time ago a 15-year-old Negro boy had been arrested on his return from a stay of two weeks in Ashburn. Frightened, cowed and very much alone, he was taken roughly, he says, to jail.

In a sworn statement from a hospital bed, he said that after arrest he was told he had insulted a white woman. He had not, and he denied it as strongly as he could. The officer then called up a number and had the boy talk into the telephone. "Does that sound like him?" he asked.

The boy said the county officer then hit him with his fist and locked him up. There was no warrant and no charge made.

He says he asked the county officer what he was charged with doing and the officer said to him that if it were up to him the boy would never see his daddy again. That's pretty hard on a boy of 15.

Waiting   Apparently there was no charge or evidence against him because the next night the boy was released — late, about 10:30 P. M.

In his statement he said that when he came down the steps from the jail two men were waiting. They both hit him and one put a sack over his head. They took him to a car. During the drive they struck him and cursed him. After a while they reached some woods and got out, dragging him with them.

Boy   Now, whatever his race, this was but a 15-year-old boy. He was, one may assume, very much afraid and in a state of terror. Any boy would have been. He was all alone and knew he might be killed.

The boy was beaten, very heavily, with a strap and a club. He was asked if he believed in civil rights. He said he didn't know what they were and had never heard of them. The odds are the men who were mistreating him so brutally didn't know what they were either. They asked him if he knew of any niggers insulting white women. He says they told him they were going to beat him until they killed him if he didn't tell. He said, truthfully, he didn't know any. They asked him who he ran around with and he told them. He is afraid they will be beaten, although the boy swears that neither he nor they have ever insulted or sought to insult anyone. He says they then asked him how old he was and he said 15 and they each whipped him hard for every year of his age. They then told him to run.

Alone   It was after midnight and dark. The 15-year-old boy tried to run, but kept falling down because he was almost unconscious and badly beaten. He says he hid in some bushes all night and the next morning, feverish and sick, asked for some water at a white farmer's house. The man gave him the water and asked him what the matter was. He said nothing was the matter. He went on to a Negro's house and these people bathed him and dressed his badly wounded back and put him to bed. They also called the deputy.

The boy and the deputy found the place where he had been whipped. They also found his shoes which had come off during the beating.

The deputy called the sheriff at Bainbridge and the boy's father, and the boy was put in the hospital at Bainbridge, with raw wounds from the beating.

The case is being "investigated."

Results   As I have said here before, the Klan or a manifestation of the Klan, is a cancer which will sicken and harm any town which does not rise to put it down.

Bainbridge is a fine city. Its colored and white populations always have got on well together. Its people do not approve of vicious ruffians taking the law into their own hands. The good people must not be afraid of the Klan element, which has pack courage, but only pack courage.

The pattern of this was typical. The law had nothing against the boy. But the outlaws, those of the Klan mentality, wanted to beat and slug someone in order to terrorize the Negro population, rather than allow the law to run down any law violation by any Negro or persons in the town, suspected of saying obscene things over the telephone, which was the offense being investigated.

Pattern   It could easily have been determined if the boy had been away. If he had been guilty it could have been proved. The boy in question was released because he was not involved.

But, the point to note is that two men knew when the boy would be released and were waiting. That is in the pattern.

What has happened here — as has happened in a few more places — is that a group of men have put themselves above the law.

Somebody at the jail let the men know when the boy would be released.

The people of Bainbridge and the county can join together and say they vote for sheriffs and for courts and they want them to handle their cases. They can demand of the sheriff that he run this down and arrest the guilty men and present the evidence to the grand jury. They can ask the sheriff why prisoners released from his jail can be picked up at the door, a sack put over their head, and then taken away by force and violence at the very door of the building which houses the law enforcement offices of the county. Many persons in the county are outraged and aroused. That's what we need.

Georgia can't go on advertising to the Nation that mobs can mock our law and our courts. We aren't the sort of people these evil persons try to make us seem.

Let the law find the guilty and try them legally, by law, and jail them by law.

We can't go on allowing violent and lawless men to dominate us. The flag of the United States and the flag of Georgia are supposed to fly over our courthouses and public buildings. Let's remember that. They are supposed to stand for law and justice.

(August 18, 1949)

The Yellow Rats of Unadilla

Easter was a beautiful day.

It was beautiful, too, in Unadilla, Ga., but there was an ugly shadow on the town.

It is a good town with fine people. It has fine homes and churches. It has a real man, too, in the Rev. M. W. Flanders of the Methodist Church.

In time Unadilla will translate those good homes, good people and churches into the power to say to the cowardly, evil-minded, wicked jerks of whom the town now is afraid, that the town no longer is afraid of them. But now they seem to need some help.

I pick this story from the Associated Press. The Camp Creek Baptist congregation of Negro Christians had set Easter Sunday as the day to honor their pastor, Rev. George Taylor, who is 87 years old and who has preached more than 50 years. He has taught them through the years that Christ's will is their law and that it will prevail against evil. The church is a small one a few miles out from Unadilla.

Threats Two white ministers had agreed to attend. But, there began to be calls. According to the story, the Rev. M. W. Flanders, of the Methodist Church, was threatened indirectly. The congregation was threatened and sent word to the white ministers that they had called off their Easter services because they didn't have the programs printed in time.

But, the Rev. Flanders (all honor to his name) got in his car and went anyhow. There he learned the truth. The real reason was summed up in three words:

"We is afraid."

That was Unadilla, Ga., on Easter, 1950.

A few yellow rats had cast their shadow over that of the cross and its meaning.

We can forget all the pretty hats — the fine sermons, the eloquent testimony to the meaning of the cross and the empty tomb — until we somehow mobilize the strength of Christianity so that any person who wishes to worship Christ is not afraid of the Ku Klux Klan or anything like it.

When Christians are afraid to be Christians — especially on Easter Day — then the cross and the empty tomb have lost meaning.

Second Time It was only a few months ago that these same evil ghouls in Unadilla burned a cross in front of the home of a man who had spent his life among them, doing good and working in every community enterprise because a neurotic, war-orphaned boy from a DP camp had spread lies in resentment against being kept in to study when he wanted to go out and play, and because of a refusal to be given bikes and all the things some other boys had.

There again, we saw the curious paralysis of fear. The town didn't like it. But the town was afraid of the unknown.

It doesn't matter if some of the law enforcement people are lined up with these rats. They are not many. They are willing to strike only in the dark. If the town will face them down they will run.

That cowardly act was on Aug. 9.

It went unopposed save for a courageous newspaper woman in the town.

KKK   Now, the rat-souled gang has set itself up as more powerful than the meaning of Christ.

The Klan is anti-Christian, and always has been, despite its cynical and depraved use of the cross — which it burns. A burning cross is a destroyed cross. Men who set it in flames violate every Christian concept. The Klan is un-American and always has been, despite its use of the flag and its hypocritical protests of un-Americanism.

It is not powerful in Georgia or the South.

It is powerful only in small towns and communities where law enforcement isn't willing to kick it in the teeth and where the people are uselessly afraid of a few small-souled, evil wretches.

I would like to see the Baptist churches of the state arrange a real celebration at the Camp Creek church. The rats might even burn it down. We should then build them a better one.

But, it seems to me that Christianity in Georgia can't allow this affront to stand. I think we should have a great Christian rally at the Camp Creek church and that every public official from the Governor on down [should] join in making it a success.

Are the yellow rats of Unadilla more powerful than the cross? Aren't we at last tired of this scum, small in number, disgracing the whole State?

(April 11, 1950)

One Day
It Will Be
Monday

Days come and go, and Monday is among them, and one of these Mondays the Supreme Court of the United States is going to hand down a ruling which may, although it is considered by some unlikely, outlaw the South's dual school system, wholly or in part.

It is a subject which, because of its emotional content, usually is put aside with the remark, "Let's don't talk about it. If people wouldn't talk about these things, they would solve themselves."

It is an old reaction, best illustrated by *Gone With The Wind*'s Miss Scarlett O'Hara who, when confronted with a distasteful decision, pushed it away with the remark, "We'll talk about that tomorrow."

But "tomorrow" has an ugly habit of coming around.

I believe it a fact that the average citizen doesn't yet have any idea that such a decision is possible, or that everything indicates that a decision — one way or the other — is close at hand.

So, somebody, especially those who have a duty so to do, ought to be talking about it calmly, and informatively.

The Cases The issue of segregation in the schools is before the court in five cases involving South Carolina, Virginia, Delaware, Kansas and the District of Columbia. There are 13 other states which would be affected.

All of these cases are brought on the basis of the 14th Amendment to the Constitution of the United States which forbids a state to adopt any legislation "which shall abridge the privileges" of any of its citizens or deny them "equal protection" under the law.

In 1896, the Supreme Court held that "separate but equal" facilities met the demands of the 14th Amendment. Failure to meet the requirements of this decision in the years that followed now has the states involved raising taxes and spending hurriedly in an effort to satisfy the "separate but equal" phase of the 1896 decision.

But, the present complainants each contend that separation itself constitutes a condition of inequality and does, in fact, abridge the privileges of colored citizens.

This, in brief, is the legal background.

The Supreme Court cannot fail to appreciate what it would mean suddenly to overturn customs and traditions, as well as a former decision by the court, all of which have had the tenure of more than half a century.

The court may very well rule that in the grade schools there is no question of "prestige," such as exists in a long-established professional or graduate school, and leave to the states the decision as to what they will do about segregation in that field.

The court can reflect the new administration policy and eliminate the dual system entirely, or, though it is doubtful, simply reaffirm the decision of 1896.

There is yet another possibility — and an important one.

The court can rule segregation unconstitutional — but allow the states affected a period of years in which to work out procedures satisfying the court's decision.

Effect Whatever happens, for some years the majority of Southern Negro children will continue to go to separate schools. There will be evasive actions and legal tests. In many communities the wiser Negro leadership, with segregation no longer sanctioned by law, will be content to maintain separate schools until public opinion accepts it.

The pattern of segregation has changed radically in the past 20 years. It is often confusing in its startling contradictions. Nowhere in the South does it follow hard and fast rules. It continues slowly to break down at the edges. But, for a long time, by gerrymandering, by abolition of school systems and other methods, separate schools will be maintained.

The vital point is — there is no reason for violence, whatever the decision. Leadership everywhere in the South must talk about this and make it clear. Anger and violence solve nothing.

(April 9, 1953)

Once A Biscuit Is Opened —

Back in the days of minstrel shows there was one end-man ballad singer whose speciality was titled: "I'm the Only Man in the World Who Can Take a Biscuit Apart and Put It Back Together Again Just Like It Was."

In a very real sense the inability to do just this is the dilemma of the Southern politicians. They have opened the Dixie biscuit for industry, labor unions, larger city populations and less rural, and yet they spend much of their time and emotions continually trying to put the biscuit back together again just like it was.

They can't. No matter how much of the molasses of tradition and recrimination they pour on it, it never will go back "just like it was."

They never blame themselves. As they angrily try to fit the old-time biscuit back together again, they blame the Supreme Court and Justice Warren. They accuse the vaguely defined "liberals" and the ADA (Americans for Democratic Action). They are sure the Communists are yet another reason why the lid won't fit back on the biscuit.

Myrdal's Book Some of them are sure the poor fit of the biscuit is due to a Swedish sociologist who wrote a really understanding book on the nation's problems of race and titled it *The American Dilemma*. It was among the several publications referred to by the court, not as an authority on law but as one by a man who had studied the effect of unequal application of the laws. Almost none have read [Gunnar] Myrdal. But they blame him. Actually his book does not condemn the South. It argues the problem is national, not regional. And if it isn't all these then surely it must be "the radicals" who prevent the biscuit from fitting together again.

All this the trained observer finds difficulty in comprehending. Every state, city, town and Chamber of Commerce in the South for years have had both thumbs up, willing to attract industry from either, or any, direction. Governors of Southern states routinely take delegations of prominent citizens to large centers of industry to present, with oratory, diagrams and statistics revealing the water supply, the labor market, transportation, and the availability of public schools.

But once it comes and the results become evident in new and unexpected pressures at the polls and in demands for services, there is contentment only with the payroll. Resentment grows against "outsiders" and agitators "from up North" who do not understand our way of life.

It is, as aforesaid, almost incomprehensible there should be such blindness, but there is.

Great Ferment Nor is that all. So fixed is attention on the problem of putting the biscuit top back again, exactly as before, there is no time for looking elsewhere and relating the great ferment of peoples everywhere for equal protection of law, for independence, and for status as a God-made human being. The explosions in Nyasaland, the Belgian Congo, Algeria, Cairo, and South Asia are associated with the impossible business of putting the lid back on the biscuit.

The astonishing spectacle of ministers of the gospel angrily defining Chrisitianity as a segregated religion; the more understandable attempt of various councils, some business and professional men, and politicians all defiantly insisting they will put the biscuit top on just like it was — or destroy the biscuit — all this is almost incredible. It is more than that. It is preposterous and for the generations of now and the future, a demonstration filled with pathos and frustration.

The kindest thing is to say that it is . . . naive to believe that after two great wars for liberty and the rule of law, and at a time when the American promise of equal protection for all citizens is being challenged by Communism, that everything would go on as before. The American promise of dignity and equal application of the laws does not apply to a select classification of individuals. Socially they may do as they please. But the law must govern all equally in all public non-private functions of life.

(April 1, 1956)

A Church,
A School

The following column was cited specifically by the Pulitzer Committee as an example of the editorial writing which won the Pulitzer Prize for Ralph McGill. It appeared originally on October 13, 1958 and was reprinted more than a decade later.

Dynamite in great quantity ripped a beautiful temple of worship in Atlanta. It followed hard on the heels of a like destruction of a handsome high school at Clinton, Tennessee. The same rabid, mad-dog minds were, without question, behind both. They are also the source of previous bombings in Florida, Alabama, and South Carolina. The schoolhouse and the church were the targets of diseased, hate-filled minds.

Let us face the facts. This is a harvest. It is the crop of things sown.

It is the harvest of defiance of courts and the encouragement of citizens to defy law on the part of many Southern politicians. It will be the acme of irony, for example, if any one of four or five Southern governors deplore this bombing. It will be grimly humorous if certain attorneys general issue statements of regret. And it will be quite a job for some editors, columnists, and commentators, who have been saying that our courts have no jurisdiction and that the people should refuse to accept their authority, now to deplore.

It is not possible to preach lawlessness and restrict it.

Gates Opened   To be sure, none said go bomb a Jewish temple or a school. But let it be understood that when leadership in high places in any degree fails to support constituted authority, it opens the gates to all those who wish to take law into their hands.

There will be, to be sure, the customary act of the careful drawing aside of skirts on the part of those in high places. "How awful!" they will exclaim. "How terrible. Something must be done."

But the record stands. The extremists of the citizens' councils, the political leaders who in terms violent and inflammatory have repudiated their oaths and stood against due process of law have helped unloose this flood of hate and bombing.

This too is a harvest of those so-called Christian ministers who have chosen to preach hate instead of compassion. Let them now find pious words and raise their hands in deploring the bombing of a synagogue.

You do not preach and encourage hatred for the Negro and hope to restrict it to that field. It is an old, old story. It is one repeated over and over again in history. When the wolves of hate are loosed on one people, then no one is safe.

Hate and lawlessness by those who lead release the yellow rats and encourage the crazed and neurotic who print and distribute the hate pamphlets — who shrieked that Franklin Roosevelt was a Jew — who denounce the Supreme Court as being Communist and controlled by Jewish influences.

The Harvest This series of bombings is the harvest, too, of something else.

One of those connected with the bombing telephoned a news service early Sunday morning to say the job would be done. It was to be committed, he said, by the Confederate Underground.

The Confederacy and the men who led it are revered by millions. Its leaders returned to the Union and urged that the future be committed to building a stronger America. This was particularly true of General Robert E. Lee. Time after time he urged his students at Washington University to forget the War Between the States and to help build a greater and stronger union.

For too many years now we have seen the Confederate flag and the emotions of that great war become the property of men not fit to tie the shoes of those who fought it. Some of these have been merely childish and immature. Others have perverted and commercialized the flag by making the Stars and Bars, and the Confederacy itself, a symbol of hate and bombings.

For a long time now it has been needful for all Americans to stand up and be counted on the side of law and the due process of law — even when to do so goes against personal beliefs and emotions. It is late. But there is yet time.

(February 5, 1969)

Gov. Battle Warned, But —

Former Gov. John S. Battle of Virginia stood to speak.

The place was Montgomery, Ala., which likes to refer to itself as the Cradle of the Confederacy. The U. S. Civil Rights Commission was in session.

The climate was, and is, an ugly one of sullen, angry defiance.

What happened was a very Southern thing. It was as stylized in ritual as a ballet. It was in the code of the Old South, tradition of *noblesse oblige*, of duty and responsibility.

Only one out of an old Virginia culture could have done it so gently and so beautifully as did Gov. Battle. His voice, as heard later on radio and television, was slow and soft, almost like a teacher speaking to boys who had been unruly.

The ritual of it was flawless.

First he evoked his ancestors. His father had been an Alabamian. Then came the Confederacy. His grandfather had been an officer in the Confederacy and subsequently had been denied a seat in the Congress because of that fact. He came, he said, as a friend. He asked permission to say that he had come back to the house of his fathers.

This was the first movement in the symphony of an ancient and well loved ceremonial rite.

The second movement followed.

Southern Sentiments Gov. Battle said that he had accepted membership on the commission because the President wanted someone who possessed strong Southern sentiments. These he had, he said.

This done, he could then address himself to his subject. He did so, sincerely, courteously, hopefully, saying:

> I am constrained to say in all friendliness I fear the officials of Alabama and of certain counties have made an error in doing that which appears to be an attempt to cover up their actions in relation to the exercise of the ballot by some people.
>
> The majority of the next members of Congress will not be friendly to the South and punitive legislation may be passed and this hearing may be used in the advocacy of that legislation which will be adverse to us in Virginia and to you in Alabama.
>
> Of course, it is not up to me, nor would I presume to suggest to any counsel or any official for he should govern for himself. But we are adjourning this hearing until tomorrow morning and may I ask of you, as one who is tremendously interested in the Southern cause, will you kindly reconsider the situation and see if there is not some way you . . . may cooperate a little bit more fully with this commission and not have it said by our own enemies that the people in Alabama were not willing to explain their conduct when requested to do so? This may be entirely out of order, but it was in my heart to say it and I hope you will take it with the spirit with which I said it.

There was real character in this, and a certain forthright recognition of duty such as another Virginian, Robert E. Lee, had emphasized.

Barren Ground   But it fell on barren ground. It has been a long time since the Battles moved to Virginia. And while he spoke from a sense of duty, the climate he addressed was seemingly that of the klavern.

But the drama of it should not be overlooked. Gov. Battle was, in his gentility, and his attention to the old code, entirely correct.

The South forever plays into the hands of those who are extremists on the other side. The people of Alabama are not, as he suggested, willing to explain their conduct when requested to do so. The Senate rules on debate will be modified because use of the filibuster has been abused. What is happening in Alabama is by no means confined to that state.

Reason, duty and common sense spoke at Montgomery.

But ears, like minds, were closed.

It will, however, be well to remember Gov. Battle's prophecy. And if it comes true, whose fault will it be?

(December 12, 1958)

The Face Of The South

It is important the South realize that it cannot permit its criminal element to become the voice and face of the region. Dynamiting of the four churches in the Montgomery area, and the homes of two ministers, smears the whole South.

This, of course, is true of the shooting into buses and all other acts of deliberate violence. It condemns us all.

The explosion of dynamite in churches is at once criminal and stupid — perhaps the most stupid act yet committed.

It blows away whatever patient effort has been made by those who are trying to steer the region through this time of travail and agony of mind and spirit. The criminal element destroys the reputations of all, both they who strongly oppose the Supreme Court's policy and those who support it. All decent people, of whatever opinion, are damaged by the burning and dynamiting of these churches and homes.

Whatever Southerners think, they cannot allow criminals to put a criminal's mask on the face of the whole South.

These criminals do not, by their violence, deter any action.

They rather encourage those determined to force through the

court's decree to attempt a more rapid rate [of desegregation of public facilities] than even the court itself contemplated. They array against the South the indignation and strength of all other regions and of all those who believe in the supremacy of law.

They are, in truth, trampling out the vintage where the grapes of wrath are stored. And it will not be they alone who will have to drink of it. All will taste of its bitterness.

Legal Roadblocks Southern leadership originally set out, according to its own pronouncements, to set up legal roadblocks to the court's decree. That policy has been reaffirmed.

None could oppose their right so to proceed.

Hence it was that there have been advanced many laws, a multiplicity of plans, and a proposal of interposition.

All have been within the legal framework.

They were delaying tactics, and were so admitted to be.

In some states the leadership frankly has said that when one plan is overturned they will erect yet another for the courts to act upon.

This is entirely within their right. The very Constitution which has been interpreted as forbidding segregation in public places on the basis of color, race, or religion, equally guarantees them the right to use the last resort of law.

It is entirely possible this policy of delay may endure across a number of years. It will be condemned by many, applauded by others. But so long as it is within the framework of the law it cannot be denied, though it be criticized.

But those who dynamite or burn churches and homes; who endanger the lives of the wives and children of ministers serving those churches, are destroying the South. There is no way to avoid this harsh fact.

Law Enforcement The trouble would seem to be that in some areas some of those in the business of law enforcement are not interested in preventing such violence. Yet, it must be apparent that if the established leadership does not apprehend and punish those guilty, they will bring down upon the whole South the moral condemnation of the nation. Whatever the South's true answer is, it will be lost in the sound of explosive blasts and the crackle of flames. Let none deceive himself on this issue. Those who are in charge of the South must halt the destruction of churches and property and punish the guilty. Those who array themselves on the wrong side of a moral issue not merely end up in defeat, but in bitterness and ruin of spirit.

But, above all, the South cannot afford, now or in the future, to permit the evil and wicked to say "We are the South."

At a time when the South is saying to the nation, "You must understand our position," it cannot afford to have the criminal element drown out their words with the destruction of places of worship and the homes of those who serve them. Yet, for the time being, at least, that is what is happening.

(January 14, 1959)

South Needs
New Mood

WASHINGTON, D.C.: Now that the new civil rights legislation is law, the South has a real opportunity for one of those great leaps forward. This the region desperately needs to make in order that its political maturity may catch up with the vast progress which goes on in the industrial field. If this is not done, the economic machine will in time slow down.

The new bill is confined in major part to voting. In all their filibuster speeches against the legislation, no Southern leader opposed the right to vote. We cannot do this. The nation carries many heavy burdens. The South has a greater share of the one at which the rights bills are directed.

Now would seem to be the critical time when all Southern leadership could join in setting an example of acceptance of the right of qualified persons to vote. This would seem a fairly simple and easy thing to do. All factions could join in it. It is simply not any longer possible to deny the right to vote. This is so fundamental in our system of government that it cannot be ignored.

It is certain that the South's reaction to the new laws, which have been called moderate by those who opposed them, will be watched very closely in the months ahead. Statements by Southern congressional leaders described this amended legislation as a victory for the Southern position. They now have, as we all do, an opportunity for a greater victory by honestly encouraging implementation of the law.

One Result   Failure to do this can have but one result. There will be more civil rights legislation introduced in the sessions of the next two or three Congresses. It will be less and less possible to oppose such legislation if the new laws are defied or frustrated.

There is every reason for the local and state leadership in the South to recognize this fact and act to prevent it. The regulations cannot be used to discriminate. The laws apply only to those qualified to vote. Many of the older persons, because of educational lacks, will never be qualified. Even in counties where there is large Negro population, emigration continues at an enormous rate. There is not, in the foreseeable future, any danger of political domination by a newly-enfranchised group.

The record of the past, and present, makes the South vulnerable. There are twenty-nine counties, fifteen of them in Mississippi, which at last reports did not permit a single Negro to register for voting. Even teachers were denied. When Alabama registrars denied teachers at Tuskegee, Ala., the right to register, the story was used around the world. The Communists employed it to prove their claims that while America promises democracy, it does not permit it.

Other Counties   There are many other counties in which a half dozen or so Negro residents have been allowed to register. This condition, too, has reduced the South's ability to reply to attacks in and out of the Congress.

The present opportunity is tremendous. It will be tragic if it is fumbled. Southerners in the Congress have said the new legislation is a victory. If this be true, there is no reason why it cannot be made into a very profound one by putting the law into effect, rather than thwarting it. Here is both a responsibility and an opportunity for the South to lift off its back a burden which grows heavier and heavier and which cannot be much longer endured. Surely, the South now can say it will encourage and assist the right to vote.

The new rights legislation also covers bombing. The full weight of all law enforcement may now be used to hunt down those reckless and vicious criminals who bomb homes, places of worship, or buildings of any kind. This, too, is progress.

But what the South badly needs just now is a new mood. The civil rights legislation provides the opportunity to create it by affirming and implementing the right of qualified citizens to vote. If we fail in this, then the public mood, already heavy, will worsen, and that will not be victory but defeat.

(April 23, 1960)

Wanted —
A New Image!

A number of news items entwine like ivy on old walls to suggest the Deep South desperately needs to busy itself with revising the image it holds of itself.

In the Congress, Southerners almost fanatically oppose a federal aid to education bill. They do this at the same time new and remorseless statistics of the National Educational Assn. show that the Deep South states have a higher percentage of military rejections for mental and educational lacks [than does any other area of the country].

Local governments in the South, for all their insistence on being left alone, in general do less for their school systems than [do] those of other regions. The average classroom teacher in the South is paid far less than those of other states. The shortage of classrooms and of competent teachers also is greater. Yet, in the Congress, Southerners fight even that federal aid which would do nothing but pay for new buildings.

Not Guilty In Montgomery, Ala., Dr. Martin Luther King [Jr.], whose name is anathema to the conservative South, especially to the extremist groups, was declared not guilty by an all-white jury in a case brought by the state charging evasion of taxes. The charge fell apart when the state's tax agent, a white man, refused to let prejudice sway the facts. Being under oath he told the truth. He admitted he had informed Dr. King he had found no fraud in his tax declaration and that errors had been made in the audit. The state's case collapsed.

The jury was out for more than four hours. No one has said what went on in the jury room, but the presumption is a majority had to persuade two or three members angrily determined to vote guilty, that such a verdict was not justified. The jury system is greatly assisted by the Montgomery action. There is evidence that the old Confederate capital, which lost a long and bitter campaign to Dr. King about de-segregating its public buses, has attained a new plateau in its cold war.

A new image of the "Dr. Kings" and of the NAACP is painfully and tediously coming into focus. They are not Communistic and are not un-American. The individuals and the organization are operating from a base of law and of court decisions. They not merely are advocating legality. What they seek already has been sustained by the courts.

The extremists who have pictured them as Communist-dominated have done their own cause great harm. It is true that the Dr. Kings and the NAACP are to most Southerners symbols of all that is wicked and wrong. But, painfully, as Montgomery has demonstrated, the new image comes into focus. Men like Dr. King will not in our time be viewed without bitterness. Nor will the NAACP.

To Know Why   But it is important for the thoughtful South to understand why it is a jury in a city which entertains violent hate of the man found him not guilty. He wasn't.

There is another fact which needs to be brought from Montgomery. The bar of that city openly admired, with much headshaking, the legal representation given Dr. King — especially by a Negro attorney, Robert Ming, from Chicago. "Negro or not, he is a master of law," said a reluctantly admiring member.

We are now at a point in the South where we cannot any longer seek to live in the past, however much we revere that past. The present is here. The future begins tomorrow. And the Dr. Kings and the NAACP are a part of this present and that future.

Our educational position is approaching that of desperation wholly apart from the racial problem.

If we and our leadership blind ourselves with false images, we can do nothing but harm to our present and our future. To recognize the truth is an urgent, if unpleasant, necessity.

(May 31, 1960)

An Essay
On Dr. M. L. King

Nothing so dismays those who hold the South in affection and its future in hope as the intransigence of many of those in positions of public office and leadership. Nor does anything so well illustrate this as the case of Dr. Martin Luther King [Jr.].

Dr. King is the latest symbol of opposition for the intractable elements. Not too long ago the symbol was the NAACP. Then, for a time, it was Thurgood Marshall, chief attorney for the NAACP. He had filed the school suits and his name had become thereby known. These symbols have faded. Dr. King is the newest.

These persons might well ask themselves just why it is that Dr. Martin Luther King, until a short time ago a relatively obscure minister in Montgomery, Ala., has become the best-known leader of Negro opinion in the United States? By what steps did he ascend to this position?

Simple Answer   The answer, while it may be painful to some, none the less is a simple one. Dr. King has attained his present position of influence because of the vulnerable acts of those who have most bitterly opposed him. He must be very thankful for them. They alone provided him with the opportunity to exert and reveal his undenied courage. As the late Mahatma Gandhi demonstrated, neither jail nor physical assaults are an answer when the moral force is on the other side.

The latest episode illustrates this point. It is extremely unlikely that any person with a driver's license from another state would have been sentenced to four months in jail for not having obtained a license in the present state of residence. And certainly none other would have been handcuffed and removed from a county jail to the state prison at 4 o'clock in the morning. This was so obvious a discrimination that the conscience of the nation was outraged against the South. Editorials, sermons, radio and television criticism, and condemnation by many organizations have followed and the end is not yet.

In their determination to get at Dr. King, his enemies have, in their frustration and anger, presented to the nation the very worst stereotype of the South. The sort of action taken against him in Georgia and Alabama confirmed all that the most false and extreme critics of the South have said.

The Result Those whose seeming witlessness in recent years have made Dr. King a national figure apparently do not care about the result of their actions. We can only presume, in the absence of any evidence to the contrary, that they wish the rest of the nation to believe that injustice and discrimination in law does, in fact, exist in the South. The Ku Klux elements may not understand it, but they are not a good advertisement for a region which wishes to attract industry, to educate its children, and to move into the future with the rest of the nation. These persons can make one, and only one, contribution. They can, by violence, delay, but at the same time guarantee Dr. King his victory.

For a long time now the would-be King Canutes of the KKK mentality have been standing on the beaches demanding that the tides of history and events retreat. But the tides have not, and will not, turn back.

Across a span of more than three years, Dr. King's extremist opposition has succeeded in making him an international symbol of a persecuted man, and a national leader most influential with his own people. If this is what the opposition set out to do, then it has succeeded.

Finally, Georgians who profess to be upset by Robert F. Kennedy's telephone call about the case should cast the first stone at those who made Georgia vulnerable to a charge of injustice. Without them there would have been no call.

(November 5, 1960)

Hatred Reaps Its Harvest

On a dark, cloudy night, symbolic of the callous, hate-filled minds involved, a Negro school in Atlanta senselessly was bombed early Monday morning.

It is too bad the nation could not see the wrecked rooms where the colored Christmas drawings of children, lovingly done, were scattered in such pitiful disorder. These childish doings cry out accusingly with a mute but trumpet-like eloquence.

The big brave men who tossed the explosive in the darkness of the night, and in the deeper darkness of their own minds and souls, have not stopped the processes of education. Their kind have appeared often in history. They were among those who cried, "Crucify Him." Their kind were among those who offered Him vinegar on the cross when He said, "I thirst." Their soul-kin were among those who tended Hitler's gas furnaces. Their kind are among the Communist terror groups. Their kind are related to those who scream filth in the New Orleans demonstrations.

In a time like this, it is fashionable for leaders of those who preach, teach and organize for defiance of law and court decisions to deplore violence and say, "We are not responsible. We do not endorse violence."

But, of course, they do.

In High Places Men and women in high places who organize groups to resist court orders, those who urge pledges of never surrendering, and who encourage those of the Klan mentality, did not toss the explosive at the school. But in a very real sense, their hands were there just the same, because, if those who are willing to commit bombings, physical assaults and other crimes of violence were not encouraged by those in established positions who curse the court, who say that American judges are Communists, who reveal their own state of mind to be that of law violators, the lawless would not become so emboldened.

But, as always, when the fruits of their planting are harvested, they recoil and say, "We deplore this. We never meant such things to happen."

And there are always those who try to suggest that perhaps it was done "by the others," by those who want to bring discredit on organizations publicly preaching defiance of law and no surrender to the orders of the government of the United States.

There are always excuses for not doing what is right, for not obeying law and the processes of courts.

So, once again, as in the bombing of the Atlanta Temple — and of schools and churches in other cities — we have a harvest of things sown. It was but a few days ago an Atlanta Klan leader publicly advocated destroying schools.

Leadership Tested Once again, Southern leadership is put to the test.

Here again we have the essence of the Greek tragedy. In the end the decent, civilized people will prevail. In the end there will be education for all children. Bombers prove nothing by bombing, or destroying a school or church. God still lives. Learning remains.

The tragedy is that even though the end of the play is known, there must be needless suffering, violence and ugly lawlessness on the loose.

It isn't always easy to be an American. There are times when we must surrender our own personal wishes, emotions, and preferences for the common good. We have had waves of prejudice move across our country at different periods in its history. They have all broken against the common sense and decency of the American who knows that his country must offer the same great asset to all of its citizens — freedom, liberty, dignity and opportunity. This must be within the reach of all citizens.

The childish drawings of Christmas — of Peace on Earth to Men of Good Will — on the floors of the bombed classrooms have a message for all whose hearts are not ruled by darkness and evil.

(December 13, 1960)

An Idyl of the KKK

As a young reporter, to whom a wad of copy paper and a soft copy-reader's pencil were comparable with an emperor's medal and a queen's decoration, I went to work at about the outset of two major evils of the twenties — the Ku Klux Klan and Prohibition.

The Klan was (and is) a racket for promoters, who got about seven dollars out of each ten they took from the suckers. It became politically powerful and pretty soon, deluded by its power, was committing murders, assaults and intimidation. Gen. Nathan Bedford Forrest had disbanded the original Reconstruction-era Klan because it had become a haven for rascals. If his ghost ever deigns to look down from heaven on earth below, he knows how right he was . . . and how unchanged things are. In Indiana the head Klansman went to the penitentiary for raping and murdering an innocent girl. In almost every other state there were a few murders and many beatings and abuses of the due processes of law.

The nation was sickened by the excesses and evil of the 20s. There was no Gen. Nathan Bedford Forrest to dissolve the Klan because it had become a haven for rascals and violence, but it nonetheless eroded away save for a few eddies here and there.

Feeble Revival   There was a feeble revival during the thirties and this was, save for a few examples of old-time lawlessness, merely a side-show. It was, in the main, a political mechanism used in some states to help out with purchasing departments.

There was an Imperial Wizard in this period who was a veterinarian. This produced the jest that he was the first man professionally prepared to handle the membership.

Looking back at this second, more pedestrian period, I guess my favorite Imperial Wizard was the Rt. Hon. Hiram Evans, known familiarly to all newsmen as "the Wiz." He was an amiable man, who never went in for violence. While he spoke pontifically and sonorously about Klan virtues, he always appeared to reporters to have tongue in cheek.

Later on the Klan seemed to feel this way, too. One Sunday they got together in an Atlanta hotel and handed "the Wiz" the black spot, somewhat in the manner of Blind Pew delivering one to the Captain at the Rainbow Inn of "Treasure Island" fame. They seemed to feel "the Wiz" had wrought more mightily in the field of asphalt sales than in the klaverns.

Nonetheless, it was this same Imperial Wizard who participated in one of the most charming idyls of the time. Yet, it, too, seemed to disenchant the members who had been more contented under the veterinarian.

New Bishop   There had come to Georgia a new bishop for the Roman Catholic diocese, a charming, intelligent and delightful gentleman, the Very Reverend Gerald O'Hara. During the days of the Klan of the 20s it had bought an old Southern mansion, white columns and all, on Atlanta's Peachtree [Road], and used it as an "Imperial Palace."

When the Klan of the 20s had collapsed under the weight of its crimes, the building was put on the market. The Roman Catholic Church, which had been one of the major targets of the KKK's brand of "100 per cent Americanism" purchased the old Klan "palace."

The building, where once the sheeted Kluxers had counted their money and from which their anti-Catholic, anti-Jewish, anti-Negro literaure had gone, became the rectory and a beautiful cathedral was erected beside it.

When the time came to dedicate the cathedral, Bishop O'Hara questioned newspaper friends about inviting the Imperial Wizard. They felt out "the Wiz" and found him agreeable. The invitation was sent and received. On the day of the ceremony "the Wiz" was there in a pew close up to the front.

Klan mentality seems to grow more stupid through the years, as the third, and present revival demonstrates. There has not been anything humorous about it since "the Wiz" departed.

(August 5, 1961)

The Path Is Of The Pickets

Notes from the Southern Scene: One watches hate-organization pickets walking up and down with a banner proclaiming that the Communists are behind integrated schools.

There is a certain pathos in the sight. It is worse when you know the picket. A man looking on says, "I remember when that one was in trouble as a four-year-old. His mother who worked, because the father was an alcoholic, and, later a petty thief who deserted his family, appealed for help with the juvenile authorities. Sullen, defiant, rebellious, the boy was then uncooperative. He was released. Soon he was back again. And the mother came in tears to ask for help again. As he grew in size he enlarged as a problem. He dropped out of school. He had been a trouble-maker there, and did not get along with other pupils. He began to develop a police record."

The promoters of hate recruit such material. They, themselves, rarely get into the picket lines or take any chances. They obtain the money from adults who themselves are psychopathic in their prejudices. They support the Nazi parties, the anti-Semitic groups, the anti-Negro mobs.

Those Who Hate The South's efforts to accept the processes of law are deterred by those who really hate. They hate everybody, Jews, Catholics, Negroes, decent, law-abiding people of any creed who work and find life at least relatively satisfying.

One feels they really hate themselves. They are convinced that somehow life has been unjust to them — that they are superior persons deprived of opportunity. (Their minds fester like boils.) They are sure it is the fault of Jews, or Negroes, or the police, the mayor, the newspapers, the "government".

Most of them are relatively young — in their twenties or thirties. They do not, as a rule, have much education. They read little save the hate sheets put out by their own, or other groups. They listen to the older ones — those who really handle the money and who give them their daily injections of hate propaganda. Their counterparts were the "black shirts" who made up Mussolini's toughs. They are kin to Hitler's Nazi guards. They are the tools, the puppets of those who really make the profits.

They manage to look as if they were all brothers . . . as, in a sense, they are. Numerically they are not many. In the riots in New Orleans, in Birmingham, Little Rock, and Montgomery, there were the haters with placards, the toughs swinging clubs or throwing stones, who had gathered there from several cities.

Sort of Status   They glory in picketing — it is a sort of status. For an hour or so they are not unknown failures, and psychologically crippled, sick persons, but objects of attention, players strutting their brief hour . . . persons of importance . . .

"Only Communists Want Integrated Schools . . ."

"Shall Moscow Run Our Schools?"

"Don't Send Your Child to School With Niggers."

There is nothing in life for them now — and nothing much ahead. Most of them have had prison experiences — and will have more. Some will slip into a whole life of crime. They will continue to live off infrequent jobs and cash handouts from those who handle the hate money. Few employers want to have violent, unstable, sick minds on their payrolls.

So, with each job lost they blame it on "the Jews, the Nigger lovers". They are sure the government is filled with Communists or else it wouldn't give jobs to Jews and enact civil rights legislation, or they are sure the courts are Communist because they ordered that Negro children have an equal right to education . . .

So, they turn out — pitiful, sinister in malice, defeated, vain, bitter, defiant . . . with emptiness and barrenness of life ahead of them . . . and bitterness and hate for the present.

(August 30, 1961)

"Cry, Beloved Country"

"The niggers here" said the sheriff, an old man with a wrinkled face, "are not interested in voting . . . the better niggers, that is . . ."

Near him were the smoking ruins of two churches destroyed because there had been voter registration meetings held in them. Down the road were houses riddled with gunshots because the occupants had been working at bringing frightened, uncertain, rural farm Negroes to the registration books.

An old image and an older myth were dying. The troubled sheriff, his familiar routine of life shaken, was a symbol of much of the Deep South states where old patterns have remained undisturbed since slavery. There had been a time when all the Negroes in the county had been "good niggers" . . . doing what they were told, not bothering with voting and not complaining.

"The people are disturbed about the outsiders," the sheriff was quoted as saying. "If they'd leave, things would quiet down again."

Churches Spoke   The churches, with the crude stone-and-brick chimneys standing amid the ashes, were mute, but not silent. They were speaking in distant cities and countries. These churches, and others like them, but yet unburned, are not like the ones in cities. They are plain and bare. When the sun is hot on them the pine smell comes out of them and resin gathers in drops along the seams. The money that paid for the timber was mostly nickels, dimes, and quarters, greasy from sweaty hands and fingers. They were brought to meetings wrapped in a bandana handkerchief and taken proudly to the pine-plank altar when donations were called for.

The burned churches will be rebuilt.

The voters' list will grow.

The legend that a rural sheriff's "good niggers" don't want to vote, or to educate their children or have the same rights — no more — than other people, was never true. It dies now, painfully but surely.

Slowly, but surely, the processes of law move. Whatever the irrelevant arguments about the 14th Amendment, or local laws to the contrary, the American Negro is a citizen.

Facts Ignored   Progress — and facts — are ignored by fanatics — the church burners, the night riders, the Klan speakers, the inflammable politicians.

In much of the South compliance with law has proceeded without trouble. In Virginia, in Tennessee, in Kentucky, in West Virginia, in

Arkansas, in Texas, and in Atlanta, Georgia, colored pupils and students have gone to school without any of the dire results which the extremist fanatics insist will happen. There is no forced "mixing" as such. Parents vote. They and their children use the parks. They go to the library for books. They ride in buses. Life goes on. Nothing happens unless violent men and women — and inflammable politics - make it happen. The best in us comes out if we give it a chance.

There are days when Southern honor and pride cry out to us — asking that the South do what is right and decent.

It is a beloved region — already hurt by evil and prejudice. There is leadership in the South which will not follow the church burners, the night riders with their guns, the haters and the preachers of violence.

We first of all are Americans ... We are all part of the great national tradition.

So, as the processes of law continue — as they will — the decisions come more and more frequently ... Is it really so difficult to allow all qualified persons to vote, to use the parks, to go to school? Are we so weak and afraid we cannot trust ourselves to do what is right — to answer honor instead of shame?

(September 12, 1962)

We Cannot Escape History

In the wake of the wholly unnecessary and brutal riots at the University of Mississippi, history and civilization focus a bright and revealing spotlight on Alabama and South Carolina. In these states the leadership in the capital, the congressional delegations, the press, the pulpit, and business community must soon give answer. The question is whether it is determined to follow the Ross Barnett blueprint of forcing federal authority to act to preserve the national integrity, or if it will provide the people with a policy of compliance with laws to meet the inevitable decisions of the future.

The eloquent and conciliatory words of President Kennedy on Sunday evening before the riots deserve to be heard again and again. The executive branch of the government did not wish to become involved in Mississippi. The politicians and White Citizens Councils of that state apparently had enough influence to create state-police resistance to federal marshals charged with carrying out a federal court order.

Primary Issue   The issue of segregation has, therefore become a secondary and relatively minor one. The primary issue has become the authority of the United States government to govern by law.

It is not reassuring to hear voices from Alabama and South Carolina encourage the violent in their states by saying publicly that both President Eisenhower, at Little Rock, and President Kennedy, at Oxford, acted illegally and in violation of state sovereignty, and states rights.

A cruel and dangerous deceit of Southern people, especially those of the Deep South states, for years has been practiced by most of their politicians. The people have been told that their states are sovereign, that they can interpose their authority in constitutional decisions. It has been this long period of deception which has conditioned the people to resist federal authority.

The Thirteen Colony Confederation that followed the American Revolution collapsed because its members were sovereign. Out of its ruins came the United States with a central government and a Constitution which, with its Bill of Rights, guarantees equal citizenship to all citizens.

Four score and seven years later, as Abraham Lincoln said at Gettysburg, a bloody Civil War was fought and the necessary federal supremacy reaffirmed. It has been further strengthened by amendments.

To Be A Nation If just one state could defy federal courts and federal authority the United States quickly would disintegrate into a chaos of factionalism and would soon fall prey to its enemies. We could not be a nation without the supremacy of the Constitution and the federal courts. Each state and the courts thereof are bound by that Constitution. Each governor, each member of the Congress and the state legislatures, takes an oath to support that Constitution and its interpretations as made by the United States Supreme Court.

The South has suffered much and will endure even more grief because of many political leaders who for years have harangued audiences with talk of nonexistent state sovereignty and who have beguiled them with a folly and falseness of the theory of interposition.

History and civilization are watching to see if still more needless and bloody pageants of defiance and resistance will be staged in Alabama and South Carolina when court orders come to them.

The national integrity certainly must come first in all of our hearts. Next in importance is education. The South, despite its sacrifice and efforts, still has less education for its children than do other regions. The future is going to belong to the best prepared. That the South, in bitterness and anger, would defy the national authority for the sake of slogans and traditions long without validity is one of the great ironies of this last half of the 20th Century.

Let it be said again, we cannot escape history.

(October 3, 1962)

A String Of Beads

West Africa: In Guinea a collector of antiquities gave as a farewell gift a string of beads. They date to the late 17th or early 18th century. They appear to be made of china. They are of good quality and not without beauty.

"These," said the giver of the gift, "were used in the slave trade."

These beads were, at one time, part of the price paid for a human being. Originally a single string was enough. By the 18th century the price was beads and a gun, or a keg of rum plus beads.

It shook one, somehow, to hold the cool beads in one's hand and to know that more than a century ago they had been a part of the price paid to sell some man or woman into chattel slavery. The hour was early morning. The sea was in sight, booming against some of the masses of red-black, iron-ore rocks which ring the Guinean coast. When the long lines of captives, brought from the inland, came to the beaches and for the first time saw the always curling, foaming sea they must have known then the acid taste of bitter, hopeless despair and deep, un-bounded terror.

Slave Trade   There are castle-fortresses along the west African coast which various slave-dealing nations built at a time when the castles were declining in Europe. The trade was brutal and ugly long before a slowly awakening conscience of humanity and of Christianity condemned it. There are stories too awful to tell. The trade at its origin was largely African and Arabic, the rival chiefs selling captives, and raiding weaker enemy tribes to obtain them. Glass and china beads, guns, and rum were the three major offers. The latter was, in a sense, worst of all in that it corrupted and depraved.

First to come from Europe were Portugal and Spain. From about 1415, as the tide of Islam retreated from the European peninsula, these nations crossed to Africa. In time they heard that in Guinea was gold. This land lay below the Sahara and was not occupied by their Muslim enemies. Henry the Navigator envisioned the great design of circum-navigating Africa and outflanking Islam. By 1471 Portuguese colonies had moved southward from Senegal to the Gold Coast. Not many years later they were at the mouth of the Congo.

Need Of Labor   The slave trade began in earnest with the 17th century. The new Spanish and Portuguese colonies in the tropical areas of the new world needed labor. As the 17th century began, the Dutch, French, and English were in the West Indies. Europe wanted sugar, a crop demanding much hand labor. The slave trade began to be more profitable than gold. The Dutch, who in 1642 had ousted the Portuguese from the Gold Coast, developed what was virtually a monopoly in slaving. By the 18th century this success had brought in the English, French, and Danes. American traders came late and were relatively few.

It is estimated that by 1600 about 900,000 enslaved persons had been landed in the West Indies and other areas in the Americas. The labor requirements of crops heavily in demand in Europe pushed the figures astronomically. Some 2,750,000 slaves were taken from Africa in the 17th century. The figures for the 18th are the highest, not less than 7,000,000. Those for the 19th were 4,000,000.

As Christianity moved against the trade, the greedy power of those in it proved strong enough to banish missionaries or to corrupt them. At one time Portugal actually defied the Vatican. By 1814 slave trading was in general outlawed but slavery continued until the 1880s when Cuba and Brazil at last abolished it. The man whose name is most connected with the period of abolition is Abraham Lincoln.

As one stood in the brief coolness of an early morning in Guinea, with the trade beads in one's hand, the symbol of them shook mind and conscience and man's historic inhumanity to man became even more hateful to consider.

(February 24, 1963)

A Matter Of Costs

Birmingham's barbarism of dogs and water hoses, following hard on the heels of that at Oxford [Mississippi], and the many instances of discrimination in other states, highlights an inescapable conclusion. It is that the nation's single most important internal problem at this place and time in history is how we deal with the minorities. To say that the security of the nation is in the final balance is no overstatement.

Historians long have pointed out that much of our national history has been a process of integrating minority groups into our life stream.

This has been largely accomplished insosfar as most of the great in-migrations are concerned. Most of these came relatively late — the Italians, Jews, Irish, and lesser, though by no means insignificant, numbers from other nations — Poles, Ukrainians, Lithuanians, Germans, *et al.* It was not until the advent of the Second World War, and the discussions and pledges of freedom and dignity for man growing out of it that we began really to face the problems of one of the oldest of Americans, the Negro, and of citizens of Mexican, Oriental, and Indian descent.

Rising Expectations There is everywhere in Latin America, in Africa, in Asia — and in the United States — a revolution of rising expectations. Since it may not be avoided, it must be faced. It is made more difficult by governors such as George Wallace of Alabama and Ross Barnett of Mississippi, as was true seven years ago when a peaceful process needlessly was turned into chaos and violence by Governor Orval Faubus' decision in Little Rock. Adding to the difficulty are refusals by lesser officials and organizations. But it should be plain to all that the issue of legitimate rising expectations is not going to be dissipated. Nor will it mysteriously disappear.

The televisions of the world are showing pictures of [Birmingham] Police Commissioner Bull Connor's tactics as examples of American inequality. The spectacle of a city attacking peacefully parading citizens with dogs and fire hoses and subjecting them to rough handling and arrest is doing this country incalculable harm. The incidents of churches and places of public business practicing discrimination are a part of the pattern which religious, business, and economic interests one day must bring to an end. This they must know. That delay frustrates resolvement of what is, after all, a fairly simple matter is plainly before us.

Certainly it will not much longer be possible to avoid court tests.

Nation Of Law We are a nation of law. Over it is the Constitution. It asserts that each citizen shall have equal protection of the law. After almost a century of ignoring this constitutional provision, there came the school decision of 1954 and subsequent court findings in this area . . . that each citizen shall have equal treatment. Critics, who were outraged by that decree, insisted each state should be permitted to treat its citizens according to its own wishes, without their resorting to the federal Constitution. They asserted that the Supreme Court actions illegally "made law". This certainly was not true. The Constitutional requirement had been there all along. It no longer may — or should be — ignored. No "rights" are being taken away. But the public rights of each U.S. citizen are being affirmed.

If discriminations, admittedly based on color, continue in the field of what is called "private business," then it is inescapable that a long, expensive — and from the viewpoint of morality and common sense, unnecessary — series of court tests will ensue. Serious questions already are being raised. Does a license issued by a city, county, or state government, to do a public service, allow the owner of such a business to exercise his whims of like and dislike in saying what customers, of all those who come in orderly manner, he will admit and what he will refuse? To be "private" does he not need to set himself up as a private club with membership? Whatever the answer, if discriminations based on color continue such court cases will be filed. They will be expensive. Morality and common sense are much less expensive than courts and ill will.

(May 9, 1963)

Bull Connor
Helps Insight

Birmingham, Alabama, by becoming a city of dreadful nights and days, managed to produce more critical world reaction than the mobs of Little Rock and Oxford, Mississippi. The vicious violence and the shocking example of hate and ill will were an affront to civilized conduct. The fact that these attitudes were more callously sustained expanded the shock reaction. Mississippi's Ross Barnett and Arkansas' Orval Faubus managed to project their personality and values and their concepts of social morality in a manner quite clear and easily comprehended.

But Bull Connor, Birmingham's commissioner of police and education, outdid them all in these categories by deed and public statements. He was pictured around the world on television. To many, unfamiliar with the South's history of prejudice and economics, Mr. Connor was quite unbelievable. But nonetheleess, there he was, and he will not be forgotten, nor should he be, since he is a symbol we need to remember.

Rarely has such a symbol had such loud and immediate endorsement from those who looked to him for leadership. Not many hours after Mr. Bull Connor denounced as gutless cowards the committee of merchants who had hammered out an armristice and an agreement to end some of the worse discriminations of segregation, two bombs were exploded at Negro residences and rifle fire damaged a third. These explosions touched off a riot in which a number of persons were injured.

It is necessary to the maintenance of one's perspective and under-

standing to note that the use of dynamite and the gunfire were exclusively confined to those white persons who, by bombing and firing
rifles under the cover of darkness, presumably were trying to demon-
strate that they were not gutless.

Mr. Bull Connor is also helpful in understanding Birmingham. The
city elected him to office for almost a quater of a century and saw
nothing incongruous in making him commissioner of education as well
of police. He had the ardent support of the city's newspapers and others
who make up what is called the power structure. Down to the hour of the
riots no single element of the city's leadership had sought to present the
alternative to Mr. Connor's policy.

The governor of the state, who let it be known in last November's
election that he hoped for the re-election of Mr. Connor, also assists us to
understand Alabama and Birmingham. The governor has pledged to
defy federal court orders in event of school desegregation. He condemned President Kennedy, who is sworn to uphold the Constitution of
the United States, for sending troops to military bases in Alabama for
use if the riots continue. The governor said, with no trace of tongue in
cheek, that the city was wholly able to control the situation.

Status Quo What Mr. Bull Connor meant to say, when he
charged the city's committee of merchants with being gutless, and what
the governor apparently wished people to understand, was that what
Alabama really was able to do was maintain the old segregated status
quo. And that is not exactly law and order.

The newspapers also took a curious position in the days before the
riots and bombings. They angrily appealed to the White House "to do
something." Mr. Bull Connor, the governor, and the newspapers, apparently reflecting what they believed to be public opinion, took the
attitude that if Mr. Kennedy would remove Dr. Martin Luther King
from Birmingham all would be well. In other words, with Dr. King gone,
things would go on as in the good old days. It would be, of course, very
easy at any time to be rid of those agitating for equal citizenship rights.
Birmingham could have achieved this by doing what was morally right
and finally what the city must do anyway. Birmingham and Alabama
are on the wrong side of the most important moral issue of this last half
of the 20th Century. Neither they nor others like them can prevail.

(May 14, 1963)

Shadow On The Schoolhouse

"I will bar the door."

One wonders if Gov. George Wallace (Alabama) realizes what a dark symbol he became when he said he would stand in the schoolhouse or university door to bar entry to those directed there by the courts of his nation — and accepted by the institutions involved.

For generations the South's children and her young men and women have had an invisible something standing in the doors of their schools — barring adequate education. Southern students have been sacrificed to lack of funds, to prejudice. Their education has not been equal to that received by children in other regions. Southern drop-out totals are higher than those of other areas. Southern teachers are paid less. The per-pupil expenditure is far below that of the more prosperous states. The South, though it tries, still spends below the national average on school plant, equipment, and teaching aids. Fewer Southern children go to high school and college.

We are in a period of crisis in education.

Social Problem   A recent report issued by the U. S. Department of Labor concluded that "unemployment among the nation's (uneducated, untrained) young is already critical and if it continues to be neglected it could develop into one of the most explosive social problems in the United States."

It is against this background that we see the governor of Alabama standing in the schoolhouse door to bar entry.

The prophets have had their say about the dangers of vanity. But the political vanity of the man who once worked his way through school, boxed in the Golden Glove contests, and whose prejudices are so intense he is willing to set an example of defiance at the highest level in the state, is more than shocking. It makes one wonder . . .

The university and college officials involved are willing to accept the applicants whom they — the universities — have found qualified. That entry of the disputed students could have been quietly, decently, honorably accomplished as was done at Clemson, S. C., a few short weeks ago is undoubted.

But, no. The governor of the state, sworn to uphold the Constitution of the United States, and knowing that the federal orders have primacy over state courts and state constitutions, has chosen "to stand in the door."

One is compelled to wonder what lights guide Governor Wallace.

One of the colleges in whose doors he will stand to bar entry is in Huntsville. Does he remember it as a small, sleepy city made prosperous by the creeping socialism of the TVA dams and cheap power that brought the textile mills?

Space Challenge Huntsville now is a city of scientists — working on missiles and the challenge of space. Some of these are foreign-born. Others are brought there from the great universities of the nation and the world. They are not interested in depriving a qualified student of an education because of his color. There would have been no student mob.

But, to have the governor of the state, while denying he wishes violence, announce he will defy the nation's orders, practically assures some sort of mob. If the governor is in defiant mood every fanatic extremist is thereby encouraged.

And Tuscaloosa? The state university has had some hard times. Its administration is not opposed to the court order. Its students have voted to accept integration. Those concerned with education in Alabama at the university and college level have not failed to see what is happening at the University of Mississippi where some 25, perhaps even 30 or more, teachers are leaving with the end of the semester in June.

The governor may attain his political martyrdom by having troops remove him from the door. It may make him the candidate of some futile Dixiecrat organization.

So what? Is it worth it to Alabama and her future?

(May 27, 1963)

Honest To God

Birmingham (Alabama) churches began a program of noon-day tolling of bells after the dynamite murder of young children to call people to programs of prayer. Reports said there was very little response — often none at all.

This lack is not unexpected. With painfully few exceptions the churches had done nothing at all before the murderous dynamiting of Sunday school attendance to give leadership in the moral dilemma and decision weighing so heavily on the city and state. Sermons preached on the morning of the modern slaughter of the innocents were, a spot check indicates, routinely irrelevant, concerning themselves with superficial admonitions of St. Paul or one of the Gospels.

Those churches that did hear of the murders of the children paused for a minute of silent or spoken prayer. This was done in several Southern cities. The repelling humor of this exhibition was that almost without exception, those who offered such prayers were churches which ruthlessly, and sometimes physically, had refused admission to Negroes appearing for worship.

Part Of Picture The sudden prayers were a part of the over-all Southern picture of Christianity at its embarrassed, or rationalized, worst. With a handful of magnificent exceptions, Christianity in the South, even in some of the larger urban centers, has supported discrimination in church and church-related schools. Some have done so with appalling honesty, saying that to have done otherwise would have offended some of those who had signed pledges for major contributions.

More and more Christians, including members of the clergy, are beginning to publish, preach and say in public discussion that modern Christianity has become chiefly a civic club ethic, not as well spelled out or promoted as that of Rotary. An increasing number of ministers privately will agree that the Christian spirit of the early church is, insofar as any use of it is concerned, quite moribund. Certainly the South's Christian churches, save for the handful of inspiring exceptions, have placed themselves on the sidelines of the great moral struggle of our time.

It is not at all surprising that the major attack on members of the National Council of Churches, who have come to grips with the inescapable moral demands of the time, have come from the South. Some have described the Council leaders as Communist-inspired. Others have adopted resolutions saying that though their local churches are members of the National Council, they, the Southern congregations, do not agree.

Genuine Pathos There is genuine pathos — and among much of the clergy a deep feeling of frustration and guilt — in the everywhere-admitted failure of Christianity to face up to a moral issue. The South is largely Protestant. The fact that the Roman Catholic Church, although itself not without its own guilt-feelings, has by and large been more forthright in its decisions has added to the frustration of the concerned Protestant clergy.

Some of them have commented in letters "The sheep are in the pulpit . . ." "The Bishop's staff no longer reminds us of a shepherd — but of a question mark . . ." "The most humiliating evidence of our shame is our almost childish pride in admitting a Negro to worship . . . this pride in what we know to be a bit of window-dressing, reveals our deeper frustration . . ."

A controversial book now being widely read by clergymen and laymen alike is *Honest to God*, by John A. T. Robinson, Bishop of Woolwich, England. Few will disagree with its assertion that for most of Christianity the image is of a "three-decker universe." God is "up there," or "out yonder." Hell is "down below." And in between is man, praying to "the man upstairs" and less and less afraid of a "downstairs hell." God is rarely "here" — he is "out there," or "up above." Man is running things just to suit himself with a set of civic club commandments.

(September 22, 1963)

Emancipating
The Southerner

President Johnson's pressure for the civil rights bill will not hurt him politically. The die had been cast before he took office. Minds already were made up on this issue. Mr. Johnson knows this.

He, and a considerable number of Southerners in the Congress, are well aware of something else.

Passage of the civil rights bill will be a sort of emancipation enactment for Southern congressmen and the South. Some of them have told him as much. They would like to have the issue of rights legislation removed from their elections. Some of them yearn to be free to present their real selves in the public eye and not always have to deny themselves the opportunity to apply their intelligence and political skills without always looking over their shoulders at the issue of civil rights.

Not long ago, after his speech on the need for a review of foreign policy and the elimination of myths and fears, Senator William Fulbright was asked why he, a civilized and able man, had voted as he had on civil rights legislation.

Candid Answer   The senator answered candidly, "So that I could remain in the Senate."

We can be glad he remained.

There are perhaps three Southern senators who are able and possessed of abilities that would have enabled them to become leaders of national opinion and thought. Two had all necessary qualifications for the presidency. Yet, each was obliged (to remain in the Senate) to pander to prejudices and positions which events were making less and less tenable.

There was in it something of the story of the young medical student

Frankenstein who created a monster that destroyed him. Southern leaders in the Congress trapped in the chains of the old one-party system, bound by the actions of their states in restricting the franchise by various stratagems, all dishonest, and therefore committed to all that was worst in the system of segregation, have for generations been at the mercy of the monster thereby created.

Tom Watson, perhaps the most dynamic of the Populist leaders, was so destroyed. In his late years he said, also with candor, that he would have been able to have become as great a national figure as Daniel Webster had there not hung over him "the dark nemesis of race."

A Proclamation   So it is no mere figure of speech to say that passage of the civil rights legislation will be an emancipation proclamation for the South and its representatives. The bill is in itself not a panacea. Its mere passage will solve little. It will for a while be strongly resisted. But it will provide a legal base from which to operate. It will do what the Congress suggested in passing the 14th Amendment — augment and broaden the intent and purpose of the amendment.

The Southern emancipation feature of the bill's passage will, of course, extend to the industrial and economic development of the Southeastern states. Corporations and industries will be able to come to the region free of the fear of reprisals, of disorders, or of inability freely to establish an employment policy.

No single act would add as much impetus to Southern development as enactment of law that will, in due time, open the public sector of life equally to all citizens . . . the right to vote, to seek a job, and to use public services. Fear of so-called "social mixing" is irrational in that it will be, as it is and always has been, a matter of personal choice. The bill does not apply to private clubs.

For the South, the door of opportunity and economic progress will be opened wider. For the Southern congressman and senator the future will be more rewarding.

(May 4, 1964)

Nobel Prize Reminds Us

Award of the Nobel Peace Prize to Dr. Martin Luther King, Jr., of Atlanta, by the Norwegian Assembly came after strong recommendation of leading Swedish members of Parliament and by many Europeans and Americans. Thirty-odd persons had been nominated.

It would be helpful if even those who oppose Dr. King would now attempt a quiet, honest evaluation of the man, of the times in which he and all of us live and have our being, and of the slow but inevitable events that mark the passing of our days and years.

The award is unique in that it rewards efforts to attain racial peace in this country and, by indirection, in all troubled areas of the world. Past recipients have labored to prevent armed conflict. Dr. King has worked in the field of human relations. In his own country, and more particularly in the South where he was born and educated and where he has labored most, he has become a highly controversial figure. Calumny, abuse, and danger have been his daily companions, despite the fact he has never advocated or initiated violence. It was his advocacy of the Gandhi-like passive resistance that won him and his followers early success and attention.

The Alternative   As others have noted, the South one day will be grateful when it realizes what the alternative would have been had Dr. King, with his capacity to stir and inspire, come preaching violence, hate and aggression. One does not like to think what the dreadful and corrosive consequences would have been.

So in evaluating the award, it is well to consider that it was given in Scandinavian Europe by the Parliament of Norway after careful study of numerous nominees. These Europeans have a view of Dr. King that is clearer than ours, which has become befogged by emotions and prejudices. The world does, however, keep a constant eye on us, as we do on it. Its peoples look at us not without sympathy as they watch 162 million Americans do what is morally and legally right about making equal the citizenship rights of 20 million other Americans. It is quite true that persons are not equal in all things. They can be equal only before the law, and historically about 10 percent of our citizens have not been.

This contradiction in our great pride in, and promise of American democracy and the rights of man has made us vulnerable to Communist propagandists. Denial of these rights has produced enormous frustrations, and as we saw in the summer, senseless riots.

American Promise   Europeans understand what is not clear to all Americans — namely, that Africa and Asia have watched Dr. Martin Luther King and seen in him manifestation of the American promise. Had Dr. King preached violence instead of peaceful resistance, the result certainly would have been a violent, anti-American reaction in much of the world. It is no exaggeration to say that Asians and Africans were fascinated with the efforts and successes of this one man working within the framework of his country's promises. Dr. King has become a symbol. As such he was seen in comparison with other symbols that arose, particularly those in Alabama, and Mississippi. These symbols were opposing legal and constitutional decisions.

The nation has much to do. The South, as a part of that nation, has a long way to go. It is the region with the greatest growth potential. Its future is delayed by an obsession with the past and by unreasonable fear of change. The Nobel Prize reminds us that the sooner more Southern communities go to work at the fairly simple problem of human beings getting along with dignity and equality before the law, the sooner our potential will be realized.

(October 16, 1964)

Not So Much Of "Old Ugly"

He was old and walked with a heavy cane. There was rheumatism in his knees and hips. He had lived a long time on a piece of land near a large Southern city. He seldom went there. But his grandson was a student at an Atlanta university.

"He (the grandson) was up to see me last week," he said. "And I told him I was proud of him and for him to keep a-goin' like he was. And then I told him, 'Son, I don't believe we are goin' to see as much of Old Ugly as we used to see.'"

The headlines have a lot of "Old Ugly" in them. But the real story out of the South now is that racial discrimination almost everywhere is abating. There is plenty of "Old Ugly" in Selma, Alabama. There is, perhaps, more of it in the rural counties adjacent to Selma. A lot of "Old Ugly" is left in the South, but it is more scattered.

"You look at the South now," said a sociologist, "and it is like looking at a laboratory technician's slide taken from an infection after a week of antibiotics. Cells of infection still are to be seen, but compare it with the slide made when the patient first was admitted to the hospital and the difference is great. In that first one the infection agents were thick and dominant."

Steady Advance Steady advance is being made in acceptance of the new civil rights law. The South now knows that its leaders who so long filibustered against it did the South and the nation a disservice — but most of all the South. Businessmen are relieved to have the law. They may prefer the old way. Most probably do. But they know the law was just and inevitable. They knew that long ago. And to their surprise they find that acceptance of it has not produced any of the evils they feared. Fear is disappearing.

There has been a considerable breakthrough in Mississippi — if we think in terms of comparison. The recent hearings of the Civil Rights Commission in the capital city of Jackson were held with dignity and with such careful attention to detail and fact that even the most defiant and angry could not object to procedures. Day after day men appeared who had been beaten, cursed, abused, shot at, and injured because of the desire to vote. More important of all was that Jackson television stations gave their audiences the commission hearings. Mississippians could sit and see the men and women who came, and hear what they said to the U. S. Commission. The effect of this showing may not be measured. But it is not superficial.

Evil Remains There has been no complete about-face in Mississippi. The evil of "Old Ugly" remains. Much of it is determined and willing to be violent. But the Mississippi power structure is now aware that they were wrong to support the White Citizens Councils — that they were badly led — and that change must be made. There is hope for decency and Americanism.

"Old Ugly" in the form of sterotype sheriffs remains in many rural counties. These sterotypes are blind — and they are followed only by the blind. Every day more persons "see."

The time is near when about all the legal devices to be employed to prevent the ballot will have been used up. Refusal of counties — such as that of which Selma is the seat — generously to assist in registering those qualified may bring on federal registrars. Here we have again another example of the deterioration and corruption of local government. It destroys itself and its integrity by such actions as those of Selma — and other areas. The vote is the greatest instrument in behalf of justice. More and more voters will be added to the rolls.

"Old Ugly" is in retreat. You don't see as much of "Old Ugly" in the South as we did even a year ago.

(March 7, 1965)

Cancer of "Southernness"

James Meredith was gunned down in Mississippi by three shotgun blasts fired by a "Southerner." This "Southerner," unemployed, known to be an uncommunicative man, driven by God-alone-knows what hatreds, fears, or inspirations from so-called "leaders" — politicians, white supremacists, preachers, state legislators or congressmen, writers of hate sheets — had never so much as seen Meredith. Yet, he reportedly told police he took his gun, drove across the river from Memphis, lay in wait in the ambush of a few shrubs beside the highway and sought to kill this man from whom he had suffered nothing and by whom he would never be wronged.

The fear of not being, maybe, after all, "supreme" can gall a man who is jobless, who finds the old "traditions" and uncertainties no more cashable in the supermarket checkout. Whatever it was that caused him to drive from Memphis to his hidden place by the highway, maybe the man who told police he did the shooting will one day make plain. Or maybe never will. The reason may be locked in his genes, in his environment, in his inner insecurities, self-doubts and the gnawing belief that maybe, after all, he is not really supreme or a superior human being.

Doubt and Fear   It is this eroding doubt and fear that is a cancer in today's "Southernness." The Barnetts, the Faubuses, the White Citizens Councils, the klans, all the racist shouters and whoopers, the "Never" sayers — all these persons and organizations have failed the insecure and all those increasingly dubious about their status as white supremacists. All these said "Never." But they didn't make good. So there is a mocking, laughing whisper in the heads of those bereft of the word "Never" that asks, "Supreme over what?" (Weep, weep for that "Southernness.")

James Meredith wrote about this in his recent book, *Three Years in Mississippi.*

> Until I was 15 I did not know my group was supposed to be the inferior one . . . There is no way for one Negro to change his basic status without changing that of all Negroes. I have long recognized the folly of advocating a change simply because it is right, because it is humane, because it is Christian, because it is in the Constitution, or for any other nonpractical reason. I am aware of another important fact. If I were a white man, I would not give up my favored position unless there was an extremely good reason. The greatest hope for a major change in the basic status of the Negro is to convince the American whites that it is in their best interests . . .

Potential Voters   Meredith went to Mississippi because he was afraid. He wanted to show the potential voters of Mississippi that they must not allow fear to stop them from registering and voting. In his book he wrote his thoughts on fear and death:

> During the first few weeks at the University of Mississippi almost all the focus was on the possibility of my being killed by the "White

Supremacists." . . . My apprehensions had been faced a long time before that. The hardest thing in human nature is to decide to act . . . The Negro in Mississippi was dead because he would not live. I was fighting to live. Where there is life there is chance. My only fear is death . . . I believe in the immortality of ideas and in the immortality of those who manifest them . . .

Meredith, walking along a Mississippi road, was manifesting an idea about the South and the nation.

What idea of "Southernness" or of civilization was in the mind of the Southerner who rose from his ambush to try and kill the man walking the road? Whom did the gunman think he was serving?

(June 10, 1966)

Look Away,
Look Away

If the band master will lift his baton we will get on with the tune — There now is rather general understanding that the old black-face "darky" minstrel song "Dixie," brought to the South in 1861 by a New York black-face minstrel show cast, is unsuited for sports and other public gatherings which include Negro citizens. Some communities, of course, persist in bad manners by defiant "what-are-you-going-to-make-of-it?" renditions of the admittedly lively and jaunty tune. But even they in time will quietly omit it.

Discussion and controversy, pro and con, stir up the "Old South" partisans, especially the professionally unreconstructed. These, by their fervor, seemingly wish the Union had been destroyed and the Confederacy perpetuated. These irrelevancies are amusing and psychologically revealing.

Great Songs One Confederate asks why not call "Yankee Doodle" bad manners? It is argued that the "Battle Hymn of the Republic" and "Marching Though Georgia" are affronts. "Yankee Doodle" is a rewrite of an old English tune dating back to the time of Oliver Cromwell. It was a popular tune of the American Revolution. "The Battle Hymn of the Republic" is one of the great national songs. It speaks for liberty and freedom and against enslavement of human beings. "Marching Through Georgia" was a song inspired by General William T. Sherman's march from Atlanta to the sea. The song ridicules no one. It celebrates a tremendously successful military operation that helped save the Union and end slavery. It seldom is played today.

Aficionados of "Dixie" should, of course, feel free to go ahead with the song. They might better enjoy it if they formed "Dixie Minstrel Clubs" and staged black-face programs with soft shoe and buck-and-wing dances. Only in this manner can they get into the original "soul" of the song. They would, of course, wear preposterous costumes. The original cast of the minstrel show which brought "Dixie" from New York to New Orleans in 1861 for performances in the large river cities, wore long-tailed swallow coats, white pantaloons, gloved hands and tattered shoes.

One of the minor but psychologically interesting bits of history was the South's addiction to the black-face minstrel shows in which white men with blacked faces portrayed the stereotype "darky." He deliberately was made a ridiculous figure, afraid of ghosts, dressed in "cast-off," ill-fitting garments; and he was a foot-shifting, shuffling "yas, suh, boss" fellow who was very good at dancing.

Minstrel Show   In reading diaries kept by civilians in the South during the Civil War one finds frequent references to "going to the minstrel show." Many communities organized their own "minstrels" and white participants would black their faces and give imitations of their concept of the stereotype darky. The South's fascination for black-face minstrels persisted into the 1920s.

It obviously is bad manners to affront Negro athletes, students and spectators with "Dixie," a song historically associated with defense of slavery and ridicule of the Negro by white men in black-face performances. One may be sure that no self-respecting Negro athlete would feel complimented if his school had Confederate flags, Confederate uniforms and a band blaring "Dixie" to remind him of ridicule and slavery. "Dixie" was never a Southern song in origin or intent.

By all means let those who can't do without it continue to have it. I do suggest, however, that only if they black their faces and put on preposterous costumes such as the minstrel show "darkies" wore will they get to the soul of it.

(July 11, 1967)

A Free Man Killed By White Slaves

White slaves killed Dr. Martin Luther King [Jr.] in Memphis. At the moment the trigger man fired, Martin Luther King was the free man. The white killer (or killers) was a slave to fear, a slave to his own sense of inferiority, a slave to hatred, a slave to all the bloody instincts that surge in a brain when a human being decides to become a beast.

In the wake of this disaster in Memphis, a great many such slaves must consider if they wish to continue serving their masters of fear, hate, inferiority, and beastliness. It is something of an irony that Dr. King was free and was hated by so many slaves. It is perhaps too much to hope, but much of the violent reaction to this bloody murder could be blunted if in every city and town there would now be a resolve to remove what remains of injustice and racial prejudice from schools, from training and job opportunities, from housing and community life in general.

Nonviolence   Dr. King's voice was the last one arguing for nonviolence. The young militants respected him enough to pledge him they would accept his leadership in the summer ahead.

And now?

The old ghost of John Brown whispers out of the by-gone years. He was a white man and a violent one. He was hanged after his foolish foray at Harper's Ferry, Virginia, in the autumn of 1859. Brown was the martyr. His death was a catalyst. His soul became a cutting edge that broke hearts and walls as the great war came on with a rush. One frets with that memory.

There are other effects of martyrdoms.

Dr. King would not want his death to be an emotion that brought on what he had all his life opposed — violence and death. Atlanta's Mayor Ivan Allen, who drove his car through a rain-swept city to the home of Dr. King and took the stunned wife to the airport where she learned that death had come in Memphis, was another symbol of the South. He, too, was a free man. He was not a slave to hate and fear. His city is not a slave city bound by such terrible chains as held the killers in Memphis.

That city, which allowed a strike of Negro garbage workers to grow into a protest against all the many remaining forms of racist prejudice, did not meet a necessary test. And so Memphis became the site of a slave uprising where death and hate opposed freedom.

The Beast   The Memphis killer and his associates have done their own race a grave and hideous injustice. They have made it possible for blind violence to be loosed. They have elevated the beast in man. They may have imperiled the negotiations that, hopefully, may be arranged to end the war in Vietnam. The slave beast does not reason. The beast, unless chained, is only a beast.

The white South — the white population in all the country — must now give answer. If injustice and inequity, if racist prejudices and discriminations now become the targets of all decent men and women,

Dr. King's death may bring about what he sought for himself, his people and country.

If this does not happen, then slaves who serve masters of hatred, fear, and evil will have to be put down mercilessly and immediately.

Out of martyrdom must come the right answer.

(April 5, 1968)

"Many Fingers On The Trigger"

Shortly after the murder of Dr. Martin Luther King, Jr., I saw his faith-sustained, grief-burdened father. "No one man did this," he said, controlling with difficulty his emotions. "There were a lot of fingers on that trigger."

Dr. King did not mean to imply there was a conspiracy, although he does not rule out that possibility. He meant that the long accumulation of hatred against his son, the many previous violent attacks against him and the many brutalities unleashed against him and his protest marches had come from a sick element of white society. Many persons, steeped in vindictive hatreds, had prepared the way for the rifle to be fired.

The Rev. James Bevel of the Southern Christian Leadership Conference (SCLC) staff has said he does not believe James Earl Ray is "guilty." The Rev. Mr. Bevel talked on this theme more fully some weeks ago at a meeting of SCLC at Frogmore, S. C. At that time his idea seemed to be that since a society of hate had produced the murder, Ray, even though he might be found to have fired the fatal shot, was not truly guilty. Since all those whose hate had contributed to the death could not be found guilty then, *ipso facto*, Ray was not guilty. . . .

But no matter who did it, the killing of Dr. Martin Luther King, Jr., was, in major part, a product of the vicious hatreds that stew in the minds of those whose racist attitudes and emotions are themselves at, or near, the paranoia state. "Daddy" King was right. There were many fingers on the trigger.

(February 1, 1969)

The Harvest
Of Hate

Flaming death out of a gun barrel — mindless, senseless, violent death — has taken another man from the ranks of those who believed in human rights and justice; a man who took that belief to the people and imposed it upon their consciences.

There is in this violent nation a long and bloody record of such murders. President John Kennedy leads the list in our time. There are others on that roll of honor, men well known and who worked in areas where all too often the days were a part of the darkness of despair. One was a lonely and courageous Negro, shot down in his own driveway in Mississippi because, as head of the NAACP, he publicly had sought to have his state accept the laws of equal citizenship; Medgar Evers died just outside the door of his home behind which waited his wife and children.

Martin Luther King was gunned down by a sniper. He, too, had spoken up for justice in areas where justice had long been ignored and mocked.

And now Robert Kennedy's name is added. He, too, had spoken up for justice. He, too, was unafraid of the cowards who betray and kill from ambush or who infiltrate a friendly group to murder.

A few lines from Edna St. Vincent Millay's poem "Dirge Without Music" seem apropos:

> Down, down into the darkness of
>   the grave,
> Gently they go, the beautiful, the
>   tender and the kind;
> Quietly they go, the intelligent,
>   the witty, the brave.
> I know. But I do not approve.
> And I am not resigned.

We are not resigned. Nor may we be.

The jackals, the cowards, the haters, the failures who hate achievers, the yapping feist pack that tries to drown out truth; those who dislike Jews, Negroes, Catholics, "liberals;" the bitter and evil persons who organize themselves and send out hate literature; the Klan types, the "States Rights" diehards, those who dynamite churches, synagogues, and homes — they are the abscesses in America's society.

Atlanta's mayor had an anonymous letter from one of those yellow rats:

> Let us hope that Bobby Kennedy dies . . . I personally cheered when John F. Kennedy was killed and will give three cheers if Bobby goes on his merry way to hell . . .

America is sick — sick with its haters . . . sick with its cowards . . . sick with its do-nothing "good people."

There is a harvest of all things sown . . . On the day Kennedy died, Georgia's governor was ecstatic in his praise of a county which had signed a petition of protest against a United States Supreme Court order requiring schools to hasten removal of the indignities and inferiority of segregated education . . .

George Wallace, a shrewd man, decided to call off his scheduled journey into the New England states to preach his prejudiced doctrine of states rights — the opposite of what Robert Kennedy of Massachusetts believed and promoted.

These two news items were straws in the winds.

The murder[s] of John Kennedy and Robert Kennedy . . . of Martin Luther King and Medgar Evers . . . of children by dynamite in the Birmingham church . . . of the civil rights workers in Mississippi . . . of the Episcopal minister in Selma; all these — and others — are harvest of things sown.

Preachments of hatred may not be restricted to one field. Daily the mails bring in insane pamphlets that declare Franklin Roosevelt was a Jew; the Supreme Court is controlled by Jews and Communists; Communism is taking over the country; the newspapers and television are "run by Jews" . . . and so on and on, *ad nauseum*.

Sirhan, who killed Robert Kennedy, hated rich people, Jews and Negroes; he filled up a notebook with his slobbering mad-dog drivel . . .

Robert Kennedy is dead. But, we are not resigned.

(June 7, 1968)

They Mourned Lost Rights

I was late. It was the 9:10 bus I boarded for the six-mile ride to the office. Two well-dressed, too-plump, matronly-looking women of about 60 were on the seat just ahead of me. Across the way two neat Negro women sat, talking and laughing over some experience. A few stops later three more Negroes got aboard. One sat up front. The other two, apparently unacquainted, took separate seats on the left, also up front.

The plumper of the two women ahead of me, sitting next to the window, said to the other, in a well-modulated voice: "We certainly don't have any rights any more."

"None," said the other, nodding affirmatively. "They have all the rights now."

They both nodded, as if to emphasize the point, and fell silent. It was so preposterous a situation and revelation, one wanted to laugh out loud. And yet it also was enormously sad. These two over-fed women, almost stereotypes of comfortable "middle-class" appearance and values, were unhappy inside. They revealed a great deal in their brief little scene. They almost surely hate "that Lyndon Johnson" and all those Yankees who have taken away their "rights" to be among the exclusive ones who once upon a time could ride in the front of the bus.

Their Presence   The Negro women opposite them were just as well dressed, were equally well behaved, had paid the same fare — but their presence there somehow meant to the two pathetic women ahead of me a "loss" of a right. "Jack Kennedy, Lyndon Johnson — all those hypocritical civil rights people — had taken away their rights." They were two of the unhappy persons who write angry letters to editors saying, "Don't white people have rights any more?" No white person has lost a single right merely because a Negro citizen has gained civil rights long denied — illegally and unconstitutionally.

The historian C. Vann Woodward has best described how segregated practices came well after the Civil War. The processes by which they became "habit," "custom," and "our way of life" are tortuous, ugly, often cruel, and always unworthy of those who imposed them. They remind us of the power of habit and custom. In some periods of history, children were sacrificed to idols. Because custom demanded it, the agonized parents acquiesced. Some, perhaps, did not even agonize. In the days of serfdom in Russia and Middle Europe, "custom" and tradition required that a serf girl who was given permission to marry must spend the first night with the nobleman, who owned the serfs — or with his son. The newly married couple was not happy about it, but it was a "right" of the owner.

Public Transport   The cost-ridden association that was the Southern custom now erodes away. Passengers sit where they find seats on public transport. They eat in restaurants when they wish and have the price. They stop at public hotels and motels.

None of the dire threats or prophecies of a few years ago have come true. No restaurants, hotels, motels, airplanes or buses have been "ruined" or hurt financially. No person has lost any "social status" by these changes. Presumably, everyone now knows that the old fears and predictions were myths. We can laugh about them now. The best part of it is that the old close relation between black and white people in the South has survived. It is there to build on. Even the two sad fat ladies, going to town to shop, were still riding the buses. They mourned their lost "rights," but they were on the bus.

(December 28, 1966)

Ralph McGill talks with Dr. Martin Luther King (*top*), father of the famed civil rights leader, at the centennial of Morehouse College in 1966. He is shown in the lower photo with Roy Wilkins (*left*) and Carl T. Rowan after the three had been awarded honorary degrees in 1965.

(*Photo Credits are on Page 210*)

A Farmer's Corn (*top*) was but one of many subjects McGill dealt with in a series of agricultural articles which earned him a Rosenwald Fellowhip for 1935–'36. In the lower picture he visits with Carl Sandburg at the latter's home in the mountains of North Carolina.

The Peripatetic Columnist impersonates a chef, visits a circus performer and her elephant, and goes on a bird shoot at the South Georgia plantation of Robert W. Woodruff.

VIPs were a routine part of Ralph McGill's world after he became nationally famous. General Lucius Clay, a Georgian who was serving as American military governor, welcomed him to Berlin in 1947 (*top photo*), and McGill and his family chatted with President John F. Kennedy (*bottom photo*) at Palm Beach early in the 1960s.

MORE VIPs: Robert W. Woodruff and McGill confer (*top left*), 1961; the *Constitution* editor leaves the White House during World War II (*top right*); and (*bottom*) Vice President and Mrs. Hubert Humphrey (*shown at left*) and Atlanta Mayor and Mrs. Ivan Allen, Jr. arrive for Mr. McGill's funeral at All Saints Episcopal Church, 1969.

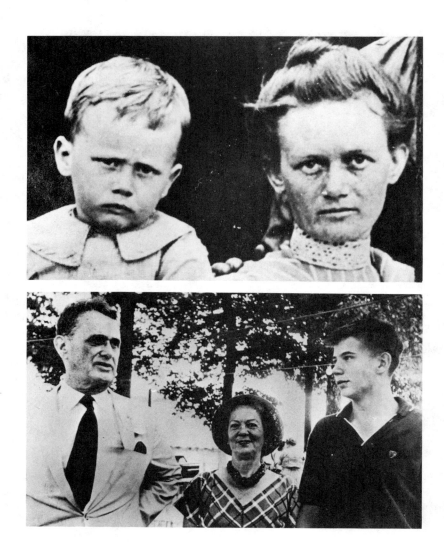

McGill And His Family. As a small boy Ralph McGill scowls as he is photographed with his mother. Years later, in 1959, he and his first wife and their son, Ralph Jr., enjoy a *Constitution* picnic.

The Second Mrs. McGill (*top left*) at a ceremony honoring her husband, who is shown (*top right*) speaking at the Democratic National Convention in 1944. Ralph McGill (*bottom*) stands beside his desk at the *Constitution*, which previously had belonged to Henry W. Grady.

1972
SHINING LIGHT AWARD
IN HONOR OF
RALPH E. McGILL
EDITOR & PUBLISHER
ATLANTA CONSTITUTION
DEFENDER OF TRUTH. TIRELESS
SOUTHERN CRUSADER AGAINST
IGNORANCE, PREJUDICE AND
APATHY. HE AWAKENED THE
CONSCIENCE OF THE NATION.
ATLANTA GAS LIGHT CO.
W S B RADIO

Text of the "Shining Light Award" Honoring Ralph McGill.

THE PRESIDENCY

For Ralph McGill, the presidency was a hallowed institution to be studied and respected. He wrote many columns about presidents past and present. His favorite was probably Andrew Jackson, but he admired Abraham Lincoln and had a special devotion to Franklin Roosevelt.

McGill also had a special feel for the majesty of Washington as expressed in "Young Queen of Capitals" and "Capital Braces for a Big Show." Harry Truman was admired for doing a good job in a tough situation. "Here Goes Private Truman" is a fond farewell to the gentleman from Missouri.

Originally, McGill had some reservations about John F. Kennedy, but these doubts were erased. In "A President with Steel" and "The Symbol of a Grave," it is obvious that Kennedy measured up to McGill's high standards.

Young Queen Of Capitals

WASHINGTON, D. C. — This is a wondrous, beautiful city. There is no capital anywhere which can match it in loveliness. London has more majestic dignity and more of a presence of history. Copenhagen is a delight. Stockholm has her own enchantment of sea and stone. Paris is Paris. But Washington is the young queen of capitals and she is now at her loveliest. In the spring her buildings seem to bloom almost as much as the flowers. The jade green of the new leaves on her many trees is a color to make one stop and look in admiring wonder.

And history is here, too. The Supreme Court Building is the center of it. Our history is one of law. It grows out of the fact that our forebears created a system of law which gave the individual dignity and responsibility. All our history radiates from the Supreme Court as spokes from the hub of a wheel.

The Supreme Court is the custodian and interpreter of the Constitution and the Constitution is the symbol of our nation. We are a young country but our Constitution is the oldest such document in the universe. Its principles inspire persons all around the world.

Tom Jefferson It was in this city that red-headed Tom Jefferson left his boarding house, mounted his horse, and rode off to the Capitol to be inaugurated as President. It always is good to take a taxi out to his memorial reflected in the pool before it. It is beautiful as a Greek temple has beauty. Jefferson had a mind which was as ordered and disciplined as the clean, architectural lines of his memorial. It was his mind, more than any other, which broke the old thought structure of his time. He shook down the foundation of rule by divine right with his contributions to the Declaration and the Constitution. There is not here the almost intangible sense of history one feels in London or Paris. But Jefferson is here. And so is Lincoln.

One can stand at Lincoln's Memorial and watch the people who come. A little girl asks, tugging at her mother's skirt, "Why is he so sad, Mama?" A boy says, "He seems about to speak. He is making a big decision and he will tell us about it."

Lincoln is here. We cannot pass the White House without thinking of him during the grim days of the Civil War when the future of the Union hung in the balance. Andrew Jackson is here. And Woodrow Wilson and Teddy and Franklin Roosevelt. Though they do not intrude on one's consciousness, fearful Buchanan and the desolate and inadequate Harding. The dry, unimaginative Coolidge. But essentially, this is the city of Jefferson and Lincoln.

Youngsters Come Spring is the time when the youngsters come. They arrive by train, plane and chartered bus. Senior classes from high schools over the nation come to see their nation's capital city. One encounters them in the corridors of the Capitol Building, at the White House, the Supreme Court, and in the chambers of the Senate and House. One wonders what image of their country they bring with them. All ages learn what we live and live what we learn.

They come from farm and city, from homes which believe in America, and from those which distrust it and its institutions.

The schoolboy patrols come. It is not always easy to meet the eyes of the Negro youngsters when we see them and the flag and remember the pledge of liberty and justice for all. The editors come in annual convention and debate the problem of the press. The Daughters of the American Revolution come, and they seem timorous and afraid of anything revolutionary.

In the spring in Washington the badges bloom as prolifically as the flowers. It is a city of badges. The hotel lobbies seem always filled with the same faces. Only the badges change.

But if one gets out of the lobbies and the convention rooms, Washington is a wonderfully beautiful city to see.

(April 28, 1960)

The Home
Of Jefferson

Out from Charlottesville, Virginia, one begins to climb a hill. Almost to the top one stops one's car and gets out at the grave of Thomas Jefferson.

There always is someone there. Someone from Maine or Texas or Oregon or Georgia or some of the other states. They stand there before the simple marble shaft, their hats in their hands, and read the simple inscription on the shaft. It says that beneath it is buried Thomas Jefferson, author of the Declaration of Independence. About him lie his relatives and one or two close friends.

One stands there and wonders at the shortness of time we have had our liberty and our freedom. There before one's eyes is the grave of the man who, along with others, took his life in his hands by signing that most revolutionary document, the Declaration of Independence. Once they signed it no man's life was safe if the British captured the owner of one of those names. One stands there and wonders at the fact that our liberties and our freedom came from the stubborn insistence of the man whose dust and bones lie beneath the shaft. It was he who opposed, in 1787, the Constitution of the United States, saying it contained no Bill of Rights. It is well to remember that Alexander Hamilton did not want those rights in that constitution and that they had to be added by amendment. No one ever gives liberties. They have to be fought for to be had and kept.

One stands there looking while the fat woman from Iowa says:

"George, I think the monument over grandpa's grave is prettier than this, don't you?"

Monticello   It is not too fantastic and it is not extravagant to say that every school boy and girl ought to see three homes of three Presidents.

One would be the home of Jefferson. High on the hill out from Charlottesville. Another would be the Hermitage, home of Andrew Jackson, some 12 miles out from Nashville. And the other would be that poor log cabin, the birthplace and home of Abraham Lincoln, which one may see on the road out of Bardstown, Kentucky.

One should tell the children the story, the full story of Jefferson. He was one of the Virginia aristocrats. With a passion for the rights of the average man. It was he who wrote, well before the Declaration of Independence, the bill of religious freedom which Virginia adopted. He was well educated. He talked French. He liked, and knew, good wines and liquors, books and paintings. He was a brilliant conversationalist. He was in France when the French revolution was gathering force. He wrote our Declaration of Independence and did not waste a word. He fought for a bill of rights to be amended into the constitution.

One should tell them also of the border captain, Andrew Jackson. One should tell them of the horse races, the chicken fights, the duels, the stubborn courage and the unwavering loyalty to the people of Andrew Jackson. One should tell them of the man man born in the log cabin of semi-illiterate parents, of the boyhood dedicated to toil and hardship, of the patient kindness and positive loyalty to the people of the rail splitter, Abe Lincoln.

One could say, having shown these three places and told the three stories:

That is America. That is the blending. That is the aristocrat, the border captain, the man from the prairies just beginning to know the plow.

They are the three men who kept for us the thing we call democracy. They are the three men whose blending of character, personality and loyalty to the rights of the people kept democracy for us. They are, between them, the story of this country.

The Fine Arts   The main house at Monticello was half finished when the revolution came. It was this war which was to cause an emperor of Russia to refuse to recognize the government of the United States because it was too radical. Jefferson was the father of it all. One may see [that] the man loved the house . . .

Behind his mantelpiece in the dining room is the dumb waiter for wine. The guide showed it. The chilled full bottles came up one side and the empties went down the other. A hard-faced, ugly woman from Indiana tossed her head and said, "H-mpif" when that was shown. She didn't think so much of Thomas Jefferson after that.

It shocked her to find the man she had seen only in marble or bronze come alive and become human.

One may see the clock which tells the day of the week. The weather vane with a connection on the front portico so one would not have to go out in the weather to see how the wind blew, the bed which one could get into from either side and which pulled up into the attic when one got out of it. There are so many things to see. He loved the house.

It sits on a high hill and one may look in any direction and see the great vista of fields, hills and mountains stretching as far as eye can see.

He wrote his own epitaph. It was found in his papers after his death. It reads:

Here was buried Thomas Jefferson, author of the Declaration of Independence, of the statute of Virginia for religious freedom, and father of the University of Virginia.

There is no epitaph in the world as great as that.

All of it is something done for all the people, and not for any special interest.

Some day go to see Monticello.

(April 28, 1941)

Asking The Pardon
Of Andrew Jackson

When Andrew Jackson lay in his bed at the Hermitage, with the shade of death waiting nearby to darken his mortal eyes forever, one of those about the bedside piously asked him if he had any regrets to express.

The dying eagle thought for a moment, marshaling his memories in his dying mind, and said after awhile, he had but two.

"What are they?" asked the pious brother, thinking to hear some regret over horse racing or card playing or dueling.

"I regret I did not hang John Calhoun and shoot Henry Clay," he said, slowly, and quite firmly, too, considering he was dying.

He was near to hanging him, too, in 1833 when John Calhoun, in South Carolina, refused to permit payment to the United States of certain custom duties at the port.

Old Hickory, who along with his friend William Crawford, of Georgia, hated the man, went cold with rage.

He sent a message that if John Calhoun did not pay the taxes he would accompany troops to South Carolina and take great personal pleasure in hanging the said John C. Calhoun.

John Calhoun thought it over. He may have thought about a certain duel or so in Tennessee.

Whatever it was he paid up.

It was not well to trifle with Andrew Jackson, especially when Andrew Jackson thought the welfare of the United States of America was at hand.

The Prophet   This week, asking the pardon of the shade of Andrew Jackson, there is to be a ceremony honoring John C. Calhoun as a prophet.

It seems that in 1845 when the name of a village of two or three hundred persons was changed from Marthasville to Atlanta, John C. Calhoun halted at the village as was his custom.

He had married well, adding a tidy fortune to his own, but it was from Georgia's gold mines at Dahlonega that he got his real wealth. It is not a pretty story the histories tell about the working conditions of slaves in the Calhoun mines, but it is one that would not have surprised William Crawford, of Georgia, and Andrew Jackson, of Tennessee.

They, had they known of it, would have said it was no more than was to be expected of John C. Calhoun.

William Crawford, probably the greatest and most able Georgian, was the one who stood off Calhoun when Old Hickory, with a fine disregard of Congress and international law moved in and captured the Spanish forts during the Seminole war. Old Hickory knew it would mean the United States would hold that territory instead of Spain, but the politicians, Calhoun among them, were willing to let the United States go if they could ruin Jackson. William Crawford prevented it. It is a pity that a stroke, probably from a cerebral hemorrage, killed him at the moment when he might have become president of the United States.

But, to get back to John C. Calhoun . . . when he was halted in the small village of Atlanta he made a prophecy. He pointed out that terrain, and rivers and mountains and the inevitable flow of trade, would cause the little village to become the focal point of a great number of railroads.

There was one then. Today every railroad Calhoun foresaw is in existence — and in the place he said it would be.

Place In History   No general estimate of the man exists. Many conflicting opinions do. Nevertheless, his place in history is secure.

John Quincy Adams wrote of Calhoun in his diary, on date of March 2, 1831:

Mr. Calhoun's friendships and enmities are regulated exclusively by his interests. His opinions are the sport of every popular blast, and his career as a statesman has been marked by a series of the most flagrant inconsistencies.

A popular saying in those days was that:

John C. Calhoun is a cast iron man who looks as if he had never been born and could not be extinguished.

He was, all of his life, something of the cast-iron and stone statues they have made of him and put up here and there. Yet he was a great and magnificent orator, the cold aristocrat.

He saw, and never doubted the issue, that the south could not live with the north and remain a slave-holding section. Others thought the issue could be compromised. Calhoun knew it couldn't be and didn't want it compromised.

He was a good prophet about railroads.

And, he too, had a death-bed statement. His last words were: "The south, the poor south."

And that prophecy, too, remains with us.

But they will put it on no plaques.

(September 9, 1945)

Rachel Reaches White House

There was a sentimental little touch to the cold and objective story saying that Rachel Jackson had at last reached the White House.

She never went there and never wanted to go, although she would have gone with the general had not death intervened. Death took her before the inauguration. She went peacefully to sleep a week before Andrew Jackson took over the reins of government.

It was a good thing, I guess, because the Washington of even that early period would not have understood this plain, simple woman, deeply religious and deeply in love with her husband.

She would not have fitted into the picture, although Old Andy, in his way, would have tried to fit her there if it meant killing a man or so who might have objected.

He was rather firm about his Rachel. After her death they got the old warrior to join the church. He joined, pain eating at his heart, knowing she would have wished it. He looked upward at the skies, hoping and believing she was looking down on him and approving. It soothed the ache in his heart to think that.

When he had joined and had been prayed over and had prayed, they suggested that he should forgive his enemies.

"I forgive them all," he said, "except those who have hurt her. They must answer to me in hell."

I always had a firm faith they did answer. I have never doubted but that Old Andy went down in the smoking caverns of hell and horse-whipped Lewis Robards and several others of that frontier set of gossips who tried to smirch a good woman's name with their lying tongues.

Duel He was a very firm man, was Andrew Jackson. He was firm in the duel that morning when he went to shoot it out with Charles Dickinson.

Charles Dickinson was a smug sort of person, I think, if I have read history aright. He was the greatest pistol shot in the west. That morning, going out to the duel, he amused himself shooting the diamonds out of playing cards at the dueling distance and leaving them stuck on trees for Jackson to see. Jackson saw them, but he gave no sign. He was patient, for an impatient man.

They got to the dueling place and there was Dickinson smiling his hard, bitter, confident smile. Old Andy was there, quiet and calm.

The word was given and Dickinson fired first.

Old Hickory just stood there.

"My God, have I missed him?" asked Dickinson of himself, and of death, whom he could feel at his elbow. He recoiled back a step as Jackson stood there, still and strong.

"Back to your mark sir," said the seconds, and Dickinson stepped [forward].

Old Hickory was not a good shot. He was wounded, too, which Dickinson didn't know. He was getting weak fast and his arm was shaking a bit, so he just shot Dickinson in the stomach, not trying for anything fancy like the head or heart, as had Dickinson.

Dickinson fell, mortally wounded, and died in agony a few hours later, all of which would have suited Old Hickory fine.

Dickinson had been speaking badly about Rachel and Old Hickory wouldn't allow that to happen, and when it did happen he ended it for good . . .

Old Hickory had been shot very near the heart. The bullet missed the heart by the fraction of an inch, and it stayed in his body the rest of his life to plague him.

They talked about Rachel because she had married Andrew Jackson before her divorce from the worthless . . . Lewis Robards was completed. He was a long way from Nashville and in the frontier of that time it was not possible to know. Also, there is evidence Robards had written her it was completed. He was a rat, I think, and it comforts me to know that Old Hickory shouldered his way into hell and horsewhipped him. Old Hickory and Rachel were married again, which was a foolish, impulsive thing to do, but Old Hickory always wanted to do the right thing.

A Fine Woman   She was a fine woman. All that she asked of life was to stay at home with "the general." There wasn't much time for that. He was away fighting the Indians and the British.

When they made him senator she didn't care for it. She stayed at home. They offered him the ambassadorship to Mexico and when he refused it she was immensely gratified. It didn't last long. One of her letters lets us see the sorrow of this plain, simple woman of the frontier:

> Through all his trials . . . I watched, waited, and prayed, most of the time alone. They talk of his being President . . . In this, as in all else, I can only say, the Lord's will be done.

The general was elected. He went off to Washington, but always there was an ache in his heart. He served two terms, breaking the power of the Bank of the United States and smashing the special privileges of financial groups which were in control of government. They hated him, calling him a dictator and saying that we no longer had democratic government but lived under the reign of one man. They cartooned him as "King Andrew, the First." He gave the government back to the people.

Today one may look upon the face of Rachel Jackson as she looks down from the gold frame in the new east wing of the White House. Howard Chandler Christy painted it. The state of Tennessee presented it. I can only wish the Tennesseans had done it ere now.

(April 25, 1943)

Portrait In A Nightshirt

WASHINGTON, D. C. — A painting of Abraham Lincoln in a white nightshirt was unveiled this week in the rotunda of the old Senate office building.

Some lay critics, a little shocked to see the gaunt bearded President in a nightshirt, were dubious. But Sen. John Sherman Cooper, of Lincoln's native state Kentucky, liked it.

This painting captured the simple dignity, the solemn earnestness and determination of President Lincoln just before the Battle of Antietam.

So it seemed to me. Too many of our great are pictured to us in marble or painted on canvas all dressed out as if prepared to give their Sunday-best front to posterity.

This picture is a part of America of Lincoln's time. Men did wear nightshirts. The effete pajama had not been invented. Men slept in their underwear or nightshirts. The old kerosene lamp, the daguerreotypes in their round, walnut frames, the four-poster bed — all these are a part of our country that has been gone a long time.

The nightshirt is a long one. Not many inches of the President's thin shanks may be seen. His left leg is crossed over the right at the knee. And on his feet are the old brocaded felt slippers mentioned so often in the stories of the war years.

His Custom   It was his custom to shuffle about the White House on nights when the war news was bad or when there was no word from a great battle known to be in progress. He liked to go and visit with the telegraph operators, sitting with them, his legs crossed and the old slipper half-falling from the crossed feet.

A telegraph operator, David Homer Bates, wrote of the President's rising from an old hair-cloth sofa, where he often waited while telegrams were being de-coded, to discover and brush from the presidential lapel a bedbug. "Boy," he said, "I've become very fond of that old lounge, but as it has become a little buggy, I fear I must stop using it."

Once the captain of the White House guards, who knocked each morning on the President's door at 7 o'clock, found Lincoln sewing a button on a shirt, which he had to wear. "Come in," he said, "wait until I repair the damage."

America was young in those years. The frontier was near. And not too many years were between young Lincoln, the railsplitter, and the President sewing on a button.

Lincoln Working   The painting depicts Lincoln working on his notes for the emancipation proclamation of September, 1862. He was not in the White House on the night pictured in the painting. He was staying for a few days at the Soldliers Home, three miles out of Washington. News came that the advantage lay with the Union Army in the Battle of Antietam. Emancipation had been debated for some weeks. Indeed, the President previously had written a preliminary draft, but had put it aside. News of the battle seemed an omen. He wrote out the notes sitting in his bedroom — much as the painting has it.

The preliminary proclamation provided for buying and setting free the slaves of the border states and colonizing of them. All freed slaves who wished could have free steamer tickets to Haiti or Liberia. It further provided that on Jan. 1, 1863, all slaves in the states "in rebellion against the Union should be then and thence forward forever free." The proclamation was made public after Cabinet acceptance on Monday, Sept. 4.

That night the President addressed serenaders from a White House balcony: "What I did, I did after a full deliberation . . . I can only trust in God I have made no mistake . . ."

Looking at the picture of the deeply intense man, sitting there in a nightshirt by an old four-poster bed, lost in the momentous notes, one feels glad it occurred as it did. A lonely man, with only the presence of God in the room, was then and there setting in motion one of the great moral movements of all time.

(March 14, 1959)

Hoover, A Story of Usefulness

Former President Herbert Hoover died peacefully and content, full of years and faith. He had outlived his critics, a rare accomplishment in itself. But what was the more remarkable was that he had, after some years of bitterness, erected a new and shining career of usefullness on the wreckage of the old.

We know from his books and the few impulsive remarks of the bitter years that the crash of his presidential career in the vast and corrosive Depression was a heavy and galling cross to bear. He felt that much of the criticism was unjust. Some of it was. But more than that, there was a time when he seemed to feel himself a target of fate, a victim of blind furies. And, in a sense, he was.

He was not a politician — and it is impossible efficiently to carry on the appalling burden of the presidency without political skills. Mr. Hoover had been engineer and humanitarian. He had taken relief to Russia. He had coped with typhus, hunger, and the chaos of revolution. He was a secretary of commerce and then President.

Since he did not understand politics he could not communicate. He lacked the ability to get along with Congress. He was not a politician and so he did not understand how to contend with the checks and balances. His legislation, some of it excellent, was therefore stalled in committees. He could not extract it. He did not know how to make the necessary moves of give and take, of public appeal, of compromise.

When the great crash came he took poor advice. He allowed himself to say to the nation that a return to prosperity was "just around the corner," and that the people must rely on "rugged individualism."

By 1932, at least 10 million persons were out of work and all who had jobs had taken substantial wage cuts. Thousands were doing part-time work. Savings painfully accumulated soon were spent. Thousands of farmers and homeowners lost their property.

Soon the real estate market was so depressed that creditors postponed taking action. Farmers were hit perhaps hardest of all. (In 1933 farm prices were 63 per cent below their 1929 level.) There were breadlines and soup kitchens in the cities. Men who had held good jobs were selling apples on street corners. The highways and railroads daily saw the tides of roaming men and women, hunting work.

Conditions did not improve. The Congress passed the outrageous Smoot-Hawley high tariff act.

Unemployment Unemployed veterans camped near Washington, lobbying for payment of a bonus. In July, 1932, panic seized the leaders in Washington. General Douglas MacArthur was sent with four troops of cavalry and four of infantry, a machine-gun squadron and six tanks. The veterans' shacks were burned.

In farm areas a rabbit was called "A Hoover dinner." When the old flivver would run no more its wheels were used to make a horse or mule-pulled "Hoover cart." Men who could not afford cigarets smoked "Bull Durham" and called it "Hoover dust."

President Hoover was willing to spend federal [money]. But he thought it should be used to strengthen banks, corporations, and railroads. A process of recovery would, he believed, begin. It was too late for that. Direct action was needed.

There was no heart in the Republican convention of 1932 that nominated him. His defeat was complete. Herbert Hoover came back from that disaster to die at 90 as a man loved and honored. He and Harry Truman had become close friends. His critics were dead or had forgiven him — and he them. The Hoover story is one of our best.

(October 25, 1964)

The Tree
Has Been Down
Six Years

"A tree is measured best when it is down." Franklin D. Roosevelt, who among other gifts had that of managing Gen. Douglas MacArthur, has been down six years now, surely a brief time as the years go, yet it seems a long, long time ago indeed that he slipped from life through the door each of us must enter.

He was many men.

To some he was the man who had a son named Elliott who was irresponsible and who persuaded a grocery chain executive to invest a small fortune in one of many ventures which never paid off. This, somehow, has been repeated and repeated and made into some sort of major crime by those who loudly trumpet Franklin Roosevelt was not, after all, God Almighty. To others he was the father of Jimmy Roosevelt who once got a lot of insurance business on the magic of the family name, but who was never too good at business or politics. His wife was Eleanor Roosevelt and the fact that she has calmly lived her life and made it one which has made the people of America vote her the greatest living American woman, seems to sadden those whose text is that FDR was God Almighty.

Homes To several hundreds of thousands of Americans he was the man who saved their homes and farms through the HOLC and through government credits of a long-time nature, which could not be granted by private banks. Millions of farmers know him as the man who brought REA into being and who lifted the burden of toil off the backs of themselves, their wives and their children. He knew what was wrong about the dust bowl. They laughed at him for planting belts of trees which now are doing the job of windbreaks. There are perhaps a quarter of a million or more new American land owners, living [on] their own land, and feeling the pride of ownership because of his tenant purchase act. The face of America is annually being changed by soil conservation processes and there are men who think of Franklin Roosevelt when they see pastures and trees growing where old eroded lands were twenty years ago. To millions of others sitting in their homes in the early thirties, with no job or one which was about to end, with paychecks part grocery orders and promises to pay, he was a voice that came out of their radio speakers and said not to be afraid.

To others he was the man who was too careless about Communists; who didn't really believe they would betray their own country; who was out-traded at Yalta. To many other Americans he was a man too friendly to organized labor and who refused to see the coercive, oppressive evils of some of its organization methods. To others he was the man who ended sweat shops and exploitation.

To several million old people he was the person who brought social security and who took away at least some of the insecurity from the last, dim years.

Leader   To some he was the great democrat of our time, a leader who knew the answers and who possessed the quality of making people follow him because they believed in him.

To some he was a man who degraded American politics. To others he was the man who gave renewed life and vitality to the political processes. To some, especially those who crossed swords with him and were wounded, he was ungrateful. To others, he was loyal to a fault.

So, Franklin D. Roosevelt was many men. That means he was complex. It means, too, he was a very able man. It indicates that he knew politics, geography, history, people, and it is safe to say, I think, that he and Winston Churchill alone, of all the allied leaders in the Great War, knew the meaning of sea power and of the great global reach of the war. They knew why there was a drive into the middle East and into Africa. They knew.

He was President during a great depression and a vast and awful war. During those years kingdoms and dynasties fell; dictators arose, came to power and were destroyed. During his time there were those who said he was a dictator and we would never have another election. Yet, when he died all our democratic institutions were intact — and still are. Once again we are facing another test, and we are doing the job in the old, painful, clamorous, accusing way. Our system alone has survived.

So — he was many men.

The tree has been down six years and they still are measuring it — and will be for years to come.

(April 14, 1951)

Capital Braces For Big Show

WASHINGTON, D. C., Jan. 18 — By late dusk of a dun, gray day which followed hard on the heels of nightlong, heavy rain, the Capital City was like a vast theater waiting for the opening of Tuesday's heralded drama entitled "Great Expectations."

All through the slow misty day the traffic mounted as thousands drove in for the inauguration, and seemingly tens of thousands more came just to see the sights and to gawk at the reviewing stand, with its simple white pillars, and at the seats still going up along the historic mile of Pennsylvania Avenue between the Capitol and the White House. Traffic whistles shrilled and weary, frustrated police fought to keep things moving.

By early evening the man who is to play the leading role in this drama of great expectations had arrived with others of the cast, and the crush about the Statler Hotel was greater even than that which came to see the deposed Gen. Douglas MacArthur when he was housed there prior to his appearance before a joint session of the Congress where he had his day in the sun months ago. Police shudder when they think of Tuesday's crowds.

Flags And Bunting I have read that Pennsylvania Avenue presents a carnival appearance. It is not so. True, the flags are there and the bunting is everywhere. And many of the persons and cars moving along it have a fiesta aspect of costume and decoration.

But, not the Avenue. She is like a staid old dowager, ribbon-bedecked and dressed to kill for the annual convention of her favorite organization, but she is not carnival. The old avenue is indeed a little worn and shabby, if one looks closely, but she has the dignity of gentility, and she is wise with years of experience. So one does not notice that here and there are threadbare spots and mended rents. She has been used to this since she was a muddy road and Tom Jefferson rode his horse along her to be the first President inaugurated in the new capital.

But there is carnival. It is in the hotel lobbies where the Republican delegations are wearing ribbons, buttons, and uniforms. The Kansas group, for example, is sporting huge, cloth sun flowers of realistic appearance.

Station Repaired   There is carnival, too, at the huge Union Station, where the terrific damage of last Thursday's runaway train which smashed into it is almost cleared away in a spectacular job of swift repair.

Almost every train brings in a band. And of course it must form and march to the street playing mightily, with the drums being assaulted savagely, and the brasses being blown until the cheeks of the buglers seem about to burst, and the cymbals clashing like shocks of doom.

Here, and at the airport, too, is frolic, fun and carnival. Fort Worth sent a group with new brooms, the sweeping straws wrapped in cellophane and the stick tied with ribbons. Never was the lowly broom so glamorized.

All day long they came, and into the night, with bands in hotel lobbies and the gaily-beribboned Republicans, happy after 20 years of wandering in the political deserts, exuberant, eager, and, on occasion, a little delirious.

But, even that is not all the Washington picture. There is sadness here, too. For many this is the end of 10, 15, or even 20 years in Washington. They have homes here and put down roots here, and they are not protected by civil service. Some of these laugh that they may not weep. The cocktail parties celebrating departure are almost as many as those before the altar of victory.

So, there is laughter here, and merriment, and sadness, and tears. But the dominant note is joy and hope. The feeling is high that somehow the change will mean something better at home, in Korea, and in the world. And that is why the great audience keeps pouring eagerly in for Tuesday's opening of the drama of great expectations.

(January 19, 1953)

"Here Goes Private Truman"

It was late afternoon, following the inauguration. There was just quiet, relaxed talk and a lot of fun in the large hotel living room, but at last someone said, "It's time to go to the train, Mr. President."

It was not really the President, but ex-President Harry S. Truman. He grinned as he stood, walked over to where his largest bag was sitting, a new aluminum air-travel bag, lifted it, struck a pose and said, "Here goes Private Truman."

His family and friends laughed, and the man who was on his way to Missouri joined in.

"Will it rain do you think?", asked one of the ladies present.

"It won't rain until Daddy leaves town," said Margaret Truman. "That's Daddy's luck. It will rain tonight or tomorrow." (And sure enough, it did.)

On the way down to the station they expected to find there some of the cabinet and close friends. It had been a heart-warming day. At lunch they had been to the home of Dean Acheson and there the neighbors had gathered in large numbers to applaud and welcome them.

President Dwight D. Eisenhower had made available the presidential private car for the journey and two secret service men went along to the train.

But, no one there wanted to do any harm to Harry Truman.

Thousands There were literally thousands there.

"I thought," said a friend, "the opposition had informed us that everyone was finished with that little so-and-so in the White House."

There were tears in the eyes of the Trumans and in the eyes of many of those present. Even trainmen were seen wiping the backs of gloved hands across their eyes. The train was held up, and there were cheers and laughter; and warm affection for the entire Truman group — including Acheson — was evident.

The nation knows now that on the entire journey homeward, unguarded and alone, the former President wandered up and down the train, finding the most interesting people in the day coaches, talking with trainmen and crowds, and coming, finally, to his home town where another warming welcome from thousands more greeted him and his family.

He had left behind even among Republicans a grudging sort of admiration. It was almost as if he had managed to attract most of the attention by his complete co-operation which made it possible for the new President to have his organization not merely ready to step into the job, but for its members to have been briefed and made acquainted with their work and responsibilities.

And, he left us, too, a fine example of the simple and yet majestic method of the transfer of power in America, which ought to give us all a great pride and confidence in our system.

Regard It is not too surprising, really, that the people suddenly feel more friendly toward Harry Truman and that his faults, which were many, are being forgiven and forgotten. They were faults of the "heart," never of the mind.

As Winston Churchill said of him a few days ago, he made "great and valiant decisions." For those decisions millions of people yet free have reason to be grateful to him.

Perhaps his greatest fault was overloyalty . . . although in these days when there is so little personal loyalty, it is difficult to term it so. But it was loyalty to friends who embarrassed him with their own lack of it, that gave him the the most grief. The mink coats, the deep freezes, the pettiness of Harry Vaughan, the scandals caused by weak and inept men appointed to jobs with the RFC and in tax offices — all these hurt him. In politics he was a Democrat, and highly partisan, and this sometimes led him to error. He did not lose China to the Communists — the Chinese did that. He stood up to Stalin — always — as in Korea. He was always willing to do more about inflation than the Congress.

So, he goes home — and it is not too surprising [that] there is affection for him.

(January 24, 1953)

A President
With Steel

For days there had been the clamor of voices saying the President had acted too late with too little. At cocktail parties, and over luncheon tables, the second-guessers had held forth in gusty conversations about what should have been done, what armies should have been unloosed, what bombing fleets should have been committed.

The more bellicose accused him directly. They shrilled like cheap fifes of tin as they cried for war and blood and for loosing the dogs of war. The Goldwater chorale group sang what sounded almost like a requiem for national glory and honor. It seemed as if it were chanting that it was much, much too late. They wanted action, not quarantine.

And then came the Kremlin decision to dismantle its burnished cylinders of nuclear death in Cuba and ship them back home. The United Nations, it was obvious, would be brought to use.

Danger   In that moment it was made plain that the President of the United States had grasped the nettle [of] danger at the most propitious moment. Had he reached earlier, it would not have been effective. The aggressive missile sites were not earlier being built. There would have been no pictures to lay before the eyes of a shocked world. There would have been no spectacle of discomfited Valerian Zorin in the Security Council, hoist by his own petard of missiles he could not deny. He was held there, for the world to see, by the insistent, eloquent, strong direction of Adlai Stevenson in what was a very real personal and national triumph of diplomatic strength and skill.

In that hour when the Soviets, never able to deny the fact of their missiles in Cuba, announced they would dismantle and remove them, it was possible to thank God, or be grateful, depending on how one reacts, for the Kennedy toughness, and again for the Kennedy mind. Once he had grasped the nettle of danger, he did not relax his grip. He had advisers about him. They were sound. But this was his decision on Cuba. It was not one inherited or long-drawn out. He looked. He listened. And in the most desolate loneliness a man may know, he made a judgement.

There is steel in the man. (His critics admit as much.) There is a toughness of mind and integrity which are not always apparent in the day-to-day pace of life and government. We demand much of a President. To govern us he must often do expedient things — without sacrificing principle — or at least not too much of it. Politics is not an exact science. Nor is government. But, let us not, in this hour of pride and gratitude, fail to note that we have a President in whom there is steel and decision. Former Vice President Nixon, a great steel company, and Gov. Ross Barnett of Mississippi, who sought to deny the rights of American citizenship, are three from diverse areas of the National life who have encountered the Kennedy toughness.

More Abuses We have done for President [John F.] Kennedy what we have done for all strong presidents whose destiny it was to govern in time of severe, and long-continuing emergency. We have subjected him and his family to abuse, to ridicule, to slander, and to the most petty and malicious calumny. He has laughed at some of it. He has winced at some which hurt him and what he was trying to do for his country.

Now, having grasped the nettle of danger and held on to it with a grip so tight the Kremlin refused to grasp it with him, he has done a very considerable service for his country and for civilization. The more extreme pack of critics will, of course, continue to yap. But, the great heart of the country will be with the President. It was willing to go to war with him. It did not want war. It wished, if it could be had, peace with honor.

Now we shall see. The Russians have not suddenly become peaceful men. They will not relish the diplomatic defeat they have suffered. There will be, somewhere, sometime, an angry riposte. The power struggle goes on. We will continue to live on a plateau of danger for many, many months. A Kennedy-Khruschev talk is in the future.

Khruschev has felt the Kennedy steel. And for the time being the health of this nation and the world is better because of it.

(October 29, 1962)

The Symbol Of A Grave

Washington, D. C.: Gates at Arlington Cemetery open shortly after 7:00 each morning. Always there are some persons waiting at the entrance nearest the grave of John F. Kennedy. On the way there, they walk between rows of headstones that stretch as far as one may see. By 8:00 o'clock the roadways are thronged. Visitors crowd about the neat white picket fence and stand mostly silent, looking at the evergreen-covered grave. A few whisper to companions. Some quietly make snapshots.

They are of all ages — those who come to pay their respects to the President whose youth, energy, imagination and intellect stimulated the whole quality of American life. The visitors do not seem to be morbidly curious. They come with respect and regret. Even when they walk away, down the curving road to the buses or taxicabs, they rarely talk. They seem to be lost in remembering some aspect of the life of the man whose grave they have so lately seen.

Unending Numbers This grave does seem to be a sort of symbol that has meaning for much of America. That it is on the minds of many is attested to by the unending numbers that go there. But there are other testimonies. When the Attorney General of the United States talked recently to the nation's editors in annual convention in Washington he used another grave in Arlington to illustrate his discussion of the civil rights bill. He spoke with quiet eloquence. He mentioned a Negro soldier from a Southern state who was killed in fighting at Viet Nam. A widow could bring her husband to Arlington and there he could be buried with other men who had died in battle, but she would have trouble getting a hotel room or eating in a restaurant in a country for which her husband had given his life.

This, in a sense, is the issue back of the demonstrations, some few of which are unwise or provocative. We have, perhaps, permitted the extremists of both races too often to obscure the central issue and the morality of it. The story of the Arlington grave reminds us of what is really at stake. Hopelessness and irrational acts that grow out of decay and the callousness of conscience remain to shame us.

Other Evidence There are still other pieces of evidence of the meaning and significance of the Kennedy symbol. In a large room in the old State Office Building adjacent to the White House, Mrs. Evelyn Lincoln is at work at the huge task of classifying the papers of the late President. She finds herself reading letters over and recalling the reasons why they were written and the discussions about them. A surprising number of college students come to see her. They sit and talk of what the man now at Arlington meant to them. Few had ever seen him, except on television, but they tell Mrs. Lincoln how he had affected their lives. Young men out of college come to talk and ask questions about John F. Kennedy. Some of these are Republicans, some Democrats. A great many say they are now running for some minor office in their several communities. John Kennedy had inspired them to do something.

So widespread was this appeal to the American people, especially its younger ones, that President Johnson, recognizing it, has established a high school scholarship honors program. Young men who do well will be brought to the White House and given national honor and attention.

It is not surprising, therefore, that the American Negro, especially the younger ones, also took faith and visions from him.

One thinks on these things coming away from the grave at Arlington.

(April 26, 1964)

CAMPAIGNS AND CONVENTIONS

Starting with Wendell Wilkie in 1940 and ending with the debacle at the Chicago convention in 1968, Ralph McGill covered each of the Presidential campaigns of his time. He made no effort to submerge his love for politics and his Democratic leanings, but his writing was objective and fair even during the Dixiecrat walkout of 1948 and the "Checkers" scandal of 1952.

To get the essence and the feel of his writing on the campaign trail, one campaign was selected for inclusion. The 1960 campaign of Richard Nixon and John Kennedy was selected because of its unique qualities, and because it shows McGill at the height of his maturity and influence.

The writing in this section is a model of concise, perceptive political reporting.

"... So Gaudy And Hilarious"

LOS ANGELES: What is it like to cover a national nominating convention? None ever said it better than the late Henry Mencken:

> ... meals bolted suicidally or missed altogether, nights spent in pursuing elusive and infamous politicians, hours wasted upon the writing of dispatches that were overtaken by fresh news ... dreadful alarm and surprises at 3 o'clock in the morning, all the horrors of war without any of its glory.

And yet, for all the sleeplessness and weariness, and for all the preposterous qualities of it, I would not willingly miss an hour of it. Nor would Mr. Mencken:

> For there is something about a national convention that makes it as fascinating as a revival or a hanging. It is vulgar, it is ugly, it is stupid, it is tedious, it is hard upon both the higher cerebral centres and the *gluteus maximus*, and yet it is somehow charming. One sits through long sessions wishing heartily that all the delegates and alternates were dead and in hell — and then suddenly there comes a show so gaudy and hilarious, so melodramatic and obscene, so unimaginably exhilarating and preposterous that one lives a gorgeous year in an hour.

Neat Suits The Democrats are better. They are not always proper and are rarely smug. The Republicans come with their neat suits and their air of respectability. They have an aroma about them of money, of expensive leather chairs in rich offices, and of propriety. The Democrats come in the most incredible costumes and decorations. They do not mind being loudly drunk in public, while a Republican always prefers to overindulge with dignity and in privacy.

The Democrats are given to impromptu parades and to grand and hilarious evenings in night clubs.

The delegates are the heart and soul of the show. They do not, however, have much real participation in decisions. Now and then a delegation will rebel, or a faction will defy the chairman. But by and large, the delegates are the creatures of the governors of their states. A few of them are chosen by direct election, but those who offer almost invariably are choices of the organization.

Caucuses Delegates are called to caucuses to hear what has been decided by their chairmen and governors. The states with the huge delegate totals, such as New York, Pennsylvania, California, New Jersey and Massachusetts, swing the greatest weight. When political writers speak of "they" it is the heads of these state organizations whom they have in mind. The managers of candidates must go to them. It is they who will win on the first ballot or the second. It is they who will determine if Kennedy is not to be nominated. This is a very simple bit of arithmetic, and political skills. Usually, as now, "they" manage to remain uncommitted. They maneuver behind the facade of a favorite son. It is "they" who have the most power. If they can hold it in reserve to be thrown into the scrimmage at the critical moment, "they" can determine a nomination.

Henry Mencken, he of the searing words and descriptive phrases, loved the delegates for their submissiveness, their good humor, their sudden angers, their faithful performances in the ritual of the demonstration parades for their favorites, for their sweating, their naiveté, their cunning, their smugness. He was intrigued by the lady delegates, especially those of great girth and depth of bosom. Observing them, badge- and ribbon-bedecked, he once wrote that they looked like British tramp steamers decorated for the queen's birthday.

There is melodrama, hilarity and vulgarity, a certain majesty and folly, and, at times, a feeling as if history is being made and decisions taken which will plague or preserve us in the dark mystery of the years to come.

(July 11, 1960)

New Frontiers
By Fast Travel

LOS ANGELES NOTEBOOK: Fingers of light searched the skies. Trumpets sounded. Bands played, and into the floodlit spotlight about the huge podium, itself encumbered with electronic devices and a small elevator to make short men tall and tall men short, came the choices of the democrats — Jack Kennedy and Lyndon Johnson.

A brief few days ago their names were regarded as unlikely ever to be linked in anything save a power struggle.

But there they were. Kennedy, 43, looked young enough to be the son of Johnson, 51. It is almost impossible to accept the fact of Kennedy's age. It is an appeal to the feminine voters. The older ones wish to mother him. The young ones think in terms of the ads for convertible cars and imagine how nice it would be to be riding along the beach with the reddish-thatched young man.

But there is a fine mind under that thatch. And there is a boldness in the approach of this mind. It may be he is bold because he always has had the poise of wealth and position. A millionaire at 21 years of age, he has been able to think and venture with confidence. And yet, this cannot be the reason. The shores of life are strewn with the wreckage of men who had wealth and opportunity and did not know how to use either.

Splendid Education He has a splendid education. He was given excellent preparatory schooling and attended one of the more notable of our universities where a student may find a superior faculty. But the world is crowded with educated men and women who have never been able to make use of what they learned.

It is something more than that. Here is a man intensely ambitious. He long ago knew where he wanted to go. He stayed with the Democratic Party. Most of the friends he had, and classmates who were of Irish ancestry, left the party of their fathers in the college years and went over to the GOP because it was, and is, the "status party."

He is mentally tough. He has one of those steel-trap minds. He is patient. He is not afraid to ask for advice, and he takes it once he trusts the source. He is, as has been said, "an organization man." He makes use of all the latest techniques for probing into the mind of man. He believes strongly in motivation. He is deeply convinced it is important the public have the proper image of him and his family, his campaign, his policy. He spares no time or expense to make this "Image" available to the public.

Religion A Factor Religion is a factor in this campaign. So, in his acceptance speech he moved boldly into it. He took note of the fact that many Protestants are angry because of persecution, real and alleged, in lands dominated by Catholics. "It is not relevant (to me and this campaign) what abuses may have existed in other countries in other times," he said. "It is not relevant what pressures, if any, might conceivably be brought to bear on me. I am telling you what you are entitled to know: That my decisions on every public policy will be my own — as an American, a Democrat and a free man."

Kennedy is an attacker. He moved quickly to the offensive. He named the election target, Richard M. Nixon. "He is a young man but his approach is as old as McKinley," he said.

Kennedy and Johnson both early pledged to stand on the party platform.

They each bound the party to continue with programs which the conservatives attack as socialistic — care for the aged, medical subsidies, help for education, and jobs.

There was, he said, the New Deal and the Fair Deal. But this is a new frontier. Kennedy will take us into it. But he will not be crossing the plains in a covered wagon. He will travel fast. And he won't bypass any fights.

He closed with a Biblical quotation which should please the Bible-loving South. It was from Isaiah:

> They that wait upon the Lord shall renew their strength; they shall mount up with wings as eagles; they shall run, and not be weary.

(July 18, 1960)

Nixon's Choice: South Or North

CAMPAIGN NOTES: If Richard M. Nixon becomes president of the United States it may well be that a preliminary meeting in New York on the evening of Oct. 4 and a breakfast meeting the next morning with Gov. Nelson Rockefeller and Sen. Jacob Javits, and others in New York politics, will be remembered as the pivot of victory.

It was at these meetings that the vice president candidly was told that New York State was in doubt. So is California. And the New York leaders frankly said that the campaign speeches of the vice president had to be tougher and required a forthright position on civil rights and the sit-in demonstrations against lunch counter segregation.

Until that time the vice president had been intrigued with the idea of winning as many, and maybe more, Southern states than did President Eisenhower. The religious issue and the hostility of the economic power structure of the cotton states to Kennedy, made the South a sort of promised land, a political Delilah to be wooed and won.

But New York has 45 electoral votes. California has 32. Pennsylvania has 32. The pragmatic gentlemen who have the job of trying to carry New York told Mr. Nixon what had to be done. He listened and he responded in a speech which students of politics will do well to remember. It was made in the center of New York's garment industry at 38th Street and Seventh Avenue where Democratic party support is traditional.

Mr. Nixon went all out in a pledge [that], if elected, he will do all within his power to hurry along the demise of second-class citizenship.

He promised he and the attorney general of the United States would do all they could to throw the weight of the government against such segregation.

On that same evening the vice president spoke in Philadelphia where the Declaration of Independence was written and proclaimed. Here again he gave primary emphasis to civil rights in a rousing speech to a capacity crowd.

Those Southerners who, in their understandable, if not admirable, frustration have been turning to the vice president because they think him soft on human rights, could not be more wrong. One almost weeps for the South to see the workings of power politics. It is wrong to deny the Negro citizen full equality as a citizen. This concept is distasteful to many persons, including many outside the South. But children must be educated and jobs must be available and in public affairs all citizens must have equal position.

The tides of history are running. And the power of Communism has been thrown on the side of the colored peoples of the world. Both Kennedy, who first stood for educational and economic rights, and Mr. Nixon have now committed themselves. They have passed the point of no return. So has the world. So has history.

Christianity and the moral code long ago demanded that we do what the pragmatic politicians now know must be done to win elections in this country. And, let me add something else, by no means all of them are cynical about it. Nixon and Kennedy both believe, out of their personal codes and out of their political realism, that this country must do what is right insofar as its citizenship is concerned if we are to survive.

There is no national hatred of the South or Southerners. There is, in fact, an admiration of the South's best contributions. But, there is no longer any national patience with Ku Klux Klanism or White Citizens Councils propaganda.

Mr. Nixon comes a bit late. But he has spoken. He is going for broke on civil rights because in 1960 that is what most Americans want for their country and because Jack Kennedy had helped himself with an early pledge to that end.

(October 8, 1960)

In Dixie Land He Takes A Stand

SOUTHERN CAMPAIGN NOTES: Sen. Jack Kennedy, taking his stand way down South in the Dixie of Georgia and South Carolina, used two texts which evoked an emotional response.

One, of course, spoken from in front of Franklin D. Roosevelt's "Little White House," at Warm Springs, was from FDR himself. It was a paragraph from his second acceptance speech made before 100,000 persons at Philadelphia:

> Governments can err. Presidents do make mistakes. But the immortal Dante tells us that Divine justice weighs the sins of the cold-blooded and the sins of the warm-hearted in a different scale. Better the occasional fault of a government living in the spirit of charity, than the consistent omissions of a government frozen in the ice of its own indifference.

This text he used for a universal appeal. It reached the farmers of the South, whose incomes have been dropping for four years. It spoke equally to those who have been pushed off the land by machines and are trying to fit themselves into urban and industrial jobs and culture for which, unhappily, most are ill-prepared.

He reminded them that Roosevelt took an America which had been allowed to stagnate in depression and had, by boldness and courage, made the nation move forward once more.

> Franklin Roosevelt . . . knew who had been omitted and ignored. And he knew who had omitted and ignored them. And he set about to help them — the forgotten man — to light the farms, to help the aged, to protect the worker, to open new doors to the Negroes, to care for the needs of millions of Americans in a thousand different ways.

And what, he asked, did the opposition say of Roosevelt's plans in 1936?

It said, Sen. Kennedy declared, that Roosevelt would destroy and bankrupt us.

The same sources today, he said, are saying in 1960 that to make America strong and set us once again on the move will destroy us and bankrupt us.

It was a skillful use of the deadly parallel.

The second text was an appeal to the new generation. Again, the inspiration was from a speech by FDR in 1936. "This generation," said Roosevelt, "has a rendezvous with destiny." [John F. Kennedy said:]

> I believe, in 1960 . . . a new generation of Americans who fought for freedom on all fronts in World War II have now come to their own rendezvous with destiny — that their generation must bear the responsibility of leadership . . .

and I want Khrushchev [of the Soviet Union] to know that a new generation of Americans has assumed leadership, a generation of Americans that is not satisfied to be second best — that wants to be first — not first *if, but, when,* or *sometime,* but first, period.

Kennedy's managers believe that the younger voters — up to 30 years of age, are especially leaning to him. This was the first clarion call to them.

The Democratic position in the South is believed to be improving. Some senators who have been silent are now publicly active. The appearance of Sen. Herman Talmadge [of Georgia] with Kennedy at Warm Springs, along with most of the congressional delegation, was significant. In Alabama both Senators Hill and Sparkman are at work. But in South Carolina and Mississippi, sullen silence is the rule. The real imponderable is the depth of the religious issue. But the outlook is somewhat brighter.

There is a growing belief that the religious issue is losing some of its force. Sen. Kennedy has repeatedly declared himself free of any pressure, of church or whatever group. The American people like fair play. They sense that much of the opposition to the senator is persecution. That some of it is honest, is true. But most of it is prejudice. But here again, no accurate evaluation is possible. This remains the imponderable.

(October 11, 1960)

Nixon — At His Best Or Worst?

Depending upon how one feels about Richard M. Nixon he was, in the third of the great televised debates [with Sen. John F. Kennedy], at his best or worst.

For those who consider his occasional piousness, and his use of emotional cliches, as in the worst possible taste, he was at his devious worst. He was again using the formula of his little dog Checkers and the good, honest "Republican cloth coat" owned by Mrs. Nixon, as so successfully employed in the television defense of his expense account in 1952. It was enormously effective then insofar as mass appeal was concerned. He has no reason to consider it any less so today.

In the third debate Mr. Nixon took advantage of the fact that former President Harry Truman used the word "hell" in a Texas speech to launch into a lengthy statement about the Nixon concept of presidential dignity. He rolled his eyes back and said, in a muted voice, that he thought of mothers holding little children up to see the president, and that the ideals of the office required it to be just like Mr. Eisenhower has maintained it.

Sweet?   This was a skillful attempt to connect himself with Mr. Eisenhower's popularity. But it also served, by indirection, to imply that Harry Truman had been as profane as a Marine Corps sergeant working with a boot company in which each man had two left feet.

It was a somewhat lengthy sermon in dubious taste unless, of course, one thinks it was tender and sweet. But, if Mr. Truman was listening one may be sure he was moved to say something more than "hell" unless, perchance, Mrs. Bess Truman was there to hold up an admonishing finger.

In the Quemoy-Matsu business, most of the facts are on Mr. Kennedy's side. Even the late [Secretary of State John Foster] Dulles, Mr. Eisenhower, and most of the generals and admirals are with Mr. Kennedy. He has never suggested surrendering the islands just five miles off the Red Chinese coast. He has quoted others as saying they are not worth defending with American lives, being so near the mainland. But Mr. Nixon has seen the political mileage in the surrrender-of-freedom charge. He presses it hard and likely will continue to do so. He was in difficulty, though, when Sen. Kennedy asked why Mr. Nixon had also not had some protest about Communistic control in Cuba, and why he was not similarly eager about freedom in Tibet, Hungary, and other areas where the Communists have taken over.

Too Fast?   One got the feeling that Kennedy, well-prepared and eager, was often so literally factual as to be over the heads of many in his audience of millions. His mind works quicker, and he leaps into his argument with such a staccato rush of thoughts that he seemingly does not stop to consider [that] his audience is not the U. S. Senate, but instead, an invisible audience of curious and interested persons who do not understand the intricate business of farm and labor legislation but are moved by references to God, mother and little children.

Mr. Nixon worked all these things in — God, mothers, and little children, and the odds are he had the best of the debate with a considerable portion of his audience. For those who put their minds to it, and were not swayed by the political emotions aroused, Sen. Kennedy seemed the more direct and prepared. He did not try for effects, nor did he resort to the stock cliches. These may be excellent qualities in an administrator, but they don't win points in a mass debate.

But, still, the odds are the debates won't change many minds. At the close of them each person thinks his man was the better. About three weeks remain — and one more debate.

(October 14, 1960)

Kennedy-Nixon Campaign
Far Cry From McKinley's

ON TOUR WITH KENNEDY: Whistle-stopping across the rich land that early Ohio settlers said needed only to be tickled with the hoe to laugh with the harvest, the weary candidate might wistfully recall the campaign ease of William McKinley of Canton, Ohio.

The astute Mark Hanna, Republican boss of his time known familiarly as "Dollar Mark," faced a Democratic Party riven by Populist defections. So he conceived the idea of a front porch campaign.

William McKinley would sit daily on his front porch, in the pleasant autumn air, and let the crowds come to him. The Republican committee paid the expenses of all delegations which wished to travel to Canton to see their nominee, hear him, and shake his hand. The obedient McKinley obeyed. He sat on his porch. And the delegations came. Sometimes he spoke as many as 20 times a day.

The GOP committee also paid to have this wisdom from the porch podium wired to the Republican newspapers across the nation. The campaign was eminently successful. A record number of 14,000,000 persons went to the polls. McKinley received more than seven million to Bryan's six and a half million. His electoral margin was 271 to 176.

But in this pleasant autumn of 1960, with the pumpkins yellow and golden in the fields, and a hint of frost to come in the early morning air, the candidates are seeking a majority of the more than 60 million anticipated ballots.

The year 1960 assigns little time for sitting on front porches. This is a pity, but true. The barbarians are at the foot of the walls about Western civilization. The candidates must go to the people.

The difference between the two campaign groups is one of the spirit. There is, in the Kennedy campaign, more enthusiasm, a larger confidence, a feeling that destiny is on their side. There is no overconfidence in it. There is, however, a feeling that the tide is set their way, and that if the candidate and his party continue an unrelenting drive there will be neither slackness nor ebb.

This quality was missing, for example, from the two [Adlai] Stevenson campaigns. It was absent, I believe, because the Democratic state organizations were not working. Today they are, with the exception of a few states such as Florida, Virginia and Indiana. There are the exceptions.

Out of this comes a sense of oneness. The morale of the Kennedy organization benefits from this as that of Stevenson's suffered from lack of it.

Sen. Kennedy's first two days of this week provide the perfect illustration. In Ohio, the industrial cities are worried. There is unemployment and indications of more of it. But of greater importance is the fact that Ohio has a Democratic governor who has created a state organization. During the years when Sen. Frank Lausche was governor he deliberately refrained from such political architecture because he had such a bipartisan following. Now there is one. And it is so hard at work that Sen. Lausche has mounted the Kennedy bandwagon exuberantly and vocally. But Florida, next on the schedule, has a party organization putting state things first and more or less letting the national ticket shift for itself.

There is no mistaking the Kennedy organization's belief that hard work will win and that genius, in politics as in art, is 90 per cent sweat. But the veteran observer tends to remind himself that a fellow named Richard M. Nixon is where he is largely because of sweaty drudgery and attention to details. If he loses it will be because of party failure and an inability to match Kennedy's astonishing personal appeal.

(October 17, 1960)

Democratic
Heart Throbs
In Florida

TOURING WITH KENNEDY: Florida illustrates a present fact of life in a presidential campaign which may already be decided or which may teeter in the balance of minds not yet made up.

Florida's local Democratic leaders are beginning to speak out for the party. Where, but a week or so ago, they were as silent and sullenly torpid as an Everglades 'gator, they now are at least going through the motions of working not merely for state nominees but for the national ticket as well.

This may not be enough. Nixon's strength in Dade County (Miami), which casts a large chunk of the total vote, is high. There are large pools of GOP strength in all the urban areas of Florida. Those who are, and have been, in charge of promotion for Kennedy-Johnson have been more concerned with their future political status than with the ticket.

We see here one of the problems for Southern Democrats in the development of a second party. Many candidates, or probable ones, seeing the increase in Republican strength, become almost bipartisan. They want the Democratic label. But they do not want to offend anyone who might give them opposition.

Sen. [George] Smathers' problem illustrates it well. He must run again in two years. If he had from the start made a vigorous swing up and down the state in an all-out effort for the nominees, he would have earned GOP opposition in the form of a Republican candidate seeking the Senate seat now held by the junior senator. But now Sen. Smathers' position is somewhat easier. He has company. It may not be enough. But hope, which thrives for a time in the thinnest sort of soil, is rising in Florida. The Democrats now will make a fight of it.

The edge remains with the vice president and present indications are it is substantial. But the long-silent Democrats at last are active. Why? Because they think Sen. Kennedy may win. There was a period after the national convention when the opinion down in Dixie was that the platform, especially on civil rights, had doomed the ticket. But after a while it became apparent the GOP platform was even more emphatic.

The religious issue was at its hottest public flame in the weeks following the Los Angeles sessions. Resentment against Sen. Lyndon Johnson was also at its peak. The politicians of the South then thought Sen. Kennedy couldn't make it.

But now the single most significant straw in the Democratic Party wind is the rising support in the South. Even Sen. [James] Eastland [of Mississippi], of whom the least said the better, has been plaintively reminding his fellow Mississippians that if the Democrats lose, he, Eastland, would not be able to protect them in committes where he is powerful. In his devious manner even Eastland is asking for votes for the nominees.

In other states, notably Georgia and Alabama, the state leadership is honestly, openly and strongly for Kennedy and Johnson. Their task has been helped by the appearance of both the candidates in the South.

The people could see that Pope John was not, as some of the preachers have been saying, right behind Sen. Kennedy. Nor did the young man from Massachusetts have a tail. The seat of his pants, to be sure, did reveal a repaired patch-spot showing, if one happened to catch the senator in a bent-over position. But this could hardly be photographed and made into a political asset as was the hole in one of Gov. Adlai Stevenson's shoes.

No one know how deep the religious issue runs. Therefore, it is not possible to say what its effect will be. There were honest questions to be asked, but most of the attack has been so scurrilous as to awaken the opposition of all those who believe in fair play.

Sen. Kennedy has pledged repeatedly his freedom from all pressures, whether of church or special interests. His testament of faith in the Constitution of the United States was especially eloquent. He is a fine young American and while those who disagree with him should support the GOP, religion certainly is not a valid reason for so doing. He is a Christian and an American. Are these no longer popular qualifications?

(October 19, 1960)

Kennedy Believes In Future Of U.S.

ON TOUR WITH KENNEDY: The campaign road is long. It sometimes is in the sky, dropping down to airports, and motorcades to the courthouse, and back again. And again it is by caravan, moving from early breakfast until 10 o'clock at night, stopping at perhaps six scheduled towns, but adding, always, a dozen or more brief halts at crossroads or small towns which simply turn out enough people to demand a stop.

Traveling with Kennedy, you watch him. What sort of man is he, you wonder, seeing him and hearing him with the shrill of schoolgirls in your ears, and the shouts of partisans. Vice President Nixon is a complex man, given to changing positions with plausible reason. He can, for example, disappoint even those who truly like him, with a pious attack on Harry Truman for using the word hell, and compound it by creating a picture of mothers lifting little babies to see a man who must not use the word hell.

This man Kennedy is, in contrast, an elemental man of almost bleak simplicity. He is, by nature or training, a person who lacks complexity. He moves to a conclusion with speed which is often too accelerated for his own good. In his speeches he drives ahead as if he had no audience. Many of his points arouse tremendous applause. He does not wait. He drives on, his right hand chopping the air. Before the applause is done he is well into his next point.

Quite oblivious to thousands before him, cheering and beating their hands together, his mind runs fast. It is too swift to be other than honest. He does not calculate. He does not have time for deviousness. He allows himself no time to consider the effect of what he answers. He knows what he thinks and believes. He may be in error. But he does not stop to consider the effect of it.

The gentle reader will pardon a personal reference. I have been covering presidential candidates since Franklin Roosevelt's second term. They all are interesting. But, none has come along like this intense young man who believes. This is his strength, and, for all I know, his weakness. He believes.

Kennedy drives his staff to frustration by discarding the text to which he already has agreed. He may see something in the crowd which inspires him. For example, he talked in Dayton, Ohio, with Mrs. James M. Cox, widow of the Democratic nominee, who, in 1920, with a young Franklin D. Roosevelt as his running mate, chose to support the League of Nations. Gov. Cox did so, even though he knew it was politically unpopular in a post-war period when an America used to isolation wanted to forget all about foreign affairs.

All the rest of that day, at crossroads, towns and cities, Kennedy was excited. He forgot texts and talked at length about what he believed. He believes a lot of things about this country. And he believes them as a man who fought for it in combat and in the routine of life. "I believe," he begins, and he then speeds up the tempo of his voice, talking into applause, chopping his hand in front of his face to the despair of the television cameramen, himself consumed with what he believes about America.

This sort of campaign is hard on those who like Mr. Nixon. They know he is aware that this nation's prestige is not as high as before. They are aware Mr. Nixon knows that the United States and the West have not won a great victory in the United Nations. And the Vice President understands that many admirals and generals whose love of country is unquestioned do not believe our defenses are invulnerable. Why, then, refuse America the truth? Why attack Sen. Kennedy with the spurious charge of "running down America?"

So it is that, looking at Kennedy, one may not know him. But one does know, without question, that here is a man who believes; a man who believes, first of all, in himself. It is a rare man today who believes in himself.

(October 20, 1960)

Democrats Sense Chance At Victory

ON TOUR WITH KENNEDY: It seemed to me, at the recent annual Al Smith dinner in New York, that my friend the Honorable James A. Farley looked a little out of place among all the Union League members present. I suggested as much.

"Listen," said Mr. Farley, "I joined up before the Union League boys came in. I told Jack not to worry about them. His votes will come from Al's old territory, not from theirs."

The Al Smith dinner for charity attracts an ultra-conservative, white-tie group. Nixon wore tails; Kennedy a black tie and dinner jacket.

The "Happy Warrior," in his last years, had come full circle. The poor boy who had worked in the Fulton fish market had become wealthy and conservative. He broke in bitterness with his party and, more directly, with Franklin D. Roosevelt. The Union League took him over.

Jim Farley, talking after the dinner, said that in his opinion the country long ago made up its mind to vote Democratic and would do so.

> Only the religious issue will prevent Jack Kennedy from making an electoral sweep as great as that by FDR in 1932 . . . There aren't any unmade minds to speak of. Maybe one out of a hundred doesn't yet know how he is going to vote. Some aren't saying, but they know.

Jack Kennedy knew that most of those at the Smith dinner were Republicans. He was at his best. He was charming, but he let them have it with both barrels. He spoke of the old Al Smith. He described the Democrats who, in 1930, doubted the GOP claims. He reminded them that President Hoover and the leading business heads derided the Democratic fears that the economy was not then as sound as it should be and that Americans were suffering and in danger.

He drew an almost cruel analogy between those days and the speeches of Vice President Nixon, who insists today that prestige is high and the economy is at an all-time peak.

The senator was almost merciless, too, when he slowly paid Cardinal Spellman a compliment for being able to bring together two political figures who long had been at odds and who differed over major principles. One could see the fat cats present purring and thinking how nice it was of him to speak of Mr. Nixon and Mr. Kennedy being at the same table. But they were quickly shocked to silence or lifted to whoops of laughter when Kennedy, with just the right pause, said he referred to

Mr. Nixon and Gov. [Nelson] Rockefeller of New York.

If Kennedy wins this election the one major error Republicans will agree upon will be that of accepting the debates. It was these which enabled the country to see how much information Kennedy possesses, how poised and expert he is on his feet, and how strongly his appealing personality comes through on television. This personality in what Jim Farley refers to as a decision by millions of Americans to vote Democratic again after eight years, explains why there is a belief in a Kennedy breakthrough. It is perhaps more pronounced in New York. The vice president's big job is in upper New York State, which is the Republican region counted on to overcome Democratic majorities in New York City. Gov. Rockefeller's advisers reportedly have told the vice president to forget all about the city and work in the state. In other big industrial states, this feeling also begins to grow.

There is, in New York, evidence of near panic or defeatism in GOP ranks not present in other states. New York at this writing seems sure for Kennedy. But, of course, one does not know what destiny or the Russians will do in the days left. An incident or an error could work a change.

And in every comment, reporters do well to note that one cannot weigh the effect of the religious issue. It is inconceivable that in 1960 many Americans will be so naive as to believe that the Catholic Church will be able to give orders to Jack Kennedy. He has said not. For years, the many Catholic governors and mayors in America have served well without such influence, but because it is an underground issue about which few persons will talk, none may evaluate it.

Meanwhile, confidence and hope grow stronger in the Democratic camp. It sees a very real chance to win. We will not know how valid it is until late on the evening of November 8.

(October 22,, 1960)

The "New Nixon"
Is On The Spot

ON TOUR WITH KENNEDY: It is known that a somewhat nervous Republican committee has been, and is, under heavy pressure from state leaders to have Vice President Richard M. Nixon "take off the gloves" and become "the old Nixon."

The vice president cautiously has been trying. His innuendoes grow more strong and accusing. But so far, he has been neither the old nor the new but a combination unsatisfactory and unconvincing to himself or his supporters. It will not be easy for him to become the old Nixon. Indeed, it may be impossible.

For at least four years there has been a considerable campaign to create the image of a new Nixon. Even Mrs. Nixon has discussed it. She has said, with the great common sense with which she is blessed, that there is not a new Nixon in the sense of a deliberate changeover. She has talked of the natural process of maturity and growth. Most persons grow. And the vice president is one who has.

All of this has, in a sense, painted the vice president into a corner. If he should become a slashing, accusing Joe McCarthy type, impugning the patriotism and anti-Communist position of Jack Kennedy and the Democrats, it would hurt him more than help. Too much time and effort have been spent in creating the image of the new Nixon. To destroy it would incur very real liability.

Also, Sen. Jack Kennedy is by no means lacking in ability to reply. No more preposterous position has ever been taken than that of the extremist Chinese lobby groups which try to say that Jack Kennedy, a combat veteran and a Catholic, is not strong enough in his anti-Communist attitude. Mr. Kennedy, the challenger, already has given evidence that he has not overlooked certain unworthy innuendoes in this field. At Jacksonville, for example, he said:

> Mr. Nixon said that Khruschev never fooled him. Well, I did not invite Mr. Khrushchev to travel around the United States with Henry Cabot Lodge as a guest of the American people. I didn't invite him to Camp David. I approved of his visit. But whom does Mr. Nixon think he fools as he goes around the country casting innuendoes, suggesting that we in the Democratic Party are not as devoted to the cause of freedom, implying that for some reason or other we were fooled by Khrushchev and he understood him all the time. I was not the vice president who presided over the communization of Cuba. Does anyone think Mr. Nixon was right when, five years ago, he said communism is on the decline in Latin America?

This man Kennedy knows how to fight back. A retaliatory punch always is ready. Adlai Stevenson never mastered the knack of immediate reply to false innuendoes and charges by candidates Eisenhower and Nixon in 1952 and 1956. But Jack Kennedy strikes back before the echo of a charge or innuendo has died. He makes what the late Secretary Dulles described as a massive retaliation.

It will be interesting to see what Mr. Nixon decides. The national committee is being urged to have him get meaner and to campaign at a low-gutter level. But there are a few top Republicans who protest. They have noted that while the vice president has big crowds, those of Kennedy generally are larger and, more important, are at a peak of near-frenzy.

Dr. Norman Vincent Peale is not too popular with the Republicans. They feel that when he presided at the anti-Catholic meeting of ministers and laymen and then crawled out of it by repudiating the statement and saying he had been almost casually present, he made it look as if, somehow, the Republicans were holding the bag. And, they protest, with accuracy, they had nothing to do with it.

Hence, this more thoughtful GOP leadership argues that the party has plenty of money and brains. It believes that a stepped-up campaign in Ohio, California, Illinois, Pennsyslvania, and other key states, with President Eisenhower playing a vigorous role, will be more effective than a reversion of the vice president to what has been called "the old Nixon." This concept represents the best minds on the national committee, but they are under increasing pressure from state and district Republican leaders who daily seem more worried. It is they who want a dirty, name-calling fight in these last two and a half weeks to halt the Kennedy breakthrough.

(October 24, 1960)

McGILL ON McGILL

Ralph McGill was able to write about himself and his feelings in a way that was both expressive and captivating.

"Dear Old Rule Days" recalls his early school days and those people who stood out in his memory. In "This Was It, This Very Room," McGill talks of his boyhood for his own son in a particularly moving piece.

In "What Happened to Him?" "Old Steps, Old Memories," "A Good Thorough Examination" and "Things Change, Charlie," McGill writes of life lived and youth lost.

"Thoughts After Climbing Fuji" is a column of achievement, of pride and accomplishment, while "Objectivity? Or the Whole Truth" distills his journalistic philosophy.

An Expert In One Field

Whatever sophistication I have has taught me humility; what experience I have had has taught me the awful facts of uncertainty.

Nevertheless, I am an expert in one field: I am an expert on Ralph McGill. Coming from an old "Blue Stocking" Presbyterian family which, in my grandmother's time, allowed no cooking on Sundays, except breakfast coffee, I always have had an immense interest in things religious. The hot breath of Calvin always is on my neck, and remorse and sorrow, hot and cold flashes and "conscience" follow my every dereliction.

Nevertheless, from my mother, who is one of the few real Christians I know, I early learned not to be afraid and not to hate or fear or dislike other persons because of their beliefs, even members of the Republican party. This made it very easy for me to get along despite a great shyness and self-consciousness. Persons always have been persons to me, during and since childhood. It did not occur to me to think of or identify a person by his religion. I honestly do not believe I have ever thought of a person as a Catholic or a Jew or a nonbeliever, but always as a person possessing the same sort of human reactions as I. A Negro's color sets him apart, but I have never understood hatred for him or discrimination of him and certainly I have always regarded a Negro as a person and therefore entitled to be so treated. This did not make it necessary to be either a "nigger lover" or anti-Negro. It involved none of the social equality argument. I simply regard him as a person entitled to complete justice and economic opportunity. All this has been entirely natural to me, southern-born, southern-educated with no trace of outside influence.

Writing as an expert on myself, I can say I have always been that way. The only influence creating that attitude of mine was the Christian religion to which I was subjected at my first childhood consciousness.

Puzzles Consequently, I invariably am genuinely and entirely unable to understand or appreciate the anti-Semitic emotions of others; the various racial hates, and the fear which some persons have of the Catholic church. It amazes me to encounter it. Likewise, all such things dismay me

There is currently in the press a charge that the Catholic church [is conducting] a campaign in this country to control or destroy freedom of press and religion and to bring about union of church and state. This seems to me the sheerest sort of nonsense. I do not recall at any time in 23 years of newspaper work any pressure from the Catholic church. Indeed, newspaper desk men or editors seldom see a Catholic priest, bishop or church official. They are very familiar with a certain type of publicity-seeking minister, but they have the good sense to know he doesn't represent the best in his church nor does he typify the Protestant ministry which, by and large, rarely "pressures" newspaper offices.

I would imagine the Catholic men in service and on the lists of those dead on the field of honor would be, on a pro rata basis, fully as numerous as that of any group. They died like the others in defense of this country and its Constitution, which plainly separates church and state and which likewise establishes freedom of press and religion.

I do recall that some time ago a Catholic organization attempted to boycott a newspaper in the east for criticism. That was stupid. It failed. I also recall the attempt of a Jewish group to boycott a New York newspaper. That, too, was stupid. During the days of the Ku Klux Klan, that group attempted to boycott papers which opposed it. The stupidity was obvious. Those things happen now and then in and from all groups where the overemotional or thoughtless get control. They cannot be described as general.

Franco   The Catholic church has supported the Franco government in Spain because of the Catholic fear of Communism. This support has certainly been most thoroughly discussed and criticized by most of the newspapers of America. I have joined in deploring and opposing this support of the Franco government. I think it is a mistake. Yet I wondered at the hysteria over the report that Franco had on his desk a picture of the Pope, of Mussolini and Hitler. He is a Catholic. I would not expect him to have the photograph of a rabbi or a Protestant on his desk. He is a Fascist and, in my opinion, a wicked enemy of democracy. Therefore he had his two Fascist heroes on his desk. But assuredly this did not mean Catholics were Fascist, as the thousands who died fighting it have so eloquently testified. It did mean Franco was, and is.

There are many features of Catholic education in Latin countries which seem to me wrong. I know that many American Catholics believe the same. But the fact that those countries have been, since the first Spanish explorers stepped ashore to claim them in name of king and church, almost entirely Catholic in religion and thought, explains it, even though it does not justify it. The many struggles to change it also are noteworthy and prophetic. But the fact they and the members of their governments are Catholic always has seemed to me to explain the desirability of the United States having an official observer at the Vatican to keep this country informed.

The Catholic church has the enormous power of unity. It moves and acts with weight and direction. It also has, because of unity, the ability to tackle major problems, as it now is tackling the race problem in the South. It can do so without fear of any of its priests or bishops being attacked by dissenting groups in the congregation. It also is engaged in a drive for members and it is getting them in large numbers.

This, I think, causes many to fear it, although I do not understand why. Others are certainly able to seek members and there is no interference with them. Religious strife is wicked.

I stand on The Book and, I trust, on my heritage and obvious facts.

(December 3, 1945)

Dear Old Rule Days?

School days, school days, the dear old golden rule days, remind me of my own years of classrooms, of teachers, and not so much of regulations but of those who imposed them.

There is today a proper questioning of rules — especially those seemingly made for the sake of rules. None questions but that there must be regulations. But the essential problem of "rules" is that they are administered by individuals who give their own interpretation and meaning of them. The martinet, unsure of himself or herself, will bend a rule to his or her interpretation. The sadist will use rules as punishment and enjoy them. There are these types of teachers who sit in each classroom with roving eye, hoping to pounce on some rule violation in order to enjoy punishing the violator. Personal "whims" or prejudices become "rules."

A Gift In my elementary years the school years ran through eight grades. I do not recall across that span but one teacher who had the gift of teaching. This gift is that of making learning understandable and worthwhile. I recall one principal who, in that long period of time, himself, out of the blue, visited classes from the fifth grade up on a mid-week day. He said, to our surprise and that of the teacher, that we would have reading on that same day each week thereafter. He read on that day some pages out of one of H. Rider Haggard's *King Solomon's Mines*. He told us that reading should be fun — that a person who learned to like reading would always have something "to do."

He created more excitement and interest in learning than all the other teachers in that great weather-stained pile of brick and stone put together.

I remember no inspiration from the others, save for the exception indicated. Some were noted for humiliating punishments.

For lesser offenders there was the penalty of remaining in after school and writing sentences on the blackboard: "I will not talk in class. I will not talk in class. I will not talk in class . . . etc." I must have had that punishment a half dozen times or more.

I must have learned by rote and wished something from the teachers, but I do not recall what it was nor do I remember them as teachers or inspirers.

Autocrat Role   School principals too often cast themselves as autocrats. Some like the role and find it easy to be tyrannical and to evidence a certain joy in punishments and in inflexible administration of rules that one autocrat makes rigid and another man may make pliable.

"If you do not behave I will send you to the principal's office . . ." This was a threat to make one tremble and grow pale.

I recall most, across a long span of years, the elementary school principal who taught that reading could be fun. He himself was so bored with the class reading books of that time that he made his own rule — we will have reading that projects excitement and interest.

At McCallie preparatory school there was a fine punishment for rule violation. One spent an hour or so picking up stones to be used in building a long wall along the campus drive. That was fun. It had meaning. We were doing something useful. We took a pride in finding the better stones. Alumni to this day go back and admire the stone walls they helped make.

There also was a teacher who had rule-breakers write a little essay about why they thought they had broken the regulation. There was no accusation — no imposition of guilt — but a friendly, "Let's see what you can write about yourself . . ."

At any rate — school can be fun, interesting and instructive.

(September 21, 1968)

Old Steps,
Old Memories

NASHVILLE, TENN. — Every time I come back here I remember a thin, shy, worried youngster who got off a day coach here one Autumn morning, saw to it that an old trunk was unloaded, hired a dray and rode with the drayman to a street address out on Garland Avenue.

I remember the train-smoke smell of the cavernous Union Station; the long steps; the noise and the bustle of that early-morning arrival and departure of trains. Going up the steps, I remembered a line which our prep school commencement speaker had said, "Don't stare up the steps, step up the stairs."

Remembering it, I tried to make of it an omen. I was there to enter Vanderbilt University. I had $25 in my pocket. I had a job waiting on tables to pay for my room and board. I was to sign notes that day through a loan fund for tuition and fees. Before that year was done I was to patch my own pants, to suffer terribly from self-consciousness, but from the moment I got there life seemed to expand for me, the horizons lifted and living became an adventurue and fun.

Much water has flown beneath the arches of the years since that day, but I never come back but that I smell the train smoke and remember with sharp clarity all the noises and the impressions of that first morning.

Football   I "went out for the team" that Fall. Those were the innocent days when the coach posted a notice on the board urging all who felt they had a little football in them to come out for the team. There had been some recruiting, all by the alumni in their various home towns. (One of Vanderbilt's greatest athletic heroes, Rabbit Curry, from Marlin, Texas, was discovered in a class game. He never played and had no idea he could make the varsity team.)

I slept in my first lower berth that Fall by virtue of making the team. We played in Chicago, Lexington, Birmingham. I believe the most acute embarrassment that team suffered, aside from some defeats, was the visit in Chicago. Alonzo Stagg and his team entertained us with a dinner the evening before the game. When dinner was done, the Chicago team sang a number of the university songs. Most of us were from small Tennessee towns where the only singing we knew was done by ladies in the church choirs, and by girls who went away to school and took "voice."

They asked us to sing some of our songs and in an agony of spirit we tried. The result was squeaky, off-key and thin. We hated ourselves and almost hated the Chicago players who sang so fulsomely and well. I remember swearing then to learn something about music. So strong was this urge I almost married a young lady who had studied to become a concert pianist and who taught me a lot about Chopin, that genius being her favorite composer. One never knows from whence inspiration will come.

Teachers Looking back at it, I can remember only three teachers who sparked my mind at all. That is a pretty good average. It is dismaying to look back at high school and college and recall those teachers who really set the mind to going in inquiry and enthusiasm.

It was Dan McGugin who taught me most in those days. He was the coach and he was also a great reader of books, student of people and their ways, and expert in American history, and a profound admirer of the ancient Greeks and their ways. I have sat many hours on rattling trains and in the living room of his house talking about things in general. One of the last visits he made anyone was to me in Atlanta not long before he died. We sat in my house and talked about Carl Sandburg's books on Lincoln — taking them down to read some favorite portion. He was a wonderful man, kind, gentle and understanding. No Southern coach has had a better won-and-lost record and there is a sort of guilt complex at Vanderbilt to this day because they moved him out and strayed off into big-time football fields and have been more or less lost there ever since.

One thinks of so many things — going back to school where books and ideas first took on tangible form.

(April 14, 1950)

"What Happened To Him?"

UNIVERSITY OF MIAMI *(By Mail)* — There are times when I think there should be a law against old school mates. I do not always entertain this feeling, but at present I have a very definite feeling they should never meet again after they have left the portals of their alma mater and gone out into the world.

I have just had a distressing experience.

After a meeting here the other afternoon I noted a lady who kept waiting around while I answered a few post-meeting questions put by some students.

At the time I noted she had a sort of glint in her eye.

When at last the students were gone she appeared before me with outstretched hand.

"I'll bet," she said, "you don't remember me?"

Now it so happens that this question annoys me and I know there should be a law against it. A severe law. Obviously, if a person recognized one, some evidence of it would show. But to ask the question and to stand there while the poor victim smirks and perspires and fumbles with words is at least a misdemeanor and, at times, a felony.

"We worked side by side in the biology class at Vanderbilt," she said.

I did remember her, although with some vagueness. We shared, I recalled, the same rabbit. There was a shortage [of] rabbits in the biology budget that year. Two students shared one rabbit between them. The rabbit smelled terribly of formaldehyde and death and my partner detested it. I always had to do the job of unwrapping the damp rags which served as shroud and to my lot fell also the wrapping of the rabbit in its shroud when class was done. My partner had some illusions about being a lady doctor at the time, but I knew she would never make it.

And so, here she was, pumping my hand and still not telling me her name. She was a bit on the fattish side and her hair was turning gray.

"Could this elderly lady be a classmate of mine?" I asked.

God Bless Our Home   I just had, it seemed, to go home with her and see her family. It was late afternoon and her husband soon would be home. She had talked about me often, it seemed. She lived only a mile from the university. She had her car.

There were two children, a daughter of 17 and another of six. They were very polite. My old classmate hurried to get me a Coke, saying that since I was from Atlanta I must have one.

The two children kept eyeing me.

At last my old classmate returned with a Coke.

"When mother was in school, children," she said, "this man was young and thin and sat beside mother in classroom."

"What happened to him?" asked the child of six.

"Why, nothing happened to him," said my old classmate . . . "He went on to school and he went into the Marines and when he came back he was no longer in mother's class. Now, he works for a famous newspaper in Atlanta."

I could see this did not satisfy the child. Indeed, it didn't satisfy me. The child knew something had happened. Certainly mother's old classmate who had been young and thin was no longer young and thin. At least that much had happened. At least she kept staring while my old classmate prodded my memory for one old classmate and another.

At last her husband arrived. He was a worried-looking little man, tired after a day at the office. He was very pleasant with the forced pleasantness he had to summon at meeting one of mother's old classmates.

I left as soon as courtesy permitted.

As I got my hat I leaned over and said to the child of six:

"You are right, a great deal has happened to me."

As I went out I added to myself, "And to mummy, too."

I felt very old. There was a twinge of rheumatism in my right shoulder and my feet hurt. The years seemed to fall in upon me.

When I got back to my room I had to rest before dinner.

I hope any other old classmates will keep this in mind.

(April 15, 1944)

A Good Thorough Examination

Regularly, once every 47 years, I believe a man ought to go to a good doctor and have a physical check-up. So I went to this doctor.

Without his clothes man is a self-conscious animal, even if lying beneath a sheet. I waited.

He came in and peered at me through bifocals. I attempted a pleasantry. He ignored it. A shorthand expert was seated at a near-by table.

"The patient," he began, looking at me as impersonally as if I were a cadaver on a table before a medical class, "is a plain, middle-aged man, obviously overweight. . . ."

He went on, beginning with my hair, the scalp, the texture of my skin, and so on.

It was not flattering. Not even the shaving mirror was as unkind and factual. Not a blemish escaped him. No detail was too small to be searched out.

He took a rubber hammer and played upon my chest the snaredrum section from Sousa's "Semper Fidelis." He whipped out a steel measuring tape in meters and centimeters and bent it about me. Lights were thrust into my eyes, ears, throat.

He held up a finger and moved it slowly toward the wall and back again. Not once did I mistake it for the wall. I was proud of that.

Electric buzzers were applied here and there. Mallets beat at my knees. He rotated my head.

All the appearances of veins, skin, blemishes — all the secrets of an overweight frame were revealed, called forth in a loud voice and set down in writing.

Humility rested upon me like a weight.

"Come back tomorrow," he said.

I went out, pausing outside the door to listen for any raucous laughter should the young lady be reading the factual description of the patient. There was none. I understood, suddenly. It wasn't funny.

Tomorrow The morrow was different. I lay still for an hour on a narrow table. It required considerable skill not to fall off. A charming young lady then appeared. A tube was fitted into my mouth. My nose was clamped. I tried very hard not to try hard. The first metabolism record apparently was exciting. The young lady asked me if I had taken any haschish for breakfast.

From then on it was a race. The gentleman with the fluoroscope peered at me, making little sounds like "tsk, tsk, tsk." The X-ray technician photographed me front and profile. He made little clucking noises. I don't know if it was my profile or what the X-ray revealed.

A young lady gashed my finger for blood, drew more out of my arm, filled tubes, made slides.

Bleeding, I was led into a room and was ordered to sit in what looked like an electric chair. Electrodes were put on my ankles and wrists.

"Relax," they said.

Murmuring "Not guilty," I closed my eyes and leaned back. The machine purred. The technician bent over it, shaking his head and muttering.

"Come back tomorrow," they said.

Verdict That night, tossing on my bed, I wondered if this was my last night. I recalled old friends already gone and wondered if they would be there to meet me. Like a drowning man, my life passed in review. Most of it I liked.

The next day I went back. Miserable, I waited in a straight chair for the verdict. The doctor came in. With pleading eyes I waited for him to speak.

"Well," he said, frowning and tapping the record with his forefinger, "there isn't anything wrong with you. Your heart, blood pressure, blood count and general health are perfect. But here is a diet. For some weeks you will be an irascible, mean person. You will eat a great deal of vegetable hay and little else. I will write it down here. You knew you were overweight. I don't know what sort of mentality it is which has to pay money to be told what it knows."

He wrote.

"Doctor," I said, "I will forgive everything save that description of the patient."

"Truth," he said, "is a virtue."

But I will be patient. One of these days when he has a middle-aged lady before him and begins, "The patient is a middle-aged, plain, unattractive-looking specimen" she will rise up and take issue with him.

Once every 47 years a man ought to go regularly and have a thorough physical examination.

(April 7, 1948)

"This Was It, This Very Room"

"This was your room when you were a boy?" he asked. The boy's father nodded, feeling his throat tighten. "Yes," he said, "this was it. This very room. And so many of us have come to your grandmother's house for Christmas you will have to sleep with me."

"I don't mind," he said. "How long ago was it when this was your room?"

"A long time ago," he said, "a long time ago."

The memories came crowding in on him. He had wept there in that bed, sorrowing over some young grief. He had dreamed mightily in it, of doing great things in those years when a man came to be 21 and more years old. In that bed he had lain awake one night wondering why the grownups there for dinner had spoken of an uncle killed in the Spanish-American War at the age of 35 as a young man. To him the man of 35 seemed ancient and ready for the grave into which a Spanish bullet had sent him. In that bed he had listened to the trains whistle as they came in around Moccasin Bend and went wailing on southward in the night and he had imagined himself on one of them riding off to some faraway place and of doing great deeds.

Nightgowns   The boy pulled on his sleepgown.

"Did you sleep in pajamas then?"

"No," he said, "nightgowns. And in winter when we wore long underwear against the Tennessee winters we slept in it if we could get into bed without getting caught."

The boy laughed. "Long underwear," he said. "I've seen pictures of it in magazines."

They were silent for a moment as the father turned down the covers.

"Did you do home work for school?"

"Yes," he said, "I did some of it in this room. That was when I was in prep school and trying to learn Latin as great Caesar himself wrote it."

"Caesar the soldier?"

"That's the one." . . . He remembered coming into that room on Saturday nights after football games, sore and tired, and sometimes depressed with the bitter taste of defeat in his mouth. He remembered, too

too, nights of exultation after victory when sleep would not come and he would lie there and savor the game all over again, remembering each play and feeling again the rasping contact and panting breath of play in the line. He remembered, too, earlier days when he had gone out of the house as a scared, scrawny boy recently moved to town from a river farm, big-eyed with wonder at the city and its streets, excited by the tempo of it, and walking to the strange school.

Illness   In that room, he had almost died from an illness never diagnosed. He recalled the moments of coming out of delirium and of seeing the anxious face of his mother over him, and now and then his father, like pictures out of focus, and then the delirium which came again like a fast-whirling vortex rushing toward him and a feeling that if it reached him he would be carried away with it, forever, and he would hear someone scream, never knowing until long later it was himself. He remembered going out of that house to college and to join recruits at the old Union Station to entrain for Parris Island.

"Boy," he said.

"Yes."

"I used to dream about you, too."

"Me?"

"Yes, I dreamed of some day coming back here with a boy like you and telling him all about the old days when I was a boy here, but that would be pretty tiresome wouldn't it?"

"Yes, I guess it would. You've told me a lot of times about how you walked to school and about going on the train for the first time. I've heard all that. Was it far to your grandmother's?"

"Not so far. Just about 30 miles to the river from here. Some times we went on a steamboat . . ."

"Well, it's late for a boy not quite 8 to be awake. What about turning out the light and both of us piping down?"

He reached over and turned out the light.

(December 26, 1952)

Thoughts After Climbing Fuji

Notes from Japan: Those who are determined to see the sunrise from the peak of Japan's Mount Fuji begin their climb from the eighth way-station not later than 2 a.m. It is almost bitterly cold. After the sultry humidity of weather at the base, this is a relief. But before the ninth station has been reached, the hands in their knitted cotton gloves, which each climber purchases at the base, are numb. The eyes weep from the whipping gusts of biting wind.

Dawn begins to lighten the sky well before the sun. This comes at a point past the ninth station for those who have begun ascent by 1 or 2 o'clock. The slow wheel of earth is about to reveal the sun. Along the way, before and after the ninth station, the exhausted lie beside the trail. Some rest for an hour or so and try again. Some turn back.

The altitude and the exhaustion suffered by those not used to such extreme physical effort cause many others to halt for frequent short rests to recover the breath. They then plod on upward, from rock to rock, or pick ways through the loose rubble of lava stones, black, brick-red and brown, until the breath goes again and the legs grow numb for lack of oxygen. One sees them sitting, their faces drawn, pulling in deep breaths until the pain goes and the legs will work again.

Ninth Station The ninth way-station, one of the stone huts which provide tea, rice, and energy candy, is but 500 feet from the peak of Mt. Fuji. But as one stares upward toward it in the dim light of a still sunless morning, it seems very distant and straight up a dark, bare, rocky slope, forbidding and austere. Those 500 feet are agony for those who come to the climb without young legs. The trail is a series of many flat rocky zigzags. One seems never to make any gain.

Many of the owners of youthful legs fall out to rest. There is not a face that does not show signs of strain and weariness. But to those who persevere, the trail at last ends between the pillars indicating a Buddhist shrine, as Fuji is.

One stands there, legs trembling, lungs laboring, and turns to wait for the sun. The dark, awesome slopes of the old volcano already are softening in the growing light. The eastern sky suddenly blurs crimson. The flaming edge of the sun appears, causing the whole sky to turn rosy, then a deeper vermillion as the round disc of day rises above the horizon and comes fully into sight.

It is a scene worth the climb. The clouds are far below Fuji's peak of more than two miles above earth. Those who dwell on the earth below have not yet seen the sun. It seems to throb with flame and to have being only for those who have earned it with their climb. Shouts go up. Tired, grimy faces, streaked with the dark volcanic dust, are rapt.

Tea To Drink Then, there is tea to be drunk, many cups of it, to wash the salty copper taste from dry mouths and to put fluid back into dehydrated bodies. The sandwiches are taken from rucksacks. Rice or hot bowls of soybean soup are purchased. There are postcards to be stamped with the peak's symbol, and date. Pictures are made. One must stand at the edge of the huge crater where once lava, ashes and flame created the mountain itself.

Everyone who made the peak is filled with a sort of exultation. The student groups raise their banners and walk up and down the short, narrow row of souvenir shops and the small rest inns where one may lie down on a wooden platform or sit and drink tea.

Talk then turns to the long journey downward. But all of it is down. And one begins to develop a wish to see the places where, not too long before, one suffered and strained to keep going. The old Buddhists who said that climbing Fuji was a cleansing experience were right. It is.

(July 8, 1962)

Objectivity?
Or The Whole Truth

For a long time now I have been a voice crying in the wilderness of journalistic teaching. I think that as newspapers generally we have not done the mass job of informing the people of the United States on matters about which they should have been informed, for the simple reason that we have been taught to worship a word —

Objectivity.

Truth, I want. But not objectivity.

I want truth and not objectivity, for the simple reason there isn't any such thing as objectivity, and cannot be any such thing.

Not only that, there shouldn't be.

Objectivity is a phantom.

In chasing it we have dulled our stories. We too often made them frightfully boring, plodding unfoldings of events, in which the words, like plowmen plodding their weary way, were strung together like mud balls when they might as well have been pearls.

No story worth reading seeks to be "objective."

Truth   It seeks, or should seek, two things — to tell the truth and to be read. If it tells the truth so dully that it is not read, then it has failed utterly, no matter how "objective" it may be rated.

If it is to be read it must inform.

To inform it must carry with it the weight of the reporter's experience, his background, his ability to use words, and his feeling for the story . . . all this along with the facts.

Any well-written story, which readers find "good," must of necessity carry with it some of the reporter's opinion. I do not mean an editorial opinion. But, in writing it he cannot fail to give certain weight and importance to the various phases of the story. He has an opinion as to what is the most important factor in it.

Opinion   This is all the more true if it be a good, well-trained, experienced reporter who is at work on the story. He, or she, uses his or her experience, or opinion, to judge and evaluate the story in putting it together.

Therefore, as it appears, it represents an opinion, or an evaluation developed out of the reporter's experience, training, and ability to write.

We simply have been making a fetish of a word.

And, in semantic confusion, we have given to that fetish-word a meaning it doesn't really possess.

We have been sending young reporters out with an admonishment that their first duty is to be dull — and unread.

So, I have been going about the country for years, crying in the wilderness, saying that we needed good writing that would inform people, and not dull, "objective" assembling of "facts."

Witness   I am moved to all this by the recent speech before the Georgia Press Institute of Floyd Taylor, director of the American Press Institute, of Columbia University.

He found newspaper stories too dull and declared there was a "Need for more beneath-the-surface news digging by reporters in order to tell the reader not only what is happening, but the reasons behind what is happening." He further admonished newspaper publishers and editors "to make their papers more informative and more readable by hiring men who are specialists in different fields." If one tells "reasons" one must have opinions and put them in the stories.

I was writing almost those same words, and speaking them, in 1938 and incorporated them in an *Atlantic Monthly* article some years ago. So, naturally, it pleases me to hear this from the newly-founded American Press Institute, which has for its purpose the teaching of how to make a newspaper more informative and better read.

The press services are doing a fine job of telling us about the Winecoff fires of the country and the day-to-day events, but they must share along with the newspapers the responsibility for the fact that Americans get more informative and interpretive articles about Europe than they do of their own country.

Politics   Also, I have been crying in the wilderness about something else. I deny stoutly the accepted dictum that politics and the editorial comment should be separated . . . if by editorial comment you mean to include factual comment.

I think one of the worst crimes we have committed as newspapers is to allow irresponsible, extravagant and willfully distorted political speeches to be printed as news while we waited — of necessity — until the next day to comment and deny on the editorial page.

There should be found a way to insert, perhaps parenthetically, when possible, the actual facts when they may be obtained from accepted statistics and records, such as the Bureau of Statistics on business, exports, imports, crops, foreign countries, and so on.

Thousands of persons, reading political speeches which we faithfully reproduce as objective news, get false information and distorted ideas as to facts which are never corrected. And the newspapers, radio and press services are responsible.

Anyhow, the fact remains that newspapers and radio haven't done the job of informing the American public as well as we should have done. Nor have our schools. And magazines. One has but to listen to the quiz programs, to read the school tests, and the various information surveys and Gallup polls to know that.

We've been trying to be so objective they haven't read us as they would had we really given them a well-told story — and the why of it.

(February 23, 1947)

Things Change, Charlie

PARIS, FRANCE — Well, Charlie, I did just what you asked me to do. I found Charmaine. I walked right down the Rue Saint Honore until I found that number and I hunted around upstairs and found the name on a brass plate on the apartment door. Sure enough, like you said, the French don't move much.

She's older, Charlie. You know you told me to be sure and look her up and say hello for you. That she was as cute as a little red wagon. Well, Charlie, she is a little older. You know what I mean. After all, it's been a few years since you were in Paris.

Yes, the cafe is still on the corner. They still put out the little tables and chairs. Fact is, Charmaine and I sat and talked about you.

You remember that day you went out to the Bois and took a basket and had a picnic? You never told me about that. I'm sorry to tell you, but at first she didn't remember you. "Charlee," she said. "Let me see, Charlee. I theenk I remember heem." So she went and got a box of snapshots. They weren't all of you. How many times did you have liberty? From what you told me, I thought this Charmaine lived only for you.

Pictures   Well, anyhow, we sorted through a lot of pictures and at last we found yours. Gee, you looked a bit funny, Charles. You looked young yourself, and I never would have known Charmaine was the same girl. She's fattened up some, Charlie. I remember how you used to tell me about her and say she wasn't any bigger than a minute. Well, Charlie, she's about 10 minutes now.

Where were we? Oh, yes, out in the Bois. I mean, looking at pictures of the picnic out in the Bois.

My, you were funny, Charlie! There was one picture where you were holding your head back and Charmaine was pouring wine into your mouth out of one of those long bottles. I had a great laugh over that.

I told her you had not forgotten her and this seemed to please her. She even dug up an old letter you'd written her. Your French was terrific, being mostly English and a few French words — all misspelled.

She asked about you. And, say, come to think of it, you don't look so blithe and gay and debonaire any more. You've changed some. I think Charmaine may have changed less than you. She said you always were the life of the party. She told me about the time you hired a cab and insisted on riding the horse. I told her that while you may have been able to stay in there and punish a bottle of Three-Star in those days, you now get silly and try to sing after the second martini.

The Daughter   The years get on, Charlie. And Charmaine is married and has a daughter who is about as big as a minute and as pretty as a picture. She had a look at the pictures and said, "Did that funny looking man call on you, Mama?" Romance, Charlie, can take a lot of belting around in just a few years.

That salad you told me about? It hasn't changed a bit. And the veal cooked with mushrooms and a special sauce? Great. Just like you said. The snails are good, too. And the French like to tell how they fooled the Germans during the occupation. They would cut up horse meat into small strips, curl it up and stuff it in the shells. The sauce was good, and the Nazi officers never knew the difference.

None of that has changed, Charlie. But other things have. France has changed. And so has Paris. I guess the whole world has changed, Charlie. And to many of us it is not for the better. After seeing the pictures and the look on your face when you were out in the Bois, I didn't look up Marie, as Al had asked. It made me sad, Charlie. There is no use going around stirring up old ghosts. You keep your memories. They are better. So let it be, Charlie, and explain it to Al.

(June 25, 1960)

Photo Credits

Portrait of Ralph McGill by Robert Templeton. *The Ralph McGill Collection, Special Collections Department, Robert W. Woodruff Library, Emory University.*

McGill and Dr. Martin Luther King. *The Atlanta Constitution.*

McGill and others receive honorary degrees. *The Atlanta Constitution.*

McGill impersonates a chef. *The Atlanta Constitution.*

McGill visits a circus performer. *McGill Collection.*

McGill shoots birds. *McGill Collection.*

McGill and Gen. Lucius Clay. *Wide World Photos, Inc.*

The McGill family with President Kennedy. *McGill Collection.*

McGill and Robert W. Woodruff. *McGill Collection.*

McGill leaves the White House. *McGill Collection.*

Vice President and Mrs. Humphrey and Mayor and Mrs. Allen arrive for McGill's funeral. *The Atlanta Journal.*

The young Ralph McGill and his mother. *McGill Collection.*

McGill and his first wife and their son. *McGill Collection.*

The second Mrs. McGill. *The Atlanta Constitution.*

McGill addresses the Democratic National Convention in Chicago, 1944. *Wide World Photos, Inc.*

McGill beside his desk at the *Constitution. The Atlanta Constitution.*

Text of "Shining Light Award". *McGill Collection.*

INDEX

Acheson, Dean, 169
Adams, John Quincy, 159
Ahoskie, North Carolina, 98–100
Allen, Ivan, 146
Arlington Cemetery, 172
Asheville, North Carolina, 39
Athens, Georgia, 66
Atlanta, Georgia, 25, 80–81, 112, 122–124, 128, 199–200

Bainbridge, Georgia, 104–106
Baldwin, Stanley, 62
Barnett, Ross, 128, 132–133, 143, 171
Baseball, 26–28
Battle, John S., 113–115
Bird Hunting, 11–12
Birmingham, Alabama, 126, 131–134, 136, 149, 198
Boll Weevil, 18–19
Boone, North Carolina, 44
Brown, Edmund ("Pat"), 75
Brunswick, Georgia, 6
Brunswick Stew, 6–8
Buchanan, James, 154
Butts, Wally, 66–67

Cairo, Egypt, 28, 111
Calhoun, Georgia, 44–45
Calhoun, John C., 158–159
Cape Canaveral, 70

Carter, Hodding, 102
Chamberlain, Neville, 38, 63
Christmas, 25–26, 54–57, 122–123, 203
Churchill Downs, 50–51
Churchill, Sir Winston, 62–64, 170
Clay, Henry, 158
Clinton, North Carolina, 20
Conner, Bull, 132–134
Cooper, John Sherman, 162
Copenhagen, Denmark, 26, 154
Cox, James M., 188
Crawford, William H., 158–159

Daniels, Josephus, 15
Dickinson, Charles 160–161
Dimaggio, Joe, 45–47
Dodd, Bobby, 66
Dulles, John Foster, 183, 191

Eisenhower, Dwight D., 129, 169, 179, 183, 191
Evers, Medgar, 148–149

Farley, James A., 189–190
Faubus, Orval, 132–133, 143
Fayette County, Georgia, 4
Football, 47–48, 66–67
Fox Hunting, 8–10
Franklin, Benjamin, 61–62

Fullbright, William, 138

Gable, Clark, 16
Gagarin, Yuri, 68, 72
Gandhi, Mahatma, 121
Georgia Tech, 66–67
Goering, Herman, 35–37
Gone With The Wind, 14–16
Grissom, Gus, 71–72, 72n

Hamilton, Alexander, 156
Hanna, Mark, 184
Harding, Warren G., 155
Hayes, Ira, 49–50
Hemingway, Ernest, 69–70
"Hermitage," 156, 158
Hess, Rudolph, 36
Hitler, Adolf, 35, 38, 195
Hoover, Herbert, 163–165
Hoover, J. Edgar, 45
Huntsville, Alabama, 126

Iwo Jima, 49–50, 63–64

Jackson, Andrew, 154, 156, 158–162
Jackson, Mississippi, 142
Jackson, Rachel, 160–162
Javits, Jacob, 179
Jefferson, Thomas, 77, 154–157, 167
Johnson, Lyndon B., 85, 91, 138, 150, 173, 177–178, 186
Jones, Bobby, 16, 61–62

Ku Klux Klan, 16, 100–102, 106–108, 121–125, 127, 180, 195
Keats, John, 54
Kennedy, Edward M., 90–91
Kennedy, John F., 74, 79, 80, 90, 128, 129, 134, 148–150, 171–173, 177–183, 185–191
Kennedy, Robert F., 90, 121, 148–149
Kentucky Derby, 50
Kruschev, Nikita, 76, 172, 182, 191

King, Martin Luther, 147
King, Martin Luther, Jr., 119–121, 139–140, 145–149

Lee, Robert E., 113, 115
Leigh, Vivian, 16
Leprechauns, 31, 33
Lewis, John L., 35
Lewis, Sinclair, 40
Lincoln, Abraham, 129, 131, 154–156, 162–163
Little Rock, Arkansas, 126, 129, 132, 133
Lodge, Henry Cabot, 191
London, 154
Long, Earl, 64
Long, Huey P., 64–65

MacArthur, Douglas, 164–165, 167
Maddox, Lester, 91
Marshall, Thurgood, 120
Mason, George, 77–78
McCarthy, Joseph R., 77, 77n
McDaniell, Hattie, 16
McGugin, Dan, 199
McKinley, William, 178, 184
McQueen, Butterfly, 16
Memphis, Tennessee, 17, 145–146
Mencken, Henry, 176–177
Meredith, James, 142–144
Michelangelo, 88
Millay, Edna St. Vincent, 148
Milledgeville, Georgia, 93, 101–102
Mississippi Delta, 17, 18, 21
Mitchell, Margaret, 15–16
Monroe, Marilyn, 45–47
"Monticello," 155–157
Montgomery, Alabama, 113, 115, 119–120, 126
Mount Fuji, 204–205
Mules, 20–21
Murphy, John "Reg," 91–92
Murrow, Ed, 84
Myrdal, Gunnar, 110–111

NAACP, 119–120, 148
Nixon, Richard M., 74–75, 75n, 171, ·
     178–180, 182–183, 185, 187–191
Nobel Peace Prize, 82, 139–141
Nurenberg War Trials, 35, 37

Oxford, Mississippi, 17, 129, 131, 133

Paris, 69, 72, 154, 208–209
Patterson, Eugene, 91–93
Pineville, Kentucky, 33–35
Pope John XXIII, 186
Prynne, Hester, 87

Ray, James Earl, 147
Reece, Byron Herbert, 57–58
Ringling, John, 64–65
Rockefeller, Nelson, 179, 190
Roosevelt, Eleanor, 75–77
Roosevelt, Franklin D., 19, 63, 80,
     113, 149, 154, 165–166, 188–189
Roosevelt, Theodore, 154
Ruth, Babe, 32, 67

Sandburg, Carl, 19, 82–86, 199
Selma, Alabama, 141–142, 149
Shepard, Alan, 67–68, 72
Sirhan, Sirhan, 149
Smathers, George, 186
Speaker, Tris, 33
Spellman, Cardinal, 189
Spring, 13–14

Stagg, Amos Alonzo, 198
Steichen, Edward, 83–86
Steinbeck, John, 82–83
Stevenson, Adlai, 171, 185, 187, 191
Stockholm, Sweden, 154

Taylor, Alf, 10
Truman, Harry S., 101–102, 165,
     168–170, 182–183, 187–188
Tuscaloosa, Alabama, 136
Tuskegee, Alabama, 118
Tutankhamen, 28–30
Tyrone, Georgia, 4

Unadilla, Georgia, 107–108
University of Georgia, 66–67
University of Mississippi, 17, 128,
     136
Vanderbilt University, 198–200

Wallace, George C., 132, 135, 149
Warm Springs, Georgia, 181–182
Washington, D.C., 154–155, 167
Watson, Tom, 139
Webster, Daniel, 139
Wilson, Woodrow, 154
Wolfe, Thomas, 39–41
Woodruff, Robert W., 61, 80–81

Young Harris, Georgia, 52–53, 58